# "FINDING BUTCH CASSIDY & THE SUNDANCE KID"

*By Marilyn Grace and Dr. John McCullough*

Love,

Marilyn Grace

Nov 5, 2018

# Finding "Butch Cassidy and the Sundance Kid"

## Solving the "Wild Bunch" Mystery with That "Darn" DNA

*by Marilyn Grace & John McCullough, Ph.D.*

# WANTED
## DEAD OR ALIVE

## The 'WILD BUNCH'

Harry Longabaugh (Sundance Kid)-Robert George Parker (Butch
Cassidy)-Ben Kilpatrick-Will Carver-Harvey "Kid Curry" Logan

### Wanted for Robbery of the BUTTE COUNTY BANK and the UNION PACIFIC EXPRESS

## REWARD OF $2500
## $500 Each

for ARREST and CONVICTION of the Robbers, and one-fourth
of any portion of Treasure recovered.

All officers are warned to use precau-
tion in making arrest. These are the most
desperate men in America.

THE WORLD TIMES the PERCHINT AND PREVENTS.
REWARD NOTICE.

STORY TELLER PRODUCTIONS

www.sundancekiddna.com

marilyngrace@gmail.com

OTHER BOOKS BY MARILYN GRACE:

Hitler Escapes To America

Amelia Earhart
*Mystery Solved*

SCREAM BLOODY MURDER
The Truth about the Life and Death of Marilyn Monroe

The ASSASINATION OF JOHN FITZGERALD KENNEDY
*MYSTERY SOLVED*

"Living Green"

"The Adventures of Fuzzy Bear"
{Children's Book}

*Cover designed by Cyndee Carr*

*For My Children*

**Marilyn Grace**

Marilyn Grace, born August 26, 1952 in Ogden, Utah. She married in 1972 and became single again in 1989. She is the mother of three children and four grandchildren. Her children are Tiffany, Sterling, Adrian, and daughter-in-law Mindy. Sterling and Mindy have four children: Brandon, Arianna, Cameron and Danelle.

Marilyn owns "Story Teller Productions" in Saint George, Utah. Marilyn's background in film made her a NATURAL to search for "Butch, Sundance, and Etta." Her journey began in May of 1997. Her nineteen-years of research has taken her so many places where "Butch, Sundance, Etta," and members of the "Wild Bunch," lived and escaped from the law.

"Finding 'Butch Cassidy and The Sundance Kid' ~ Solving the 'Wild Bunch' Mystery with that 'Darn' DNA," is Marilyn Grace's second book. Her first book, "Living Green, A Gentler Way," gives helpful tips on how to live a healthy lifestyle.

William Henry Long, (also known as Bill) married Luzernia; widow of Silas Morrell. Luzernia had seven children and one of her young sons drowned in a stream just behind their homestead in Fremont, Utah. After the death of her husband, who suffered three years from a back injury, she is courted and then married William Henry Long, a horse breaker at the Hogan Ranch in Loa, Utah. Bill and Luzernia had two girls: Florence Viola and Evinda Ann, born in Fremont, Utah.

Bill and Luzernia's daughter, Florence Viola, (Viola) wrote a letter asking, "Who is my father?" She could not find any record of his birth or where his people came from. This started the search for Bill Long's identity, later leading to the discovery that William Henry Long is an alias for Harry Alonzo Longabaugh, "The Sundance Kid."

"BUTCH CASSIDY & THE SUNDANCE KID" the movie, inspired Marilyn Grace to find the TRUTH about the WESTS most FAMOUS OUTLAWS!

Marilyn Grace is an Historical Researcher, Writer and Film Producer. She makes her home in sunny St. George, Utah and lives close to family in the area.

"FINDING BUTCH CASSIDY & THE SUNDANCE KID" lead to even more UNSOLVED MYSTERIES. Marilyn's new books are; "HITLER ESCAPES TO AMERICA," "SCREAM BLOODY MURDER, The Truth About the Life and Death of Marilyn Monroe," "JFK ASSASINATION, Mystery Solved," "AMELIA EARHART, Mystery Solved," "ADMIRAL BYRD'S SECRET DIARY," and "CHINA'S 256-YEAR-OLD MAN," will be her next books and movies.

Marilyn Grace feels that her wonderful children are her greatest accomplishments and works with Tiffany, Sterling, Mindy, her daughter-in-law, and with Adrian, at STORY TELLER PRODUCTIONS by Marilyn Grace.

She has a love for travel and will create a "WILD BUNCH CRUISE" with Marilyn Grace, Collin Raye, and B.J. Thomas. The "UNSOLVED MYSTERY CRUISE" will also feature Marilyn Grace, Collin Raye, and B.J. Thomas. EVERYONE WILL BE INVITED! FUN!

## John M. McCullough, Ph.D.

Dr. John M. McCullough received his Ph.D. from the University of Illinois in 1972. He has a forty-year career as a physical anthropologist, ecological genetics, as well as human variation, and has specialized in the Americas, Yucatan and Europe. He has traveled the world and been involved with the research for over 300 cases involving human remains. John has also worked on many high-profile cases such as the Allred Murder Case and the Ted Bundy murders in Utah.

Dr. McCullough has been personally involved with "The Sundance Kid Project" since November of 2007. His skills and experience have been invaluable to the research for our project; Dr. McCullough's extensive accomplishments are included in Chapter Ten, "Getting Scientific."

Dr. McCullough likes to be called John, and has stated that of all the remains he has examined, William Henry Long is the strongest and most physically fit individual he has examined to date. He also explained that William Henry Long had a very active life. Bone fractures and wear and tear corresponds with those of an individual that rode horses and did extensive farm work.

John lives in the heart of Salt Lake City, Utah. He adores his family; his wife Chris, his daughter Lily, and two sons, Evan and Jay. John also has two wonderful grandchildren.

## Timothy Kupherschmid, MBA, MFS

Timothy Kupherschmid is an entrepreneurial-minded executive with more than 20 years of forensic DNA experience. He has extensive international experience in French and English speaking Africa. Mr. Kupherschmid holds an MBA from Western Governors University, a master's degree in forensic science (MFS) from the George Washington University and an AB degree from Bowdoin College in biology and environmental studies. Mr. Kupherschmid has worked as a senior DNA analyst at the Armed Forces DNA Identification Laboratory (AFDIL), served as the Laboratory's Director of the Maine State Police Crime Laboratory and had been the Forensic Technical Director at Myriad Genetic Laboratories, Inc.

Most recently, Mr. Kupherschmid is elected to the Board of Directors of the American Society of Crime Laboratory Directors (ASCLD). He served on this volunteer Board from 2005-2008. Current and past professional memberships include American Academy of Forensic Sciences (AAFS), Scientific Working Group on DNA Analysis Methods (SWGDAM), Maine Medico-Legal Society, Maine Management Service, NDIS (National DNA Index System) Audit Review Panel and the Utah Valley University Biotechnology Program Advisory Board.

Mr. Kupherschmid has given hundreds of scientific presentations and has numerous scientific publications. He achieved world acclaim for discovering the DNA of an African Princess (see article on Sorenson Forensics website). Mr. Kupherschmid is active with the Salt Lake Chamber of Commerce and the World Trade Center Utah.

Without Tim's help and sending William Henry Long's DNA to an undisclosed lab back east, we never would have been able to receive DNA from his degraded bones. Tim has really gone over and above the "call of duty!"

# INTRODUCTION

In 1997, I saw the NOVA documentary, "WANTED: Butch and Sundance." I lived with my elderly mother in Provo, Utah and I raised my last child on my own. I could only find part-time work and I felt very lost and alone, longing for a better life. In the Nova documentary, the DNA did not prove that the bodies from Bolivia were "Butch and Sundance." Suddenly I thought, WHERE DID THEY GO?

People have asked me how I have stayed with hunting for "Sundance, Butch, and Etta," for nineteen years. Why did I stick with it for so long, and why didn't anyone else think to look for them in the United States?

As a senior in high school, I went to a fabric store and purchased some navy blue knit material so I could make a new outfit. I showed my pattern and material to my mother and she said, "Oh, that is not the right material for that pattern, it will turn out awful." My feelings were hurt, I went to my room and sewed all night long. In the morning, I showed my mother my new outfit and she is very impressed. She admitted that she had been wrong. My mother used to say, "Just make Marilyn mad and she will clean the whole house!" When someone doubts that I can do something, I rise to the challenge and work even harder to prove them wrong. My mother must have made me mad on purpose because I cleaned our house a lot! In my home, I do not have any projects that are just sitting around. If I want to sew something, I stick with it until it is done. This is the only explanation for never giving up the search for "Butch Cassidy & The Sundance Kid." I always finish what I start!

While working on the "The Sundance Kid Project," I have been very upset because people have doubted our TEAM could solve the mystery. Many nights I would just dig in staying up until 2 a.m. working on a problem. I have gone on-line, drawn maps, checked dates, gone over research, and the solution to the problem finally came to me. Finding out what really happened to "The Wild Bunch" became fixed in my mind and I did not quit until I found the answers. I would spend all my spare time doing research and purchased any book that I thought would give me a clue. My "WILD BUNCH" library grew and grew.

I stalled with my research by June of 2007, when a friend of mine introduced to a popular documentary, "The Secret." I became completely captivated by the film! How could "The Secret" to getting what you really want in life have been so guarded? There were so few people that knew about "The Secret." Rhonda Byrne is the author and she explains how to magnetize what you really want in life. I went out and bought the DVD and the book. Watching the DVD every day, again and again began to shift my thinking. I went from thinking negative thoughts to positive thoughts, because of the information I received from "The Secret." It changed my LIFE! She also wrote, "The Magic," "The Power," and "The Hero." They are part of our Company Culture. We LOVE Rhonda Byrnes books!

I would like to mention more books and bestselling authors that have helped me with my life. The first is Richard Paul Evans, who has written many award-winning books. "The Christmas Box" is one of my favorite story's that became a TV movie. You can truly understand the Saviors atonement. All of Richard's books have such a positive message.

Self-help and motivational books have been a major influence in my life. The list could go on and on. I always have a book on my nightstand that I am reading and studying daily. The more knowledge we acquire, the better we do in life. I want it all—THE GOOD LIFE! There are more books that I love and have been a major part of my life. The information is so empowering and life is easier when you know how life works.

I highly recommend you check out Byron Katie, "The Work." You can go to youtube.com and watch her videos. She has four questions and a turnaround.

Dr. Stephen Covey is my former neighbor in Provo, Utah. He authored, "7 Habits of Highly Effective People." His son, Stephen M. R. Covey wrote, "The Speed of Trust." These are wonderful knowledgeable books and are worth your time and investment.

Tal Ben-Shahar, Ph.D., is the author of "Happier." You can have all the money in the world and still not be happy. Learn skills for a HAPPY LIFE!

Another book that influenced me tremendously is "The Passion Test: The Effortless Path to Discovering Your Destiny," by Janet and Chris Attwood. If you want to know your destiny, take the test!

Peg and Sherm Fugal co-authored "Chicken Soup for the Latter-day Saint Soul." Peg worked with Robert G. Allen of the famed "Nothing Down" series. Jack Canfield, authored the first "Chicken Soup for The Soul." His current book "The Success Principles," will ROCKET your career!

"The Kind Diet" by Alicia Silverstone is one of my favorites. Applying the principles, she teaches will help you to create a healthy and happy lifestyle. Another book I look forward to writing is, "Aging with Grace." I must write a book on everything I have learned from Alicia and other "Happy Millionaires."

The documentary, "BUCK" by Cindy Maahl is WONDERFUL! "The Man Who Listens to Horses," and "Horse Sense for People," by Monty Roberts, are both excellent! Being GENTLE is the only way to truly win! Watching Robert Redford's movie, "The Horse Whisperer," will help you understand a gentler way of dealing with horses and people. I love the song, "Looking for A Soft Place to Fall," and I have memorized the words to the song because I love it so much. What a wonderful life lesson movie. Everyone is longing for a "soft place to fall" in this world we live in.

I had always worked a day job while working on my dream of finding "Sundance." I worked nights for a newspaper agency in Salt Lake City, Utah... when I collapsed. My heart just hurt and I became exhausted. My beautiful friend Lara Chamberlain picked me up and drove me to a clinic on a Saturday. My doctor said that women do not do well working night shifts and that the night work had literally worn out my heart. He said to call work and let them know your doctor does not want you to work for three days. He then told me to give two weeks' notice and quit. He became very serious about my never working nights again. He said that it could lead to an early death.

I did what my doctor said and I gave my two weeks' notice. It felt like I jumped off a cliff like Paul Newman and Robert Redford in the movie, "Butch Cassidy & The Sundance Kid." On faith alone, I set out to change my life. Twenty-eight wonderful people showed up from my church to help me move out of my home and I put my things in storage. I rented a room with a friend and found temporary work as a gardener. It seems that I have a talent for arranging flowers in flower beds and I regained my strength and health in a short time.

A month later, I found Judy and Jerry Nickle through their website. For years, Jerry had suspected that William Henry Long, his step-great grandfather, could have hidden the fact that he is... "The Sundance Kid." My background in film-making made it a NATURAL to document this amazing story.

I created a vision board when I first saw "The Secret" and have added photos of William Henry Long and "The Sundance Kid," side by side. Robert Redford's role as "The Sundance Kid" in the movie, "BUTCH CASSIDY & THE SUNDANCE KID," is brilliant! I have communicated with Robert Redford and asked that he narrate our documentary. We had not been on KSL 5 News when I asked him to narrate. Robert Redford said he appreciated me thinking of him, but that he has so many movie projects and commitments that time would not allow him to narrate. How could he possibly know what we have discovered?

My vision board is in a place where I can see the pictures of William Henry Long and "Sundance." When I want to "feel good," I hum the theme song to the movie, "Butch Cassidy & The Sundance Kid." Morning, noon and night, I am visualizing not only to complete books and documentaries on the subject, but to do another movie on what really happened to "Butch Cassidy & The Sundance Kid," along with "Etta Place." I knew if we found "Sundance," it would lead to solving the whole mystery.

Robert Redford has been quoted as saying, "I owe my fortune to 'Butch Cassidy & The Sundance Kid.' Paul Newman and Joan Woodward helped me get the part, for which I am very grateful. We have become life-long friends."

They did not die in Bolivia! The last scene of the movie is all wrong, but how could I prove it? That is when I started to pull together our TEAM!

My favorite shows are ELEMENTARY, MONK, NCIS, NUMBERS and BONES. I have gone to the library, checked out all the DVD's and have watched all the series. I cannot get enough of solving crimes. The science used in solving crimes just fascinates me. You can have a theory as to what happened, but when you get the scientific analysis to verify your hypothesis, there is nothing better.

The photo analysis, name analysis, body analysis, examining the remains of Bill Long, as well as DNA, has been the most exciting time I have had in my life. I knew if we could solve the mystery, my life would improve! My life has changed dramatically, from living with my mother in Provo, Utah... to writing a book and creating a film on "The Sundance Kid."

Our TEAM has been on the news three times with John Hollenhorst of KSL 5 News. We have been interviewed by Geoff Liesik of the Deseret News and have made the front cover. The Deseret News doubled their readership the day they published "The Sundance Kid Story."

It's a WONDERFUL LIFE! My children are all grown and I spend my time working on the final clues. Writing this book with Dr. John McCullough has been so wonderful. I have loved every moment and I'm excited to do more research for the next book.

This book is for YOU! The fact that you would be willing to read our story means that you are a "WILD BUNCH" enthusiast. What an adventure! We have all had the time of our lives!

If YOU don't do it now, when do you plan on making your dreams come true?

*Marilyn Grace*

***Note:*** *A few years ago, my son Sterling Holmes invited me to a solar convention in Milford, Utah. The state of Utah made the news for building a wind farm. My son attended the event because he and his partner own "Solar Unlimited" in Cedar City, Utah. Sterling Holmes now owns his own solar company in Cedar City... "STERLING SOLAR." His former company furnished the solar panels for the loud speakers. My son invited me, and I loved meeting new people and spending time with my son on such a special occasion. Sterling feels a sense of purpose for his life, by helping folks go off-grid and by working to help change the world to "GREEN." Sterling and I were visiting with everyone at the event when Governor Jon Huntsman came by. Governor Huntsman started shaking hands with everyone and as he shook my hand, I jumped right in and introduced myself; "My name is Marilyn Grace and I am a documentary film-maker. You may have seen the news where our TEAM exhumed the body of 'The Sundance Kid' in Duchesne, Utah." Governor Huntsman became very excited. He said that he had seen the news. "Is that for real?" he exclaimed. I assured him we did exhume "Sundance" and explained how I had been working on solving the mystery since May of 1997. He brought over his assistant and introduced us. She gave me her card and the Governor asked me to put together a report with all our research. He then said, "Finding the Sundance Kid would be wonderful for the State of Utah." I agreed and told him that I would put together a notebook of our research, and then his entourage left.*

*Sterling and I were so excited! Sterling said he would help with designing the cover and felt that the cover should look like leather that is old and worn. We were thrilled to work together creating an "Evidence Notebook" for the governor. I had all the evidence written up for Governor Jon Huntsman... I realized I had the beginning of a book... "Finding Butch Cassidy & The Sundance Kid ~ Solving the 'Wild Bunch' Mystery with that 'Darn' DNA." Then Governor Huntsman left as governor to be the Ambassador to China, therefore I did not send him a copy of our evidence. We finally have a book and so much has happened since then.*

*We have the full sample of DNA for Bill Long and we have been introduced to Kurt and Joan Callow. I hired a private detective, Don Brooks. He found Kurt and Joan who own the property at 122 Jacobs Street in Mont Clare, Pennsylvania, the birth place of Harry Alonzo Longabaugh, "The Sundance Kid." We have made friends with Brent Ashworth who is a collector of rare signatures, documents and photos of the "Wild Bunch."*

*The completion of this book is the most significant work I have ever accomplished. Many events have taken place that helped us complete our project. They have led our TEAM down a path that has been so full of marvelous and exciting adventures.*

*There are more books to write and we are collecting information on an on-going basis. It is time to wrap up what we have. We need to spread the news that we have found Butch Cassidy, The Sundance Kid, and Etta Place.*

*Life is wonderful! We hope you enjoy our research!*

# ACKNOWLEDGEMENTS

## My Family

**Tiffany and Luis Montalvo,** (Daughter and Son-in-Law)
**Sterling Cory Holmes and Mindy,** (Son and Daughter-in-Law) Grandchildren: <u>Brandon</u>, <u>Arianna</u>, <u>Cameron</u> (Cami) and <u>Danelle</u>.
**Adrian E. Holmes,** (Son) With some SPECIAL THANKS, I dedicate this book to you, Adrian. Thank you, son, for your help! Your help in the beginning made all the difference. This project would not exist without you. I LOVE MY FAMILY!

## Team

**LONGABAUGH'S**
**Andrea Blakley:** I met Andrea on line and she introduced me to Sue Balsamo. Andrea is related to the Longabaugh's and she has a website. Type in SUNDANCE KID on the Web and it will take you to the site. Check it out! Great Work!
**Sue Balsamo:** Sue lives in Philadelphia and has indulged me for hours on the phone, and has helped me with major clues for the book. Thank you, Sue! Thanks for the information and pictures of the graves. She sent information on "Sundance's" Family: Josiah Longabaugh (father), Ann (mother), Samanna and Emma (sisters). The photo's she sent are included in the book. So... generous of you to help!
**Fritz and Edward Longabaugh:** They were the first of the Longabaugh Family to help with our search. Fritz is a Minister in New York and Edward is his father. They sent stories, genealogy, and have offered to let us test their DNA for the male line of Longabaugh's. Thank you Fritz and Edward!
**George Longabaugh Junior and Senior:** They gave their DNA for testing. Still need a more direct descendant, but thanks you guys!

## Special Thanks

**Linda Weaver Clarke, husband, George Clarke (Editors):** They came to help at the very end of the project and pushed me to do better.
**Sara James:** Sara is such a "love," her help has saved the day!
**Michael Karr:** Our Director. Outlaw name is "HOLLYWOOD!" Thanks Mike for all your time and effort.
**Tim Kupherschmid:** DNA Expert and Executive Director at Sorenson Forensics and Biotechnology, Salt Lake City, Utah. He did more than I have time to tell. He worked MIRACLES with his contacts for the DNA. Our CSI Guy!
**Cary Mac Arthur:** THE BEST! She is so remarkable, smart and professional. Cary worked miracles.
**Wendy Mair:** She edited the name analysis, time line, body analysis, and more! My friend since 2005. Wendy has helped so much.
**John McCullough, PhD:** Our Anthropologist on the project and professor of anthropology for 40 years at the University of Utah; my partner and friend. Thank you, John! He is our SCIENCE GUY! Could not have done any of this without his help!
**Jerry and Judy Nickle:** Executive Producers, Jerry is the step-great grandson of William Henry Long. For many years, they suspected that he is "The Sundance Kid."
**Tracey Obenauer:** My coach in New York City. I love and appreciate Tracey so much! She has helped me grow. I am a better person because of Tracey's guidance.
**James and Mary Petty:** Genealogists and owners of Heirlines Family History. Pulled off the impossible - they found the living Longabaugh, Carl Schuch.

**Carl and Delia Schuch:** Carl is the living descendant of Ann Place Longabaugh (Sundance's mother). He allowed me to take two mouth swabs for DNA when I went to their restaurant in Rancho Mirage, California. Lots of laughs on that one. We have stayed in touch and have made a friendship.

**Annette Sly:** She helped with contacts for the project in June 2007. Thank you, Annette.

**Jessica Moore Smith:** Thank you Jessica for having a cool head and helping us find "The Sundance Kid." Forever Grateful!

**Kelly Taylor:** Our friend and scout in Fremont, Utah. You can go for the ride of your life! Kelly owns an extreme horseback-riding adventure company. This adventure is for brave-hearted souls who love the "Wild Bunch Country."

**Susan Treadwell:** My friend and neighbor - they say "A friend is on your side in a struggle." So, glad Susan is my friend!

**Cyndee Carr:** Our creative designer and "Master of the Machines." Without Cyndee, we would never have completed this "beautiful," updated book. I Love You, Cyndee!

# Family of William Henry Long

**Betty Bird:**  A great grand-daughter of Luzernia and Bill Long.  She lives in the State of Washington.  Betty has been so helpful to tell us family stories her mother told her.  Betty told me about Matt Warner, former member of the Wild Bunch and Sheriff of Price, Utah.  Her mother told her twice that she suspected that Matt Warner murdered Bill Long.  Bill did not want Matt writing a book about the Wild Bunch.  Betty is so fun, she makes me laugh.  Thank You, Betty!

**Jody Defa:**  The great great-grandson of William Henry Long, a.k.a., "The Sundance Kid."  He lives in Heber City, Utah.  Jody welcomed us into his home with his sweet wife and children.  His girls sang songs for us and entertained us and helped with many stories.  So... grateful to Jody!

**Etta Forsyth:**  She is the step grand-daughter of Bill Long. Etta, 93 at the time and is from Duchesne, Utah.  Etta is in her 20's when her Uncle Billy died.  She came to the grave for a while when we exhumed his remains.  Major stories from Etta!  She filled in the blanks of his mysterious life.  She loved Grandpa Billy!

**Pat Lingwall:**  Direct descendant, great grand-daughter of William Henry Long and Luzernia.  Pat is so generous with her time and stories.

**Yvonne Martinez:**  Betty Bird and Yvonne Martinez are sisters.  Yvonne came to the cemetery when we exhumed William Henry Long in December, 2008.  She is such a sweetheart.  Betty and Yvonne also helped with research on Matt Warner, a former member of the "Wild Bunch."  Thank You!

**Ray McDonald:**  Sister of Sherma Payton and our beloved friend.  She passed away after filming in January, 2008.  God Bless You!

**Jerry, Georgia and Rod Morrell:**  They allowed us to film their stories; they are relatives of Luzernia and Silas Morrell.  Rod has really supported our book.  Thank You!

**Elva O'Neal:**  Mother to Gaylen Robison and is the grand-daughter of William Henry Long.  She helped with so many stories.  SHE IS A STAR!

**Sherma Payton:**  My Treasure in Tremonton and a dear friend... Sherma contributed the Bill Long photo, Viola letter, as well as Bill's sister's picture.  PRICELESS!

**Diann and Jerry Peck:**  Etta Forsyth is Diann's mother.  Diann and Jerry shared their home and guest room as well as photos and stories.  I Love You!

**Gaylen and Idonna Robison:**  Gaylen is the great grandson of William Henry Long.  Elva is Gaylen's mother and Bill Long is Elva's grandfather.  Elva is Viola's daughter.  Gaylen and his wife Idonna, gave us many important stories!  THE LONE TREE DANCE by Art Davidson is their find.

**There are more folks to thank and you know your role... Thanks everyone!**

# MY LIFE STORY

Sharing "My Life Story" will help you understand how much I love history and most importantly, "The 'Wild Bunch' Mystery!" My mother June enjoyed reading "The Wild Bunch" by James Horan. We watched the movie, "BUTCH CASSIDY & THE SUNDANCE KID" together and both read the book. How can you escape the stories about "The Wild Bunch" when you live in Utah? Everyone seems curious as to whether "Butch and Sundance" died in Bolivia, or returned to the States?

They filmed the "Hollywood" movie, "Butch Cassidy & The Sundance Kid" here in Southern Utah. I live in St. George, Utah. Just three months ago, I traveled to Grafton, Utah where they filmed the bicycle scene. Paul Newman and Katharine Ross are riding around the "turn of the century" house while Robert Redford is sleeping inside. The song, "Raindrops Keep Falling On My Head," (sung by B.J. Thomas) plays throughout the scene. Paul does some crazy stunts on his bicycle and he crashes into the fence. An angry bull chases him and his life is in danger! "Etta and Butch" jump on the bicycle for a quick get away!

What a blast to finally see the set where over 40 years ago, they filmed "Hollywood's" most successful movie, "Butch Cassidy & The Sundance Kid." What a "fantastic" day! Movies are in my blood and I cannot get enough of "The Wild Bunch."

Growing up in Clearfield, Utah… my mother always grew an organic garden. Every summer our family would make homemade strawberry milk shakes, fresh from the garden. My mother taught home economics at Roy High. My mother could cook, restaurant quality, and she is not only a seamstress, but did upholstery and tailoring. We lived in Clearfield until I turned 16, and then we moved to Rexberg, Idaho.

My father Rex purchased a three story, Idamont Hotel, and turned it into a boy's dorm for 70 college students. In 1968, I am the only girl living in a boy's dorm. I became completely overwhelmed with the turn of events and I felt like my whole life had been turned upside down. My two older sisters were attending college at Brigham Young University in Provo, Utah. I have a younger brother and my family lived in the hotel. My heart broke when I left the only home I had ever known and moved to Idaho.

I vividly remember my father throwing my shoes in a chest of drawers and then the moving company lost the chest of drawers, and "MY SHOES!" My father insisted that I go to school the next day and all I had to wear were old tennis shoes. What a scene to show up in the principal's office with old worn out shoes. Looking back on my teenage years, I can laugh, but at the time I could have just crawled into a hole and stayed there… I felt so humiliated!

In 1970 I graduated from Madison High and won an art scholarship to Ricks College, now renamed BYU-Idaho. I studied interior decorating and advanced tailoring. My courses in decorating and tailoring were my favorite, but when it came to biology, I just could not do the whole "cutting up frogs" thing! I ended up dropping out of biology. I loved college and did well there.

Then I married my college sweetheart in 1972, who just happened to be one of the 70 males in my father's dorm. We are the parents of three beautiful children. My daughter Tiffany is married and lives in Hollywood, California. My middle child Sterling is married to Mindy and they have four children, Brandon, Arianna, Cameron and Danelle. My youngest son Adrian lives in Austin, Texas. Even though my marriage ended in 1989, I stay connected to my family. I spend a lot of time with my son Sterling and his family who live just an hour away in Cedar City, Utah. Sterling and Mindy have been a great support since May of 1997 and we have shared each other's joys and helped each other when things were not so smooth. We are "family!" We love and support each other!

When our documentary TEAM made the front page of "The Deseret News," my son Sterling bought copies and showed them to all the folks at his work. What an exciting day for our family.

When we were on KSL EVENING NEWS with John Hollenhorst in 2008, my son Sterling and his wife Mindy stayed up to watch the interview. Mindy said they both fell asleep; it had been a very busy day. When the news came on, "A body has been exhumed in the Duchesne City Cemetery that is believed to be the Sundance Kid," they both woke up and were glued to the television. They were so excited that their "Mother" had been featured on the evening news. They called me right after the interview ended... so thrilled to see me on TV! Our TEAM changed history that day.

Back to my parent's boy's dorm in Rexburg, Idaho. My mother and father moved to Provo, Utah when they received a financial settlement from the Bureau of Land Management, after the Teton Dam flooded and destroyed the boy's dorm. The Teton Dam failed at 11:57 AM on June 5, 1976. My father had a cabin in the mountains, and my mother stayed on the 3rd floor until she received a settlement. I lived in Provo, Utah with my husband and two small children, so my parents bought a home right across the street from the Provo Temple. They lived there for 32 years, until both passed away.

Their home is just 20 minutes away from Robert Redford's, "Sundance Ski Resort." My favorite memory of "Sundance" is going horseback riding on my 28th Birthday. On that day, Robert Redford's children, Jamie and Amy, were working at the stables and saddled my horse for me; they were just kids when they worked there. How could I not see that they were Robert Redford's children with that "mop" of strawberry blond hair? Then I headed to "Stewart Falls" where the spray of water takes your breath away. "Sundance Resort" is my favorite place on earth! When you are in the mountains you get a "natural high" from being at such a high elevation. I dream of one day owning my own home in "Sundance," surrounded by nature. I would love it if my family joined me in "Sundance" to create more special memories.

My mother loved the "Wild Bunch." I now own her copy of "The Wild Bunch" by James Horan. Did they die in Bolivia or return to the United States? I started my research at the BYU Library in May of 1997... reading everything I could get my hands on about the "Wild Bunch." I read everything in the entire library and I now have an extensive library of my own. I have read every book ever written on "Sundance, Butch, and Etta."

It is now March 27, 2017... years later and I have worked with Dr. John McCullough our anthropologist and a terrific film crew. Our Team has worked with many experts that have helped us to solve the mystery.

"Sundance Resort" is where I love to play, but the "Sundance Film Festival" in Park City, Utah is where I worked on my career as a film maker. I have enjoyed attending the "Film Makers Lodge" during the Festival. Meeting Robert Redford and listening to his wisdom and knowledge on film making has been an opportunity of a lifetime.

It has all come full circle and we have enough research to prove our case. "Sundance and Butch" did not die in Bolivia! Two American Yankees were killed in Bolivia and Percy Siebert, an American Engineer working for the Bolivia Tin Mines, said that the two American bandits were "Butch and Sundance." He told the authorities that the two dead outlaws were "Butch and Sundance," but he had not physically identified the bodies. Percy probably knew where "Butch and Sundance" were... at the time. Percy became friends with Robert LeRoy Parker, "Butch Cassidy" and Harry Alonzo Longabaugh, "The Sundance Kid." He knew how much they wanted out of the outlaw life, so he lied to the authorities to help them escape. The Pinkerton's were also tired and frustrated at never being able to capture the outlaws, so they closed the books on the case.

William Henry Long is the missing piece; his family hid him out among the Mormon communities of Loa, Fremont, and Duchesne, Utah. Lula Parker Betenson said that her brother, Robert LeRoy Parker, (Bob) came back to visit the family in 1925. Bill Long disappeared for four days in 1925; no one dared ask where he went. Grandma Long said it is about a woman and it's "okay" with her; then she went in her room and pulled her apron over her head and pouted for four days, until Bill returned.

It in 1925, at Josie Bassett's 50th birthday party, they dared to be re-united in Indian Canyon outside of Price, Utah. Sundance, Butch, Etta Place, Matt Warner, and others, had a "secret" rendezvous with the "Gang" to celebrate Josie's birthday. Everyone kept watch to make sure they didn't get caught. They must have had one "Heck" of a party! Then they slipped back into their "Secret Lives!"

I have kept a journal since June, 2007. I have written daily all the events that have taken place to solve the mystery. I absolutely love doing research, moving the project forward, and hunting down clues. We have worked as a TEAM and it is time to share our research! The physical evidence is complete, we have DNA and DNA Genealogy to prove our case.

My favorite part of the story is where "Butch Cassidy" has a face lift in Paris, France. It makes sense that Robert LeRoy Parker... so, recognizable... he could not return to the United States unless he altered his appearance.

Harry Alonzo Longabaugh knew he could return to his family in Fremont, Utah because his family and friends would never betray his identity. Ann Bassett, "Etta Place," returned to her parent's ranch in Browns Park on the Utah/Colorado border. They all "three" returned to the United States and lived out their lives to a ripe old age.

"The Bassett Ranch" is where Ann and "Sundance" first started dating. I believe Ann to be Harry's first love at age 17. Ann lied to her family and friends to hide the fact that she became, "Etta Place." The "Trio" had so many adventures together as friends and lovers, but if they valued their lives, they could not be seen together "ever" again!

"My Life Story" has been changed forever and what an adventure I have been on while solving "The Wild Bunch Mystery!"


*Marilyn Grace*

# CAST OF CHARACTERS

**Josiah Longabaugh and 4 year old son Harry**: Josiah Longabaugh married Ann Place in Pennsylvania. They had 5 children and their youngest son, Harry Alonzo Longabaugh, became the West's most notorious outlaw "The Sundance Kid." Harry Alonzo Longabaugh, born "about spring" of 1867 in Mont Clare, Pennsylvania.

**Ann Place Longabaugh:** Annie Place... "The Sundance Kid's" mother. Ann... a religious woman and died when "Sundance" is young.

**Harvey Sylvester Longabaugh:** Harvey Sylvester is "The Sundance Kid's" brother. Harvey's oldest son is William Henry Longabaugh... (William Henry Long) born October 28, 1893. William Henry Long appears at the Hogan Ranch in Loa, Utah, October 1893. The William Henry Long/William Henry Longabaugh connection.

**Samanna & Emma Longabaugh**: Harry Longabaugh's sisters as well as William Henry Long's sisters. They are the same people. (Dr. John McCullough's photo comparison. They are the same women, just pictures of Samanna and Emma when they were young and middle aged women. William Henry Long's photo is when they were young.) Donna and Paul Ernst own the picture of Samanna and Emma when they are older.

**George, Mary & Walter C. Longenbaugh Families**: At age 14, Harry Longabaugh helped Cousin George and his pregnant wife Mary, along with their two-year-old son, Walter, cross the plains in a covered wagon so they could homestead in Cortez, Colorado. Longenbaugh is spelled with an "en" but they are still related.

**William Henry Long:** William Henry Long appeared at the Hogan Ranch in Loa, Utah, in 1893. He had the clothes off his back and had a job as a horse breaker for 2 dollars a day.

**Silas Morrell:** A Mormon Pioneer that married Luzernia Allred and settled in Fremont, Utah. Silas and Luzernia were the parents of 7 children.

**Luzernia Allred Morrell:** After Silas Morrell dies, Luzernia is courted and marries William Henry Long and they have two girls of their own; Viola and Evinda.

**Florence Viola & Evinda Ann Long:** The daughters of Luzernia and Bill Long. As adults, Viola and Evinda want to know if William Henry Long is their father's real name. Luzernia's genealogy could be traced back to James Allred, "The Prophet Joseph Smith's" body guard, but nothing that their father had told them can be verified. Viola wonders if his name is "Long?" (See Florence Viola letter)

**Irwin Robison:** Clara Morrell's husband and Etta's father.

**Clara Morrell Robison:** Luzernia and Silas Morrell's daughter and wife of Irwin G. Robison. Clara and Irwin name their daughter "Etta."

**Etta Robison:** Daughter of Clara and Irwin Robison. "Etta" is teased by Grandpa Billy Long that she had been named after "The Sundance Kid's" girlfriend, "Etta Place."

**Cussin' Charlie & Aunt Mary:** Mary is Luzernia and Silas Morrell's oldest daughter. She married Charley and they nick named him, "Cussin' Charley" because every other word out of his mouth is a swear word. Charley joined Grandpa Billy Long and ran with "THE WILD BUNCH." Cussin' Charley is an outlaw with Grandpa Billy Long.

**Butch Cassidy:** An alias for Robert LeRoy Parker, a Mormon boy from Circleville, Utah. Butch Cassidy formed "The Wild Bunch."

**Sundance Kid:** An alias for Harry Alonzo Longabaugh of Mont Clare, Pennsylvania, Butch Cassidy's first member of his gang.

**Etta Place:** An alias for Ann Bassett, "Queen of the Cattle Rustlers" of Browns Park on the Utah/Colorado border, "Sundance's" first love.

**Percy Siebert:**   Head of the Bolivian Tin Mines and Robert LeRoy Parker and Harry Alonzo Longabaugh's employer.  He said the bodies of two bandits in Bolivia were "Butch and Sundance" so they could escape.

**Matt Warner:**  Former member of "The Wild Bunch" and became sheriff of Price, Utah and authored the book "Last of the Bandit Riders."

**Ann Parker & William Thadeus Phillips:**  Photo Comparison.  Ann Parker is Robert LeRoy Parker's (Butch Cassidy) mother.  William Thadeus Phillips is an alias for "Butch Cassidy."  Notice the family resemblance.

**Silas Morrell Family:**  Silas and Luzernia have a photo taken with their 6 children just before Silas passes away.  Silas suffered with a broken back.

(See Photo Album)

# FOLLOW THE CLUES

There have been motion pictures, documentaries, and books produced about "Butch Cassidy & The Sundance Kid." Many heated debates have taken place among those obsessed with unraveling the mystery of how they died. "The Sundance Kid's" real name is Harry Alonzo Longabaugh... a larger-than-life outlaw who carried on a notorious affair with an attractive and equally infamous female outlaw, "Etta Place." Many believed, and the major motion picture portrayed that "Butch Cassidy" and his partner in crime, "Sundance," died in a gun fight in Bolivia, November 6, 1908. The rumors abound that their deaths in South America did not take place at all! "Butch and Sundance" secretly returned to the United States to live out the rest of their lives in obscurity.

Did "Sundance" return to the part of the United States that he is most familiar with and become an ordinary rancher? Did he settle down and live out the rest of his years as a loving husband, father, and grandfather; speaking of his past to no one while taking the secrets of his outlaw life with him to the grave?

Some of the descendants of a man buried in 1936, in a cemetery in Duchesne, Utah believe so. They, along with others, are passionate about solving the mystery of "The Sundance Kid." We have all come together, each bringing a piece of the puzzle to find out, if indeed, William Henry Long really is Harry Alonzo Longabaugh, "The Sundance Kid."

I first became interested in trying to solve this puzzle after watching the NOVA documentary: "WANTED: Butch and Sundance" in 1997. Clyde Snow, an anthropologist from Oklahoma, had gone to Bolivia to exhume what he thought were the bodies of "Butch and Sundance." The skeletal remains were flown to the Oklahoma State Coroner's Office in Oklahoma City for examination. Chris Boles, a Molecular Biologist, did the DNA testing and determined that the remains were not those of the two famous outlaws.

Among those who asserted that "Butch and Sundance" were not killed in Bolivia... Butch Cassidy's sister, Lula Parker Betenson. In 1975, just a few years before she died, wrote a book entitled, "Butch Cassidy, My Brother." In her book, she made clear that she would be breaking a forty-year silence, to set the record straight about her legendary brother. Lula clarified details about her outlaw brothers visit with the family in Circleville, Utah in 1925, many years after they were supposed to have been killed in Bolivia.

I became fascinated! I could not stop wondering what really happened to these famous outlaws. After I read everything about them, I started contacting individuals who were descendants and others, just as eager to figure out the real ending to the story of America's most famous outlaws. I kept following the clues and I interviewed anyone I thought could help. I started collecting information and began putting the pieces together. In 2000, while living in Heber City, Utah... I finally decided that I had gathered enough information. I knew it would be a matter of time before I would be able to complete my quest of finding out what really happened to "Butch and Sundance."

Now I needed to hire a director who would help me develop the project. I started interviewing directors and found Michael Karr. We had arranged for a meeting to discuss our project. At our first meeting, I shared with Mike my own background in film making and the essence of the project I had been working on. Mike loved the idea and became equally enthused with the prospect of helping create a documentary about the world-famous outlaws.

In June 2007 I came across a website of a man who believed that his step great-grandfather could be... "The Sundance Kid."  On the web-site... a picture of his step great-grandfather, William Henry Long, of Loa, Fremont, and Duchesne, Utah.  William Long's picture next to a picture of "The Sundance Kid" in the famous "Fort Worth Five" photo... similarities were remarkable.  I immediately contacted Judy and Jerry Nickle and I talked to them about my own desire to find out what really happened to "Butch and Sundance."

One month later, I found myself in remote Loa, Utah as guests of Judy and Jerry Nickle.  Jerry told me that he has long suspected that his step great-grandfather, William Henry Long, may be... "The Sundance Kid."  It dawned on me as I interviewed and met with other descendants of William Henry Long that solving the mystery would be more than just a documentary, but that it would also put the pieces of their family's historical puzzle together.  For three generations, the family has had no idea who Bill Long really is or exactly where he came from.  Now I became determined to find out exactly what happened!

The Nickle's invited me to a family reunion to meet all the folks that knew William Henry Long the week of July 4th, 2007.  I arrived in Loa, Utah and checked into Loa's only motel, "Snuggle Inn." The next day I found myself on a four-wheel drive excursion.  Our group bumped around the rugged terrain that "Butch and Sundance" knew like the backs of their hands.  We were in search of legendary gold! Family stories tell of a map that William Henry Long drew revealing the exact location of hidden treasure.  Bill Long had hidden "gold coins" many years before.  He said he's too old to go out in such desolate country and find the treasure on his own.  The "gold" is hidden by a double rock formation. We searched, but could not find the treasure.  The terrain, rugged and so daunting; we finally decided to turn back.  We headed back to our comfortable motel for a hot bath and dinner.  We had fun talking about how we all had "Gold Fever!"

I stayed in Loa for seven days and worked out all the details for producing a documentary about William Henry Long's life.  We met with Michael Karr our director a month later and we began filming on September 15, 2007.

What a wild ride our TEAM has been on and what a fun beginning to see where Luzernia and Bill Long lived and raised their family!  I loved all the stories!

We have followed the clues and when it is all said and done, we have discovered that the "real treasure" is in making new friends and discovering the truth about what really happened to "Butch, Sundance, and Etta!"

*Marilyn Grace*

# CHAPTERS

# CHAPTER ONE
## Butch, Sundance, & Etta

Robert Leroy Parker, born on April 13, 1866 in Beaver Utah. He is better known as "Butch Cassidy" and is the most notorious outlaw in western history. As leader of the "WILD BUNCH GANG," he became history's most successful outlaw and robbed an equivalent of 2.5 million dollars in about a ten-year span of time. The Pinkerton Detective Agency pursued him to the point that he is forced to flee with an accomplice, Harry Alonzo Longabaugh, known as "The Sundance Kid," and Longabaugh's girlfriend, "Etta Place." The trio fled to Argentina and then to Bolivia to escape capture or death.

Ann Campbell Gillies and Maximillian Parker, English Immigrants who came to the Utah Territory in the late 1850's as Mormon Pioneers are the parents of Butch Cassidy.

Ann Gillies, the mother of Robert Leroy Parker, alias, Butch Cassidy, lived and is born in Tyneside Newcastle, North East England and moved to America with her parents in 1850. She married Maximillian Parker in Utah.

Maximillian Parker's parents were Robert and Ann (Hartley) Parker, also lived in England. Robert Parker, born March 29, 1820 in Burnley, Lancashire, England and died February 24, 1901 in St. George Utah. Robert Parker is buried in the Washington, Utah cemetery, alongside his wife Ann, born on March 22, 1819 in Lancashire, England. Ann died on January 25, 1899 in Washington, Utah. I have pictures of their headstone and I live in St. George, Utah right next to Washington, Utah. What a surprise to see "Butch Cassidy's" grandfather and grandmother buried in my home town.

Robert and Ann Parker lived on Victoria Road in Preston, Lancashire, England. Thomas Parker is Robert Parker's father and he had entered a business relationship with a cousin by the name of John Dickens, father of the future novelist Charles Dickens.

Their business failed and both Dickens and Parker were sent to Marshalsea Prison in Southwark. Family stories state that Robert Parker ended up on the streets of London, starving and homeless. He would beg and steal to support his mother. Family members believe that Charles Dickens used Robert Parker as the main character in his novel, "Oliver Twist." I had to include that part of Butch Cassidy's history because "Oliver Twist" is one of my favorite movies. The music is just wonderful! "Where Is Love?" is such a BEAUTIFUL SONG!

While working as a master weaver in the woolen mills in the city of Manchester, Robert Parker joined The Church of Jesus Christ of Latter Day Saints, also known as the Mormon's.

In 1855 Robert Parker brought his wife and children to the United States and arrived in Utah with the Martin handcart company of Mormon Pioneers.

Ann and Maximillian Parker named Robert Leroy Parker, after his grandfather. Robert Leroy Parker is the oldest of 13 children. Butch Cassidy grew up on a ranch in Circleville, Utah south of Salt Lake City, Utah.

Robert Leroy Parker left home in his teens, and while working on a dairy farm, he met his mentor and cattle rustler, Mike Cassidy, (an alias for John Tolliver "J. T." McClammy). Shortly after his association with Mike Cassidy, Robert LeRoy Parker changed his name to Butch Cassidy, in honor of his friend Mike Cassidy who died in a shootout.

### 1880 –1887 — First incidents, becoming a robber

Around 1880 Butch Cassidy went to a clothier shop in another town. He found the shop closed and he took a pair of jeans and some pie. He left an IOU promising to pay on his next visit. The clothier pressed charges and he is acquitted by a jury for his first offense is minor.

He moved to Telluride, (Nick named, "To Hell You Ride") Colorado and continued to work on ranches until 1884. Butch may have been in Telluride to seek work but perhaps to deliver stolen horses to buyers. He returned to Telluride in 1887 and led a cowboy's life in Montana and Wyoming where he met Matt Warner. Matt owned a race horse. They raced horses at various events and they divided the winnings between them.

### 1889 – 1895 — Early robberies, going to prison

Cassidy and Warner robbed a bank on June 24, 1889 with two of the McCarty Brothers at the San Miguel Valley Bank in Telluride in which they stole approximately $21,000. They fled to Roberts Roost in southeastern Utah to hideout.

The Hole-in-the-Wall is a natural geological formation which afforded outlaws protection and cover from the law. The Wild Bunch Gang could rob a bank and head to The-Hole-in-the-Wall and they knew they were safe. Law enforcement knew that if they tried to go after Butch Cassidy and his gang, they were dead men. Cassidy purchased a ranch in 1890 near Dubois, Wyoming. It is possible that Cassidy only purchased the ranch for stealing horses and cattle. The operation never became successful.

Our TEAM at Story Teller Productions had a book signing for "Finding Butch Cassidy & The Sundance Kid" at Willow Creek Ranch at The Hole-in-the-Wall, July 2nd and 3rd, 2012. I can see how they could hide from the law. It is so remote! We had such a wonderful time at Willow Creek Ranch. The Hole-in-the-Wall is the only reason they were able steal 2.5 Million Dollars equivalent in our day. The relay horses and heading to the Hole-in-the-Wall guaranteed their success.

Butch Cassidy became romantically involved with Ann Basset, a rancher's daughter. Her father Herb Bassett did business with Cassidy and supplied him with fresh horses and beef. That same year Cassidy is arrested at Lander, Wyoming for stealing horses and possibly for running a protection racket that included the local ranchers. Then Cassidy is imprisoned in the Wyoming State Prison in Laramie, Wyoming. He served 18 months of his two-year sentence and release, January 1896. He promised Governor William Alford Richards that he would not again offend in the state in return for a partial remission of his sentence. Upon his release, he became involved with Ann Bassett's older sister Josie Bassett. Then he returned to his romance with Ann.

### 1896 – 1897 — Leaving prison and forming "The Wild Bunch"

Cassidy's mug shot from the Wyoming Territorial Prison in 1894 and his photo in the famous FORT WORTH FIVE photo are in our photo album.

When Cassidy is released from prison, he associated with a circle of criminals, most notably his closest friend Elzy Lay, Harvey "Kid Curry" Logan, Ben Kilpatrick, Harry Tracy, Will "News" Carver, Laura Bullion, and George Curry, who formed a gang known as "The Wild Bunch." Cassidy's criminal activities escalated. There is no historical record of any of its members of the Wild Bunch being charged with murder.

Cassidy, Lay, Harvey Logan and Bob Meeks robbed the bank at Montpelier, Idaho on August 13, 1886 escaping with approximately $7,000. He recruited Harry Alonzo Longabaugh, alias, "The Sundance Kid," a native of Pennsylvania, into "The Wild Bunch."

Ann Bassett joined Cassidy at Robbers Roost in early 1897 for an off and on again romance. Elzy Lay and Lay's girlfriend Maud Davis joined them. They all hid out there until early April, when Lay and Cassidy sent the women home so they could plan their next robbery. Cassidy and Lay ambushed a small group of men in the mining town of Castle Gate, Utah on April 21, 1897. They ambushed a small group of men carrying the payroll of the Pleasant Valley Coal Company for the railroad station to their office, stealing a sack containing $7,000 in gold. They fled to Robbers Roost.

Their most famous robbery took place on June 2, 1899 when the gang robbed a Union Pacific overland flyer near Wilcox, Wyoming. The robbery became famous and which resulted in a massive man hunt. Many notable lawmen of the day took part in the hunt for the robbers. The law never found them.

Following the Wilcox robbery, both Kid Curry and George Curry shot and killed Sheriff Joe Hazen. Tom Horn, a noted killer for hire and a contract employee of the Pinkerton Detective Agency... obtained information from explosives expert Bill Speck that revealed that they had shot Hazen, which Horn passed on to Pinkerton Detective Charlie Siringo. The gang escaped into the Hole-in-the-Wall. Siringo is sent to capture the outlaw gang. He became friends with Elfie Landusky, who started going by the last name of Curry. By alleging that Lonny Curry, Kid Curry's brother, had gotten her pregnant, Siringo intended to locate the gang.

Elzy Lay and others were involved in a train robbery near Folsom, New Mexico on July 11, 1899 which Cassidy may have planned. Cassidy may have been directly involved, which led to a shootout with local law enforcers in which Lay, Cassidy's best friend and closest confidant, killed Sheriff Edward Farr and posse man Henry Love, leading to life in prison in the New Mexico State Penitentiary.

The Wild Bunch Gang usually would split up after a robbery and head to "The Hole-in-the-Wall" hideout, "Robbers Roost," or Madame Fannie Porter's brothel in San Antonio, Texas. The Hole-in-the-Wall hideout has been assembled at Old Trail Town in Cody, Wyoming. The cabin, built in 1883 by Alexander Ghent.

## Failed attempt at amnesty

There is the possibility because of the loss of Lay, that Cassidy approached the Governor of Utah, Heber Wells, (Utah had joined the Union in 1896) to negotiate amnesty. Wells appears to have declined amnesty for Cassidy and instead suggested that he approach the Union Pacific Railroad to persuade them to drop their criminal complaints against him. The meeting for amnesty never happened. Butch felt like he had been stood up, so his attempt at amnesty never came about.

E. H. Harriman the chairman of The Union Pacific Railroad subsequently attempted to meet with Cassidy through former member of the Wild Bunch, Matt Warner, who had been released from prison. Cassidy, Longabaugh and others robbed a Union Pacific train near Tipton, Wyoming on August 29, 1900 violating Cassidy's earlier promise to the governor of Wyoming not to offend again in the state. That ended all hope of amnesty for Butch Cassidy.

In the meantime, there were attempts to arrest Kid Curry's brother Lonny Curry at his aunt's home on February 28, 1900. Lonny died in a shootout that followed and his cousin Bob Lees ended up in prison for rustling in Wyoming. Kid Curry and Bill Carver were pursued by posse out of St. Johns, Apache County, Arizona after being identified as passing notes possibly from the Wilcox, Wyoming robbery on March 28, 1900. A posse caught up with them and shots were fired, during which Deputy Andrew Gibbons and Deputy Frank LeSueur were killed. Carver and Curry escaped. George Curry is killed in a shootout with Grand County, Utah Sheriff John Tyler and Deputy Sam Jenkins on April 17. On May 26, Kid Curry rode into Moab, Utah and killed Tyler and Jenkins in a brazen shootout, in retaliation for the killing of George Curry and for the death of his brother Lonny. On September 19, 1900 Cassidy, Longabaugh and Bill Carver traveled to Winnemucca, Nevada where they robbed the First National Bank of Winnemucca. They robbed a total of $32,640. In December, Cassidy posed in the famous Fort Worth, Texas for the now-famous Fort Worth Five Photograph; which depicts Parker, Longabaugh, Harvey Logan (alias Kid Curry) Ben Kilpatrick, and William Carver. The photo began to be used by the Pinkerton Detective Agency for its latest wanted posters.

Kid Curry and a group of men had gathered to rob the Great Northern train near Wagner, Montana on July 3, 1901. They took $60,000 in cash. The gang split up and gang member Will Carver is killed by one pursuing posse led by Sheriff Elijah Briant. On December 12, 1901 gang member Ben Kilpatrick is captured in Knoxville, Tennessee along with Laura Bullion. Kid Curry killed Knoxville policemen William Dinwiddle and Robert Saylor on December 13, and Curry escaped. In a bold move, despite being pursued by Pinkerton agent and other law enforcement officials, Curry returned to Montana where he shot and killed rancher James Winters who is responsible for killing his brother Johnny years ago.

## 1901 — Travel to South America

Butch Cassidy and The Sundance Kid fled to New York City on February 20, 1901 with Etta Place, Longabaugh's female companion. They boarded the British steamer Herminius with the destination of Buenos Aires, Argentina. Butch Cassidy posed as James Ryan, Etta Place's fictional brother. Cassidy settled down with Longabaugh and Place in a four-room log cabin on a 15,000-acre ranch, purchased on the east band of the Rio Blanco near Cholila, Chubut province in west-central Argentina, near the Andes.

## 1905 — His last years and his biggest robbery, evading the law

Two English-speaking bandits, who may have been Cassidy and Longabaugh, robbed the Banco de Tarapaca y Argentine in Gallego, 700 miles south of Cholila, near the Strait of Magellan on February 14, 1905. They escaped with a total of what would be worth at least $100,000 today, the pair vanished north across the bleak Patagonian steppes.

On May 1, 1905, the trio sold the Cholila ranch because the law began to hunt them down. The Pinkerton Agency knew their location for a long time, but the rainy season had prevented their assigned agent, Frank Dimaio, from traveling there and making an arrest and capturing the trio. Governor Julio Lezana issued an arrest warrant, but before it could be executed, Sheriff Edward Humphrey's, a Welsh Argentine... friendly with Cassidy and infatuated with Etta Place, tipped them off.

Butch, Sundance, and Etta, fled north to San Carlos de Bariloche where they embarked on the steamer "Concor" across Nahuel Huapi Lake and into Chile. However, by the end of that year they were again back in Argentina; on December 19, 1905, Cassidy, Longabaugh, Place and an unknown male (possibly Harvey Logan) took part in the robbery of the Banco de la Nacion in Villa Mercedes, 400 miles west of Buenos Aires, taking 12,000 pesos. Pursued by armed lawmen, they crossed the Pampas and the Andes and again reaching the safety of Chile.

Etta Place decided that she wanted out of the outlaw life and would travel back to San Francisco with Longabaugh.

A letter written by Sundance, found in 1997... written in 1905... to their neighbor on their ranch states, "Etta and I have had it with this place. We are leaving for San Francisco never to return again."

Longabaugh went back to Bolivia and Butch and Sundance obtained work at the Concordia Tin Mine in the Santa Vera Cruz range of the central Bolivian Andes. Their main duties included guarding the company payroll.

## Butch Cassidy's Death

The facts surrounding Butch Cassidy's death are uncertain. On November 6, 1908 near San Vicente in southern Bolivia a courier for the Aramayo Franke and Cia Silver Mine took the company's payroll, worth about 15,000 Bolivian pesos, by mule. He is attacked and robbed by two masked American bandits. They were believed to be Cassidy and Longabaugh. The bandits then proceeded to the small mining town of San Vicente where they lodged in a small boarding house owned by a local resident miner named Bonifacio Casasola. When Casasola became suspicious of his two foreign lodgers, as well as a mule they had in their possession which came from the Aramayo Mine, identifiable from the mine company logo on the mule's left flank. Casasola left his house and notified a nearby telegraph officer who notified a small Bolivian Army cavalry unit stationed nearby, which is the Abaroa Regiment. The unit dispatched three soldiers, under the command of Captain Justo Concha, to San Vicente where they notified the local authorities. On the evening of November 6, the lodging house, they were surrounded by three soldiers, the police chief, the local mayor and some of his officials, who intended to arrest the Aramayo robbers.

When the three soldiers approached the house the bandits opened fire, killing one of the soldiers and wounding another. A gunfight then ensued. At around 2 a.m., during a lull in the firing, the police and soldiers heard a man screaming from inside the house. Soon, a single shot rang out from inside the house, whereupon the screaming stopped. Minutes later, another shot.

The standoff continued as locals kept the place surrounded until the next morning when, cautiously entering, they found two dead bodies, both with numerous bullet wounds to the arms and legs. One of the men had a bullet wound in the forehead and the other had a bullet hole in the temple. The local police report speculated that, judging from the positions of the bodies; one bandit had probably shot his fatally wounded partner-in-crime to put him out of his misery, just before killing himself with his final bullet.

In the following investigation by the Tupiza police, the bandits were identified as the men who robbed the Aramayo payroll transport, but the Bolivian authorities didn't know their real names, nor could they positively identify them. The bodies were buried at the small San Vicente cemetery, where they were buried close to the grave of a German miner named Gustav Zimmer. Although attempts have been made to find their unmarked graves, notably by the American forensic anthropologist Clyde Snow and his researchers in 1992, no remains with DNA matching the living relatives of Cassidy and Longabaugh have yet been discovered.

# Claims of post-1908 survival

However, there were claims, such as by Cassidy's sister Lula Parker Betenson that he returned alive to the United States and lived in anonymity for years. In her biography "Butch Cassidy, My Brother," Betenson cites several instances of people familiar with Cassidy who encountered him long after 1908, and she relates a detailed impromptu "family reunion" of Butch, their brother Mark, their father Maxi, and Lula in 1925. In 1974 or 1975, Red Fenwick, a columnist at The Denver Post told writer Ivan Goldman, then a reporter at the "Post," that he had been acquainted with Cassidy's physician. Fenwick said she is a person of absolute integrity. She told Fenwick that she had continued to treat Cassidy for many years after he supposedly had been killed in Bolivia.

In his Annals of the Former World, John McPhee repeats a story told to geologist David Love in the 1930s by Love's family doctor, Francis Smith, M.D., when Love is a doctoral student. Smith stated that he had just seen Cassidy who told him that his face had been altered by a surgeon in Paris, and that he showed Smith a repaired bullet wound that Smith recognized as work he had previously done on Cassidy.

In an interview with Josie Bassett, sister to Ann Bassett, in 1960 she claims that Cassidy came to visit her in the 1920s "after returning from South America" and that "Butch died in Johnnie, Nevada, about 15 years earlier. Another interview with locals of Cassidy's hometown of Circleville, Utah also finds claims of Cassidy working in Nevada until his death.

Western historian Charles Kelly closed the chapter "Is Butch Cassidy Dead?" in his 1938 book, "Outlaw Trail," by observing that, "If Cassidy is still alive, as these rumors claim, it seems exceedingly strange that he has not returned to Circleville, Utah to visit his old father Maximillian Parker, who died on July 28, 1938, at the age of 94 years." Kelly is thought to have interviewed Parker's father, but no known transcript of such an interview exists.

## Aliases

Butch Cassidy

- George Parker
- George Cassidy
- Lowe Maxwell
- James "Santiago" Maxwell
- James Ryan
- Butch Cassidy
- Santiago Lowe

# William T. Phillips
## (1863 – 1937)

Dr. John McCullough of the University of Utah Anthropology department did photo transparencies of William T. Phillips and Butch Cassidy. With science, Dr. McCullough proves that they are one in the same person. Butch Cassidy... so recognizable... he could not come back to the United States or he would be captured or killed. The photo comparison proves that William Thadeus Phillips went under the knife for drastic plastic surgery. He had his nose, ears and jawline changed. Dr. John McCullough puts his 40-year career and reputation on the line that Butch Cassidy is William T. Phillips.

The "Flash of Genius" that solved the mystery: "When I started studying THE BANDIT INVINCIBLE 200-page document, I realized that William Phillips said that Butch went to Paris, France and had a facelift. I then compared the transparencies of Phillips and Cassidy and I could see that the eyes matched, the measurements matched, but the nose, ears and jaw line did not match.

Also, Phillips chin has a distinctive WELT that is vertical and very unusual. I did research and found the plastic surgeon that would have been able to do the surgery in 1907. Dr. Louis Ombredanne (March 5, 1871 – 1956) is a French pediatric and plastic surgeon born in Paris. He is the son of general practitioner Dr. Emile Ombredanne.

In 1902 he became surgeon to Parisian hospitals, becoming a professor of surgery in 1907. Dr. Louis Ombredanne... on the cutting edge of plastic surgery because of all of the wars. He created a prototype of an inhaler as a safe anesthetic device after two fatal anesthetic accidents.

Butch Cassidy went to Paris, France and had drastic plastic surgery to hide his appearance. William Henry Long, an alias for Harry Alonzo Longabaugh, The Sundance Kid, came back from an 8 to 10-year absence speaking fluent French.

Butch and Sundance went to Paris, France for an estimated 1 to 2 years. Butch Cassidy returned to the United States and went to Spokane, Washington. Phillips married Gertrude Livesay. They married in May of 1908. Butch Cassidy arrived in Spokane in 1907.

William Thadeus Phillips founded the Phillips Manufacturing Company. Things went downhill during the 1929 Great Depression and Phillips lost his business and is close to being bankrupt. He made a few desperate trips back to Utah and Wyoming in hopes of finding buried cashes, but came back empty handed. I think Sundance found the gold coins first.

In 1929 he wrote 'The Bandit Invincible' The Life of Butch Cassidy. He tried to sell the 200-page manuscript, but now one purchased his treatment. He could not reveal he is Butch Cassidy, so no one wanted his manuscript.

Phillips is diagnosed with stomach cancer and died July 20, 1937 in Spokane, Washington.

Private Collector Brent Ashworth of Provo, Utah owns the original 'The Bandit Invincible' document that is typed on William T. Phillips letterhead.
(Photo Gallery shows a picture of "The Bandit Invincible" by William T. Phillips.)

Our research proves with science, that William Thadeus Phillips is an alias for Robert Leroy Parker, alias, Butch Cassidy."

*Marilyn Grace*

(Photo Gallery includes transparencies completed by Dr. John McCullough)

# Sundance Kid
(About Spring of 1867 – November 7, 1908)

Harry Alonzo Longabaugh, better known as The Sundance Kid, became a member of Butch Cassidy's "Wild Bunch" in the American Old West. Longabaugh likely met Butch Cassidy (real name Robert LeRoy Parker) after Parker is released from prison around 1896. Together with the other members of "The Wild Bunch" gang, they performed the longest string of successful train and bank robberies in American History.

After pursuing a career in crime for several years in the United States, the pressures of being pursued, notably by the Pinkerton Detective Agency, forced Longabaugh, his girlfriend Etta Place and Cassidy to abandon the United States. The trio fled first to Argentina and then to Bolivia, where Parker and Longabaugh were probably killed in a shootout in November 1908.

(I like "probably" killed in a shootout in November 1908. We have the photo transparencies and the science. THEY DID NOT DIE IN BOLIVIA!)

# Early life and career

Harry Alonzo Longabaugh, born in Mont Clare, Pennsylvania in the spring of 1867, the son of Pennsylvania natives Josiah and Annie G. (Ann Place) Longabaugh. The youngest of five children (his older siblings were Ellwood, Samanna, Emma and Harvey). Longabaugh is of mostly German ancestry and part Welsh. At age 15, Longabaugh traveled westward on a covered wagon with his cousin George. In 1887, Longabaugh stole a gun, horse and saddle from a ranch in Sundance, Wyoming. While attempting to flee, he is captured by authorities and convicted and sentenced to 18 months in jail by Judge William L. Maginnis. During this jail time, he adopted the nickname of "The Sundance Kid." After his release, he went back to work as a ranch hand and in 1891, as a 25-year-old, he worked at the Bar U Ranch in what is today Alberta, Canada. The Bar U Ranch at that time in history is one of the largest commercial ranches.

In 1892 Longabaugh is suspected of train robbery. Again in 1897 there is a bank robbery along with five other men. He became associated with a group known as the "Wild Bunch," which included his famous partner Robert LeRoy Parker, better known as "Butch Cassidy."

Although Longabaugh, reportedly fast with a gun and is often referred to as a "gunfighter," he is not known to have killed anyone prior to a later shootout in Bolivia, where he and Parker were alleged to have been killed. He became better known than another outlaw member of the gang dubbed "Kid," Kid Curry (real name Harvey Logan) who killed numerous men while with the gang. "The Sundance Kid" could possibly have been mistaken for "Kid Curry." Many articles referred to "The Kid." Longabaugh did participate in a shootout with lawmen who trailed a gang led by George Curry to the Hole-in-the-Wall hideout in Wyoming and is thought to have wounded two lawmen in that shootout. With that exception, though, his verified involvement in shootouts is unknown.

Longabaugh and Logan used a log cabin at what is now Old Trail Town in Cody, Wyoming as a hide-out before they robbed a bank in Red Lodge, Montana. Parker, Longabaugh, and other desperados met at another cabin brought to Old Trail Town from the Hole-in-the-Wall country in north-central Wyoming. That cabin had been built in 1883 by Alexander Ghent.

Historically, the gang, for a time had been best known for their relatively low use of violence during the course of their robberies, relying heavily on intimidation and negotiation; nevertheless, if captured, they would have faced hanging. However, that portrayal of the gang is less than accurate and mostly a result of Hollywood portrayals depicting them as usually "nonviolent." Several people were killed by members of the gang, including five law enforcement officers killed by Logan alone. "Wanted Dead or Alive" posters were posted throughout the country, with as much as a $30,000 reward for information leading to their capture or deaths.

They began hiding out at Hole-in-the-Wall, located near Kaycee, Wyoming. From there they could strike and retreat, with little fear of capture, since it is situated on high ground with a view in all directions of the surrounding territory. Pinkerton detectives led by Charlie Siring, however, hounded the gang for a few years.

Parker and Longabaugh, evidently wanting to allow things to calm down a bit and looking for fresh robbing grounds, left the United States on February 20, 1901. Longabaugh sailed with his "wife" Etta Place and Parker aboard the British ship *Herminius* for Buenos Aires in Argentina.

## Sundance Kid's Death

The facts concerning Longabaugh's death are not known for certain. On November 3, 1908 near San Vicente in southern Bolivia, a courier for the *Aramayo Franke y Cia* Silver Mine guarded his company's payroll, worth about 15,000 Bolivian pesos, by mule, when he is attacked and robbed by two masked American bandits who were believed to be Longabaugh and Parker. The bandits then proceeded to the small mining town of San Vicente, where they lodged in a small boarding house owned by a local miner named Bonifacio Casasola.

When Casasola became suspicious of his two foreign lodgers (a mule they had in their possession... from the Aramayo Mine, and bore the mining company's brand) Casasola left his house and informed a nearby telegraph officer, who notified a small Bolivian Army cavalry unit (the Abaroa Regiment) stationed nearby. The unit dispatched three soldiers under the command of Captain Justo Concha, to San Vicente, where they notified the local authorities. On the evening of November 6, 1908, the lodging house is surrounded by a small group consisting of the local mayor and several officials, along with the three soldiers from the Abaroa Regiment.

When the three soldiers approached the house where the two bandits were staying, the bandits opened fire, killing one of the soldiers and wounding another. A gunfight then ensued. Around 2 a.m., during a lull in the firing, the police and soldiers heard a man screaming from inside the house. Soon, a single shot heard from inside the house, after which the screaming stopped. Minutes later, another shot.

The standoff continued, as locals kept the place surrounded until the next morning when, cautiously entering, they found two dead bodies, both with numerous bullet wounds to the arms and legs. One of the men had a bullet wound in the forehead and the other had a bullet hole in the temple. The local police report speculated, judging from the positions of the bodies, one bandit had probably shot his fatally wounded partner-in-crime to put him out of his misery, just before killing himself with his final bullet.

In the following investigation by the Tupiza police, the bandits were identified as the men who robbed the Aramayo payroll transport, but the Bolivian authorities did not know their real names, nor could they positively identify them. The bodies were buried at the small San Vicente cemetery, where they were buried close to the grave of a German miner named Gustav Zimmer. Although attempts have been made to find their unmarked graves, notably by the American forensic anthropologist Clyde Snow and his researchers in 1991 no remains with DNA matching the living relatives of Parker and Longabaugh have been discovered.

This uncertainty has led to many claims that one or both survived and eventually returned to the United States. One of these claims that Longabaugh lived under the name of William Henry Long in the small town of Duchesne, Utah. Long died in 1936 and is buried in the town cemetery. His remains were exhumed in December 2008, and subjected to DNA testing. The results, though inconclusive, did not support the claim that he's Longabaugh.

(Our TEAM exhumed the remains of William Henry Long in the Duchesne City Cemetery to obtain DNA for DNA Genealogy. We now have the conclusive report. Continue reading, "THAT 'DARN' DNA." The photo transparencies of William Henry Long and The Sundance Kid are a perfect match.)

In 1909, a woman asked Frank Aller (US Vice-Consul in Chile) for assistance in obtaining a death certificate for Longabaugh. No such certificate has been issued and the woman's identity is unknown, but she is described as attractive, leading to speculation that she is Longabaugh's girlfriend Etta Place.

## Aliases

- The Sundance Kid
- Frank Smith
- H.A. Brown
- Harry A. Place (his mother's maiden name is Annie Place)
- Harry Long
- Longabaugh
- Frank Boyd
- Frank Jones
- Kid
- James Ryan
- H. A. Brown
- Scramble

# Ann Bassett

(Born: May 12, 1878 - May 8, 1956 died in Leeds, Utah)

Also, known as **Queen Ann Bassett**, she is a prominent female rancher of the Old West, and with her sister Josie Bassett, had been in an associate of outlaws, particularly "Butch Cassidy's Wild Bunch."

## Early Life

Ann Bassett, born to Herb Bassett and Elizabeth Chamberlain Bassett near Browns Park, Colorado but grew up in Utah, the second of two daughters. Her sister Josie, born in 1874. Herb Bassett, twenty years' senior to his wife Elizabeth Chamberlain Bassett, and the couple moved to Browns Park sometime around the earlier part of 1888. Herb Bassett had a profitable cattle ranch which straddled Utah, Wyoming and Colorado. He often did business with notable outlaws of the era such as Butch Cassidy, Harvey "Kid Curry" Logan and Black Jack Ketchum, selling horses and beef for supplies.

The park, as Browns Park is known, had been a haven for outlaws long before Butch and the boys started running stolen livestock through there. For decade's stolen horseflesh were trailed through the park to thriving mining communities in Eastern Colorado. Both Ann and Josie Bassett were attractive young women, well taught by their father in the arts of horse riding, roping, and shooting. Both were educated early on in prominent boarding schools, were intelligent and articulate in their speech, but chose to return to the life of ranching. Many accounts state the sisters always preferred "cowboying" to being a lady.

By the time, Ann Bassett turned 15, she had become involved romantically with Butch Cassidy. Her sister Josie became involved with Elsy Lay. Outlaws Ben Kilpatrick and Will "News" Carver, who were both later members of the Wild Bunch gang, also dated the sisters. These associations were what first exposed Bassett to outlaws.

## Association with Outlaws

In 1896, several wealthy cattle barons in the area made attempts to purchase the Bassett ranch from the Bassett's. When the Bassett's refused, the barons began to rustle their cattle. Ann and her sister Josie, in turn, rustled cattle from them. This led to a feud and resulted in the cattlemen bringing in killer for hire Tom Horn, to deal with what the cattlemen deemed to be criminals. Horn eliminated several known rustlers during that time but took no action against the Bassett's. While he also killed two rustlers in 1900, Isom Dart and Matt Rash, (a sandy haired Texas cowboy) who were known to be associated with the Bassett family, this... unrelated to the Bassett conflict with their neighbors.

By 1896, Josie Bassett became heavily involved in a relationship with Elzy Lay, Cassidy's closest friend. Josie had also been involved with Cassidy shortly after his release from an eighteen-month prison sentence, during which time Ann dated Ben Kilpatrick. Then Elzy Lay began a relationship with a woman named Maude Davis. Josie became involved with Will "News" Carver and Ann returned to her involvement with Cassidy. Through their relationships with the outlaws, and in exchange for their supplying the outlaws with beef and fresh horses from their ranch, the two sisters could get assistance from Cassidy and his gang in dealing with certain cattlemen who were pressuring them to sell. (The Bassett woman seemed to be involved with everyone...)

This association worked as a deterrent that kept cowboys hired to harass the sisters from doing so, for fear of retribution from the outlaws. There had been a report that Kid Curry, easily the most feared member of the "Wild Bunch" gang, once paid a visit to several cowboys known to be employed by the cattlemen, warning them to leave the Bassett's alone. That cannot be confirmed, but although the problems with the wealthy cattlemen's association continued well into 1902, by late 1899 the problems were rare, and there is little pressure placed on the sisters to sell their ranch. Despite the seemingly constant changes in romantic partners by both the Bassett sisters and the gang members, there is no report of there ever being any animosity because of this, and it seemed to simply be the accepted way that things were.

Although both sisters were taking part in the fight against the powerful cattlemen's associations, it is Ann that became best known, with newspapers as well as friends dubbing her "Queen Ann Bassett." In early 1897, Bassett joined Cassidy at "Robbers Roost." Elzy Lay, having ended his relationship with Josie Bassett, joined them with his girlfriend and future wife Maude Davis. Reports of the day stated, Bassett and Davis were two of only five women ever allowed into the "Robbers Roost" hideout, the other three being Josie Bassett, the Sundance Kid's girlfriend Etta Place, and "Wild Bunch" gang member Laura Bullion.

By April, 1897 the two women were sent home so Cassidy and his gang could concentrate on their next robbery. Cassidy would continue his romantic involvement with Ann Bassett off and on for another four years, seeing her whenever he traveled near her ranch. The total length of their relationship is estimated around seven years, but had been interrupted often with his being away, and for an eighteen-month period when in prison starting in 1894, during which time she started a romance with Ben Kilpatrick.

By 1903, Bassett had married a rancher by the name of Henry Bernard. Shortly after the marriage, she is arrested for cattle rustling. She stood trial, but acquitted and released. The marriage lasted six years, ending in divorce, with Bernard helping Bassett and her sister Josie in maintaining their ranch.

By 1904, most of the outlaws associated with the Bassett girls were either dead or had been captured by lawmen. Ann Bassett never saw Cassidy again after he first departed for South America. Several other outlaws from lesser known gangs drifted in and out of the ranch, usually visiting only to obtain beef or fresh horses, and have a place to stay for a few days. Elzy Lay reportedly visited the ranch again in 1906, shortly after his release from prison, before moving on to California where he lived out the remainder of his life as a respectable businessman. Herb Bassett died on July 30, 1918.

## Ann Bassett In Later Life

Ann Bassett remarried in 1928 to cattleman Frank Willis. The couple remained in Utah, where they maintained a ranch. She remained there for the rest of her life. Willis reportedly loved her dearly, and the two worked closely together in their business. Before she died, she requested that she be cremated, and that her remains be spread across her hometown in northern Utah. However, Willis is alleged to have grieved greatly over her death, and unable to complete that task, keeping her ashes in his car for the remainder of his life. When he died in 1963, friends and family were the ones who buried her ashes in an undisclosed area in Browns Park. They both died in Leeds, Utah.

# The alleged Ann Bassett-Etta Place connection

Ann Bassett has often been accused of having been Etta Place, the girlfriend of The Sundance Kid, and who mysteriously disappeared from all public records in 1909 not long after his death. Speculations that Bassett led a double life, dating Cassidy as Ann Bassett, and dating The Sundance Kid as Etta Place. This would mean that she had been involved with both outlaws at the same time, apparently with their full knowledge, but by 1900, when in their company, she simply went by the name of Etta Place.

Ann Bassett and Etta Place would have known one another and were alleged to have been at the "Robbers Roost" hideout at the same time on more than one occasion. Pinkerton reports give almost identical descriptions of both women, listing both with classic good looks, articulate speech and intelligence, the same hair color, describing both as being good with a rifle and riding a horse, and describing both as being promiscuous with both having taken several lovers. When comparing the best legitimate photograph of Place with the best photograph of Bassett, the two women could be mistaken for one another. Both are pretty, with similar facial features, hair color, and physical build. Michael Rutters' book "Bad Girls" details how Bassett often faked a New England accent to appear more cultured. Similarly, Place is said to have indicated that she had been raised on the East Coast, though she never revealed an exact location. (Ann Bassett attended school back east when young.)

Dr. Thomas G. Kyle of the Computer Research Group at Los Alamos National Laboratory, who had previously performed many such comparisons for government intelligence agencies, conducted a series of tests on photographs of Etta Place and Ann Bassett. Their features matched and both had the same scar or cowlick at the top of their forehead. He concluded that there could be no reasonable doubt they were the same person.

Author and researcher Doris Karren Burton indicates in her 1992 book "Queen Ann Bassett: Alias, Etta Place," that when Bassett is absent from historical records, Place is actively traveling with Cassidy and The Sundance Kid/Harry Longabaugh, and when Place is absent from historical records, Bassett is visible.

However, Burton did not account for documented instances showing Bassett to have been in the United States while Etta Place is known to have been in South America. While Place is in South America with Cassidy and Longabaugh in 1903, Bassett is arrested for cattle rustling in Utah. Furthermore, she also recently married. On the other hand, Place had departed for South America with Longabaugh in August, 1902 not to return to the United States, specifically New York City, until the summer of 1904. During that time, Bassett had married, incarcerated, tried, and released over a span of several months in 1903. Finally, Bassett never claimed to have been Etta Place, even in her memoirs.

(No, she did not claim to be Etta, but her photo comparison is a match. There were 3 Etta Place women that Butch and Sundance would switch places to keep Ann Bassett safe. Dr. John McCullough puts his reputation on the line that Ann Bassett is "Etta Place." They would take a woman with them and call her "Etta" to help Ann escape the outlaw life. FUN! We can compare the photo of the woman in South America with the photo of Ann Bassett. We never give up... SCIENCE DOES NOT LIE.)

# Etta Place

(Born *circa* 1878, date of death unknown)

Etta became a companion of the American outlaw "Butch Cassidy" (real name Robert LeRoy Parker) and "The Sundance Kid' (Harry Alonzo Longabaugh) both members of the outlaw gang known as "The Wild Bunch." Principally the companion of Longabaugh, little is known about her; both her origin and her fate remain mysterious. Despite Longabaugh and Parker's fame, by the mid-20th century, the mysterious vanishing of Place has sparked the most interest.

The Pinkerton Detective Agency described her in 1906 as having, "...classic good looks, 27 or 28 years old, 5'4" to 5'5" in height, weighing between 110 lb. and 115 lb. with a medium build and brown hair."

## Life with the Sundance Kid

Pinkerton Detective Agency memorandum dated July 29, 1902... She is "said to be from Texas," and in another Pinkerton document dated 1906, she is described as "27 to 28 years old," placing her birth around 1878. This is confirmed by a hospital staff record from Denver, where she received treatment in May 1902, which reports her age as "23 or 24," (therefore again, *circa* 1878) although both records may transpire to be from the same original source, the hospital staff.

Even her real name is a mystery; Place is the maiden surname of Longabaugh's mother (Annie Place) and she is recorded in various sources as Mrs. Harry Longabaugh or Mrs. Harry A. Place. In the one instance where she is known to have signed her name, she recorded it as "Mrs. Ethel Place." The Pinkerton's called her "Ethel," "Ethal," "Eva," and "Rita" before finally settling on "Etta" for their wanted posters. Her name may have become "Etta" after she moved to South America, where the locals could not pronounce "Ethel."

In February 1901, Etta Place accompanied Longabaugh, whom she may or may not have married, to New York City, where at Tiffany's jewelers they purchased a lapel watch and stickpin. Their photo had been taken at a studio in Union Square on Broadway, she posed with him for the now famous DeYoung portrait, one of only two known images of her. (I went to New York and went to the exact same location in 2009 and had a stranger take my picture. Fun!) She then, on February 20, sailed with him and Parker who posed as one James Ryan, her fictional brother, aboard the British ship "Herminius" for Buenos Aires in Argentina.

There she settled with the two outlaws on a ranch which they purchased near Cholila in Chubut Province of west-central Argentina. It comprised a four-room log cabin on the east bank of the Blanco River. Under a new law of 1884, they were granted 15,000 acres (61 km$^2$) of adjacent land to develop, 2,500 of which belonged to Place herself, who has the distinction of being the first woman in Argentina to acquire land under the new act, as land ownership had hitherto been almost the exclusive preserve of men. However, on March 3, 1902, she and Longabaugh sailed on the "SS Soldier Prince" from Buenos Aires to New York City, probably to visit family and friends in the US. On April 2, they registered at a Mrs. Thompson's rooming house in New York City. They toured Coney Island and visited his family (originally from Mont Clare, Pennsylvania, but by then living in Atlantic City, New Jersey). They also possibly traveled to a Dr. Pierce's Invalid Hotel in Buffalo, New York, for (unspecified) treatment. They then traveled west, where again they sought medical treatment, this time in Denver, Colorado. They returned to Buenos Aires from New York on July 10, 1902, aboard the steamer "Honorius," posing as stewards. On August 9, she arrived with Longabaugh at the Hotel Europa in Buenos Aires, and on the 15th she sailed with him aboard the steamer "SS Chubut" to return to their ranch.

In the summer of 1904, she made another visit with Longabaugh to the US, where the Pinkerton Detective Agency traced them to Fort Worth, Texas and to the St. Louis World Fair, but failed to arrest them before they again returned to Argentina. In early 1905, the trio sold the Cholila ranch, as once again the law began to catch up with them. The Pinkerton Agency had known their precise address for some months, but the rainy season prevented their assigned agent, Frank Dimaio, from traveling there and making an arrest. Governor Julio Lezana issued an arrest warrant, but before it could be executed, Sheriff Edward Humphreys, a Welsh Argentine who became friendly with Parker and enamored of Place, tipped them off. The trio fled north to San Carlos de Bariloche, where they embarked on the steamer "Condor" across Lake Nahuel Huapi and into Chili.

By the end of that year, however, they were again back in Argentina; on December 19, Place took part, along with Longabaugh, Parker and an unknown male, in the robbery of the Banco de la Nacion in Villa Mercedes, 400 miles west of Buenos Aires. Pursued by armed lawmen, they crossed the Pampas and the Andes and again into the safety of Chile.

Etta Place had long been tired of life on the run and deeply lamented the loss of their ranch. At her request, therefore, on June 30, 1906, Longabaugh accompanied her from Valparaiso, Chile, to San Francisco, California, US, where she apparently remained while he once again returned to South America. No evidence reports Longabaugh and Place saw one another at all between 1906 and his alleged death in 1908.

## Concluding Thoughts

"Etta did not leave Butch and Sundance. Anne Basset is married and back in Browns Park, Utah. The fake "Etta" is setting things up to go to San Francisco where Sundance had a brother Elwood. They were robbing enough money to go to Paris, France so Butch Cassidy could have a facelift. Remember there were 3 different Etta's so Ann Bassett is back in the United States and a different woman uses the name, "Etta Place."

George Longabaugh, a cousin to The Sundance Kid, has a relative that I talked to who is a veterinarian. The veterinarian went to Paris and found a café with a picture of Etta and Sundance. It is not the famous picture of Etta and Sundance, (Wedding Picture) but a different photo. The veterinarian on vacation talked to the café owner and inquired about the photo. He said that everyone knew that Sundance and Etta came to Paris around 1905 – 1906. Dr. McCullough visited Paris in 2012 but Paris is just so large. We want to contact the veterinarian again and have him help us find the café and prove that Butch, Sundance, and Etta went to Paris, France. Fun Stuff!"

*Marilyn Grace*

# The Mysteries of Etta Place

Those who had met Place claimed the first thing they noticed about her is that she is strikingly pretty, with a very nice smile. She is cordial and refined and an excellent shot with a rifle. It is said that she spoke in an educated manner. Many believed she's originally from the East Coast, although she never revealed an exact location.

Eyewitnesses indicated years afterward that Place is one of only five women known to have ever been allowed into the Wild Bunch hideout at Robbers Roost in southern Utah. The other four having been Will Carver's girlfriend Josie Bassett, who also became involved with Parker for a time, Josie's sister and Parker's longtime girlfriend Ann Bassett, Elzy Lay's girlfriend Maude Davis, and gang member Laura Bullion.

She is speculated to have once married a school teacher, and at least one person claimed she is a teacher who abandoned her husband and two children to be with Longabaugh. He claimed that she met the gang while working as a prostitute is widely considered the most likely scenario. There have also been claims that Place became lovers with Parker first, becoming involved with Longabaugh later, and that she met them both while working in a brothel as a prostitute. Both of those claims are possible, as members of the "Wild Bunch" gang often alternated girlfriends.

Possibly, she met Parker and/or Longabaugh in the brothel of Madame Fannie Porter in San Antonio, which is frequented by members of the "Wild Bunch" gang and which resulted in several gang members meeting girlfriends who later traveled with them, including Kid Curry's meeting of prostitute Della Moore. Gang member Will Carver also began a relationship with one of Porter's "girls," Lillie Davis, and Wild Bunch female gang member Laura Bullion is believed to have worked at the brothel from time to time. None of the women working at those places during those times ever declared to have known her.

## Identity

Many theories have been advanced over the years as to her identity. It has been suggested that her real name is said to have been Ethel and she has been identified with Ethel Bishop, who lived at a similar establishment around the corner from Fanny's at 212 Concho Street. On the 1900 Census, Bishop's occupation had been given as an unemployed music teacher. She is 23 then, born in West Virginia in September 1876. The Ethel Bishop hypothesis neatly combines the stories that she is a schoolteacher or that she had been a prostitute and a school teacher at the same time.

Another conjecture is that she is a cattle rustler named Ann Bassett (1878–1956) who knew and operated with the Wild Bunch at the turn of the 20th century. Both Bassett and Place were attractive women, with similar facial features, body frame, and hair color. Bassett, born in 1878, the same year Place is thought to have been born. Dr. Thomas G. Kyle of the Computer Research Group at Los Alamos National Laboratory, who had previously performed many such comparisons for government intelligence agencies, conducted a series of tests on photographs of Etta Place and Ann Bassett. Their features matched and both had the same scar or cowlick at the top of their forehead. He concluded that there could be no reasonable doubt they were the same person.

However, the dates do not match up when alleging to be Ann Bassett. Bassett, a former girlfriend of Parker's and there are several documents to show that Bassett, is in fact in Wyoming during much of the time when Place should have been in South America. In fact, Bassett is arrested for rustling cattle, and entered her first marriage while Place is in South America with Longabaugh and Parker. However, the most conclusive evidence is that from 1902 to the summer of 1904 Etta Place is in South America, whereas in 1903 Ann Bassett had been arrested and for a time incarcerated in Utah.

A once-popular theory held that she could be Eunice Gray, who for many years operated a bordello in Fort Worth, Texas, and afterwards ran the Waco Hotel there until her death in a fire in January 1962. Gray once told Delbert Willis of the Fort Worth Press, "I've lived in Fort Worth since 1901. That is except for the time I had to high-tail it out of town. Went to South America for a few years until things settled down." Willis conceded that Gray never admitted or even claimed to be Etta Place; he merely made that connection on his own, given the similarities of their age, and the period in which Gray said she went to South America coinciding with Place's time in South America. Gray is a beautiful woman, but there were no known photographs of her from that period to compare with the one known high-quality photograph of Place. Willis believed that Place and Gray held a striking resemblance to one another, but for many years there has been no way of testing his assumption. More recently, amateur genealogist Donna Donnell found Eunice Gray on a 1911 passenger list from Panama. It has been reported in 2007 that following that lead she tracked down the niece of Eunice Gray (real name Ermine McEntire), who had two photographs of her: one taken in her high-school graduation dress circa 1896 and another taken in the 1920s. Comparing the photos with one of Place, both agreed that Eunice Gray is not Etta Place.

## Life after Longabaugh

There is still considerable debate over when her relationship with Longabaugh ended. Some claims indicate that Place ended her relationship with Longabaugh and returned to the United States prior to his death. Other claims indicate that the two were still involved in a relationship, and that she simply returned due to her tiring of life in South America.

As for her life after Longabaugh's death, some indications are that she returned to New York City, while others indicate she moved back to Texas and started a new life there. A Pinkerton report indicates that a woman matching Place's description had been killed in a shootout resulting from a domestic dispute with a man named Mateo Gebhart in Chubut, Argentina, in March 1922. Another report indicates she committed suicide in 1924 in Argentina, while yet another report indicates that she died of natural causes in 1966.

In 1907, she is still known to have been living in San Francisco. In 1909, a woman asked Frank Aller (US Vice-Consul in Antofagasta, Chile) for assistance in obtaining a death certificate for Longbaugh. No such certificate has been issued and the woman's identity is unknown, but she is described as attractive, leading to speculation that she's Longabaugh's girlfriend Etta Place.

There have been various claims, in addition to those already mentioned, about her life after Longabaugh died. One claim is that she returned to her life as a school teacher, living the remainder of her life in Denver, Colorado, while another story claims she lived the remainder of her life teaching in Marion, Oregon. There is no evidence to support either story. There are also various claims that she returned to prostitution, living out the remainder of her life in Texas, or New York, or California. Again, those claims have no supporting evidence, and are merely rumor.

Author Richard Llewellyn claimed that while in Argentina he found links that indicated Place had moved to Paraguay following the death of Longabaugh, and that she had married into wealth. There also were rumors that Etta Place is in fact Edith Mae, wife of famous boxing promoter Tex Richard, who retired to a ranch in Paraguay shortly after promoting the famous fight between Jack Johnson and Jim Jeffries in 1910.

Author and researcher Larry Pointer, who up until the late 1970s spent more time researching and chasing leads to Etta Place than any other researcher, wrote that it, "...is one of the most intriguing riddles in western history. Leads develop only to dissolve into ambiguity." He recorded each lead in his 1977 book, "In Search of Butch Cassidy."

## Longabaugh's alleged son

Robert Harvey Longabaugh (February 21, 1901-December 18, 1972), who claimed years later to be the son of Longabaugh, claimed that Etta Place is Hazel Tyrone, a half-sister to his mother, Annie Marie Thayne. Robert Longabaugh claimed throughout his lifetime that his mother, Thayne, had been involved in a relationship with Harry Longabaugh, and further claims that the rumors that Etta Place had been a school teacher are confused with his mother who had been a school teacher when she became romantically involved with Longabaugh, aka, "The Sundance Kid." Robert Longabaugh is the reason that the town of Marion, Oregon comes into question, due to his claim that it's in Marion that his mother taught school. In his claims, he stated that Etta Place became involved with Longabaugh after his mother told him she became pregnant.

However, the claims made by Longabaugh become very clouded and confusing, with dates that don't match up, as he often cited facts that were inconsistent with earlier claims made by him, and he often changed his story. He spent part of his life in jail in Fresno, California, where he first came to public notice due to his claims. He even claimed that he had been a pallbearer at Butch Cassidy, aka, Parker's funeral years after Parker's alleged to have been killed in Bolivia and that Cassidy's buried in Spokane, Washington.

Researchers have been unable to verify any of his claims. In researching his claims about his mother, there is some evidence that she did once teach school, but also some indications that she's a prostitute. There has been no evidence to support her having a half-sister named Hazel Tyrone, aka, Etta Place. Researcher Donna Ernst pointed out that Robert Longabaugh possibly is related to Harry Longabaugh, but unlikely that he is Harry's son, and even less likely that he knew anything whatsoever about Etta Place.

Research has also detected that Robert Longabaugh possibly had been told by his mother that Etta Place, in reality is her half-sister, and that her real name had been Hazel Tyrone. Robert Longabaugh's stories were believed to have been completely fabricated by him. There also is no evidence to support that Harry Longabaugh had never been in the Oregon area during the timeframe when Robert Longabaugh alleged his mother began an affair with him. There is no mention of Annie Thayne in any reports about the gang from the day, and Pinkerton detectives, who have historically been the best source for the movements of gang members, have nothing indicating a relationship with any woman other than Etta Place after 1899.

Robert Longabaugh died in a fire in Missoula, Montana on December 18, 1972. His death certificate lists his father as being Harry Longabaugh, and his mother as being Annie Marie Thayne. There is no record of his birth certificate. There were no other available documents to show any other connection to Longabaugh or Place, other than his own claims.

## Fact timelines generally accepted by historians

- 1899-1900: Ethel is living in Texas and being courted by Harry A. Longabaugh, alias the Sundance Kid, a.k.a. Harry A. Place. Some stories claim Etta is a housekeeper or possibly a prostitute in Fannie Porter's sporting house during this time.
- December 1900: Place and Longabaugh marry, with him using the alias of Harry A. Place, shortly after he is photographed in the famous Fort Worth Five photo.

## Last Thoughts

The research that you just read is everything that has been stated from various researchers for over 100 plus years. The stories go on and on about Etta Place. The photo transparencies are science and we have Ann Bassett as the real "ETTA PLACE."

There were three Etta Place woman that were switched out to protect Ann Bassett. More research needs to be completed, but I talked to an historian, Doris Karren Burton, in Vernal, Utah and she believes Etta is just as wanted as Butch and Sundance, so to throw off the law, they would have different woman take her place.

Many years ago in 1997, I talked to Doris and she has since passed away. I am looking forward to writing more books on Etta. She is the most mysterious of all of them. We have the science to prove Etta is Ann Bassett. The photo transparencies Dr. John McCullough completed are perfect.

*Marilyn Grace*

# CHAPTER TWO
## Sundance

Harry A. Longabaugh, born in the "spring" of 1867, at 122 Jacobs Street in Mont Clare, Pennsylvania. At that time in history, Pennsylvania did not require birth records. The Longabaugh Family Bible is the only known source of Harry's birth. They were members of the Baptist Church, they did not practice infant baptisms and therefore, there are no church records. "Sundance's" sister Samanna, owned the Family Bible with family names, days, years and months of the children of Josiah and Ann (Annie) Longabaugh. Josiah and Ann's children are: Elwood Place, Samanna, Emma, Harvey Sylvester, and Harry Alonzo Longabaugh, "The Sundance Kid." All the children have a day, month and year listed when they were born. It is strange that Elwood, Samanna and Harvey have their full birthdays listed, but Emma only has the year she's born and Harry A. only has "abt. spring" {about spring} 1867. Didn't they know the day their child came into the world? Verification of any records came from memory or family stories.

From 1865 to 1870, Harry's parents, Josiah and Ann (Annie) were living in Port Providence, a small Village in Upper Providence Township, Pennsylvania. Mont Clare is a few miles north of Port Providence. Why is Harry born in a 10-room boarding house in Mont Clare? Harry Longabaugh may not have been born in the Longabaugh family home? Harry is listed among the children in the 1870 census records as three years old at the time.

In the 1880 census, Harry is listed as being 13 years old. Samanna is married and no longer living at home. Harvey, age 15 and Harry were not living with the family in Phoenixville. The two brothers were apparently earning room and board away from home and family. Harry is found listed as a hired servant, boarding with Wilmer Ralston and his family in West Vincent, Pennsylvania. Mr. Ralston farmed over 100 acres along what is now route 113 and lived ten miles from where Harry's parents were living.

Harry's family were described… "very poor" or "poor farmers" and the family moved seven times, or so, in ten years. They never owned their own land and rented farm property. Today, we would consider their lifestyle as being very unstable. On Sunday, the entire family attended the First Baptist Church in Phoenixville, located across the street from their home in 1882. The extended family, including Harry's grandparents, aunts and uncles and a large number of cousins, would attend church together.

Harry… a very unsettled spirit, a "wanderlust." He is not close to his relatives. Harry and Samanna, his sister, were extremely close and remained so even after she married in 1878. He enjoyed playing with her small children and they adored their "Uncle Harry."

Samanna kept the business ledgers for her husband and made notations among the purchase orders. One entry reads, "Phoenixville, June 1882 – Harry A. Longabaugh left to seek employment in Ph. and their (sic) to N.Y.C. from their (sic) to Boston and from their (sic) home on the 26 of July or near date. Phoenixville, Aug. 30th, 1882, Harry A. Longabaugh left Home for the West. Left home at 14 – moved west with Cousin George Longenbaugh." (See Young Sundance Kid Photo in Brent Ashworth Collection)

George Longenbaugh and his family were living in Shelby County, Illinois. They decided to move west to Colorado in a covered wagon. George invited Harry to join them and he accepted. Harry had to have been an immense help to George, his pregnant wife Mary, and two-year old son Walter. George raised and bred horses and Harry worked beside him.

The George Longenbaugh (spelling slightly different, but they were cousins) ranch comes within a 75-mile radius of the members "Butch Cassidy" recruited for his gang. Harry is probably one of the first to join "Butch." Young and impressionable, Harry is in the wrong place at the wrong time with a half-dozen outlaw partners that lived in the area when he started his life of crime. At age 17, Harry Alonzo Longabaugh, along with Robert LeRoy Parker, Will Carver, Harvey Logan, Ben Kilpatrick, Matt Warner and others, were outlaw partners; the beginning of "The Wild Bunch!"

In 1887, Harry Alonzo Longabaugh, convicted of horse theft and sentenced to 18 months "hard labor" in the Sundance, Wyoming Jail. Because of this jail time and a newspaper article that said, "They laid him down in Sundance," he earned the nickname, "The Sundance Kid." Harry served his time and upon his release he immediately rejoined the gang. They began hiding out at a place called "Hole-in-the-Wall" located near Buffalo, Wyoming. From high on a mountain top, they could strike and retreat with a clear view in all directions with little fear of capture.

Hollywood produced the 1969 blockbuster movie, "Butch Cassidy and The Sundance Kid," starring Paul Newman and Robert Redford. "Butch Cassidy and The Sundance Kid" celebrated its 40th anniversary in 2009 and is very popular all these years later. The movie portrayed them as happy-go-lucky, "non-violent" Robin Hoods that stole from the rich and gave to the poor. They were just out for a good-time and a free-wheeling life-style. There were five law enforcement officers that were killed by Kid Curry alone. Wanted posters were distributed throughout the country with as much as $30,000 dollars as reward money for their capture, "Dead or Alive!" If captured, they would most likely have been hanged.

The amount of money the gang robbed would add up to two and a half million dollars in our time, considering inflation. They were famous from coast to coast. Their relay horses would allow them to escape the law. Pinkerton detectives, led by Charlie Siringo hounded the gang for years, but "Butch and Sundance" were never captured. "Sundance" is famous for saying, "They'll never take me alive!"

"Butch and Sundance" tried to go straight and asked for amnesty. The negotiations were fouled up and instead of going straight they decided to escape the pressure of the Pinkerton's by fleeing to South America. On February 20, 1901, Longabaugh, "Cassidy," and "wife?" of "Sundance," "Etta Place," sailed on the British Ship "Herminius" for Buenos Aires, Argentina. The three bought a ranch in Patagonia and settled down as ranchers. It's not long before the Pinkerton Detectives were on their trail and they were forced to liquidate all their belongings. They had to quickly sell their hacienda and ranch to escape the law.

"Butch and Sundance" were reported to have been killed in a shoot-out. The killings took place on November 6, 1908 after robbing a Bolivian mining company payroll in San Vicente, Bolivia ending with their "alleged" deaths.

Our TEAM of experts now has new evidence that "Sundance and Butch" returned to the United States and Longabaugh, (Sundance) died in 1936. Follow the clues that our TEAM has gathered and decide for yourself!

**Harry Alonzo Longabaugh's aliases:**

| | | |
|---|---|---|
| The Sundance Kid | Frank Smith | Frank Jones |
| Harry Long | Frank Boyd | Kid |
| Longabaugh | Harry A. Place | James Ryan |
| Harry Alonzo | H. A. Brown | Scramble |

# Pinkerton's National Detective Agency.

FOUNDED BY ALLAN PINKERTON, 1850.

ROB'T A. PINKERTON, New York. }
WM. A. PINKERTON, Chicago. } Principals.

GEO. D. BANGS
ALLAN PINKERTON

JOHN CORNISH, Ass't Gen'l Sup't., Eastern Division, New York
EDWARD S. GAYLOR, Ass't Gen'l Sup't., Middle Division, Chicago
JAMES McFARLAND, Ass't Gen'l Sup't., Western Division, Denver

Attorneys — GUTHRIE, CRAVATH & HENDERSON, New York

TELEPHONE CONNECTION

**OFFICES.**

DENVER,
NEW YORK,
BOSTON,
PHILADELPHIA,
MONTREAL,
CHICAGO,
ST. PAUL,
ST. LOUIS,
KANSAS CITY,
PORTLAND, ORE.,
SEATTLE, WASH.,
SAN FRANCISCO,

## Representing American Bankers Association.

# $6,000 REWARD

THE FIRST NATIONAL BANK OF WINNEMUCCA, NEVADA, a member of THE AMERICAN BANKERS' ASSOCIATION, was robbed of $32,640 at the noon hour, September 19, 1900, by three men, who entered the bank and held up the cashier and four other persons. Two of the robbers carried revolvers and the third a Winchester rifle. They compelled the five persons to go into the inner office of the bank, where the robbery was committed.

At least $31,000 was in $20 gold coins; $1,200 in $5 and $10 gold coins; the balance in currency, including one $50 bill.

### THE MEN WERE NOT MASKED AND CAN BE IDENTIFIED.

The robbers are described as follows:

No. 1 (who entered the cashier's office and forced him, under threats, to open the safe).

AGE, about 35.
HEIGHT, 5 ft., 9 or 10 in.
WEIGHT, 160 pounds.
EYES, blue or gray.
NOSE, fairly long, but thin.
COMPLEXION, light.
HAIR, light flaxen.

BEARD, full, flaxen or blonde, and moustache light weight.
HANDS, (No. 7 glove) very small and much freckled on backs.
FEET, small.
OCCUPATION, probably cowboy.

Remarks: Walked as if lame at the hip. This may have been assumed. Has small veins, which show quite distinctly on globe of cheeks.

No. 2.

AGE, about 35.
HEIGHT, 5ft., 7 or 8 inches.
WEIGHT, 145 to 155 pounds.
BUILD, medium.

EYES, blue or brown.
HAIR, brown.
MOUSTACHE, moderately heavy, brown in color and drooping.

No. 3.

AGE, 25 to 30.
COMPLEXION, dark.
WEIGHT, 155 to 160 pounds.
BUILD, medium.

HEIGHT, 5ft., 9 or 10 inches.
EYES, dark brown.
FACE, smooth.

Remarks: Very determined expression in face. Smelled like a polecat. Think his hair was colored for the occasion. Two of the bank employes say he had a scar on one side of cheek, something like a wrinkle or life line.

PINKERTON REWARD POSTER
for the Winnemucca bank robbery

Chicago-Misc.
List of dead criminals, associates, etc.          N.Y.   Chi.   Phi.   Bo

                                                    S.F.   J.H.S.   St.L.   Seat

                              Denver, February 26th 1910.

Jas. McParland, Esq.,
        Manager, Denver.          E. E. P.

Dear Sir:-                        FEB 27 1910
          Referring to Gen'l Supt. Schumacher's letter of January 6th
under the above title by Mr. Borcutt, copy of which was sent to the
above listed offices; I desire to call your attention to the fact that
this list contains the name of George Parker, alias George Cassidy,
alias Thos. Cassidy, alias George Ingerfield, alias Butch Cassidy.  I
would like very much to have further information concerning the death
of this man and to be advised when and where he died and the cause of
his death.
          During the past year he was reported by a number of people
who knew him, as having been seen in Wyoming and also in Utah, and we
have more recent information through our New York office that he, in
company with others of the Wild Bunch, has been committing hold-ups
and robberies in South America.
          I do not think it advisable to remove any pictures from our
gallery unless we are absolutely certain that the person is dead.

                    Yours truly,

          W-S                              Supt.

          ~ ~ ~ ~ ~ ~ ~ ~ ~ ~ ~ ~ ~ ~ ~ ~

                                          All Officers.

Denver-Criminal.
History No. 1061.
Harry Longbaugh, alias Harry Alonzo,
alias Frank Jones, alias Frank Boyd.
Train & Bank Robber.

                              Denver, Colo. Mar.1, 1910.

          Please add the following to the above named
history:

          From a correspondent at Vernal, Utah, we learn that
Harry Longbaugh has a warm friend keeping a saloon in
Ogden, Utah, named Jack Egan. Egan and Longbaugh were
in Vernal, also Price, Utah and went from Price, Utah,
to Baggs, Wyoming, in July, 1901.

After a thorough investigation and from information received, GEORGE PARKER (right name) alias GEORGE CASSIDY, alias "BUTCH" CASSIDY, alias INGERFIELD; and HARRY LONGBAUGH, alias "KID" LONGBAUGH, alias HARRY ALONZO, are suspected of being two of the men engaged in this robbery.

"BUTCH" CASSIDY is known as a criminal principally in Wyoming, Utah, Idaho, Colorado and Nevada.

On July 15, 1894, he was sentenced to two years' imprisonment in the Wyoming penitentiary at Laramie, from Fremont county, for grand larceny, but was pardoned January 19, 1896.

HARRY LONGBAUGH, alias "Kid" Longbaugh, also known as Harry Alonzo, served 18 months in jail at Sundance, Cook county, Wyoming, when a boy, for horse stealing.

In December, 1892, Longbaugh, Bill Madden and Harry Bass held up a Great Northern train at Malta, Montana. Bass and Madden were tried for this crime, convicted and sentenced to prison for 10 and 14 years respectively.

HARRY LONGBAUGH escaped, and has been a fugitive from justice since.

On June 28, 1897, under the name of Frank Jones, Longbaugh participated with Harvey Logan, alias Curry, and Tom O'Day and Walter Putney, in the Belle Fourche (S. Dak.) bank robbery. All were arrested, but Longbaugh and Harvey Logan escaped from jail at Deadwood, October 31, 1897.

Governor Heber Wells (present governor) of Utah, in 1898, offered a reward of $500 for the arrest of "Butch" Cassidy for the robbery of Paymaster Carpenter of the Pleasant Valley Coal company, at Castle Gate, Utah, in 1897.

For the arrest, detention and surrender to an authorized officer of the State of Nevada of each or any of the men who robbed the First National Bank of Winnemucca as herein stated, the American Bankers' Association offers a reward of $1,000, to be paid upon identification of the prisoner or prisoners.

For the arrest, detention and surrender to an authorized officer of the State of Nevada of each or any of the men who robbed the First National Bank at Winnemucca as herein stated, that bank offers a reward of $1,000, to be paid upon identification of the prisoner or prisoners, and will in addition, in proportionate shares, pay 25 per cent of all money recovered.

Persons furnishing information leading to the arrest of either or all of the robbers will share in the reward.

In case of an arrest immediately notify Pinkerton's National Detective Agency at the nearest of the above listed offices.

# CHAPTER THREE
## William Henry Long

The Morrell and Long Family could not complete any genealogy for William Henry Long when he passed away in 1936. William Henry Long lied about his family background to hide his true-identity. The family all knew that William Henry Long is an outlaw that ran with "Butch Cassidy's Gang," but they didn't know which outlaw.

Sherma Payton is a great grand-child of Silas and Luzernia Morrell. Sherma's mother described William Henry Longa as a really... handsome man with the most beautiful blue eyes. Sherma and her brother Jerry Morrell, on several occasions, tried to find out from Josie Bassett, (from Brown's Park and dated "Butch") who he is, but she would never tell.

Silas Morrell passed away and Bill courts and marries Luzernia; they had two girls, Florence Viola and Evinda Ann. Jerry Nickle, (step-great grandson of William Henry Long and great grandson of Silas Morrell and great grandmother, Luzernia Morrell) explained that Aunt Viola lived close by in Midvale, south of Salt Lake City, Utah. In 2002, Judy and Jerry Nickle went to a Jackson Family Reunion. A family member had a picture of Bill Long as a young cowboy. There's an auction for the picture and Jerry won. He now owns one of Viola Long's copies made at the Briggs Photography Studio in Lewiston, Idaho. Sherma Payton owns the original photo of William Henry Long. Diann and Jerry Peck own a copy that the family passed down from Etta Robison Forsyth, Diann Peck's mother.

Jerry had trouble sleeping one night and around midnight, he went to his computer and started searching for clues about Bill Long's true-identity. He found cousins that also wanted to know about William Henry Long. Jerry met Pat Lingwall and Troy Morrell on-line. They started sharing information to see if they could find William Henry Long's real name.

Judy and Jerry live in Gilbert, Arizona; they own a construction company. In 2002 – 2003... Jerry semi-retired and started working on the William Henry Long mystery. Jerry credits his son Ryan for helping him to ease out of the business. Jerry started to compare the picture of William Henry Long with the famous "Wild Bunch" photo of the "The Fort Worth Five." "Sundance" to Jerry, looked the most like William Henry Long.

Jerry put up a website with side-by-side photos of William Henry Long and Harry Alonzo Longabaugh. He asked for any information regarding Jerry's step-great grandfather, William Henry Long. In June of 2007, I met Judy and Jerry because of the information posted on their website. I shared my film background along with my own search for "Butch and Sundance." I explained that I have been searching for our famous "outlaws" since May of 1997. That is the beginning of our TEAM coming together to investigate the William Henry Long story. We hired the services of Sorenson Forensics in Salt Lake City, Utah. Tim Kupherschmid, the Executive Director, helped exhume William Henry Long, buried in Duchesne, Utah. We now had DNA to compare to Ann Place Longabaugh, "The Sundance Kid's" mother. Tim Kupherschmid is the one who recommended our forensic scientist Dr. John McCullough from the University of Utah Anthropology Department.

Dr. McCullough has worked on many high-profile cases for the State of Utah. John has been on the staff of the Anthropology Department for forty years. Dr. John McCullough worked with the police to solve the Allred Murder Case, as well as the Ted Bundy Murder Case. His photo analysis and forensic work has helped to put many criminals behind bars.

On November 15, 2007 Dr. John McCullough did the photo comparison of William Henry Long and Harry Alonzo Longabaugh, a.k.a., "The Sundance Kid." His report proved to be a 99.9% match. The reason there is a .1% difference is because of the different angles of the two photos. The heads are turned just slightly. We will be doing a computer-generated photo comparison and we can get a 100% match. John also did an analysis of William Henry Long's sisters pictures, compared to "The Sundance Kid's" sisters picture. They proved to be the same people. What is William Henry Long doing with a picture of 'The Sundance Kids' sisters? Our TEAM now had the science to prove the theory that William Henry Long is really, "The Sundance Kid."

What an exciting day for all of our TEAM! History literally changed. Jerry's family finally received an answer to their question, "Who is my step-great grandfather?" He is "The Sundance Kid!" We have all had to be so secretive and now we finally could talk about this amazing discovery. Family members on the Morrell and Long side have all been notified. Family members have given us photos, documents and research that have helped solve the case. As a family, they are all thrilled to know the true-identity of William Henry Long. They now have roots and can trace their ancestry!

Judy and Jerry Nickle, Marilyn Grace, Michael Karr, Tim Kupherschmid, Dr. John McCullough and James Petty, our genealogist, joined forces! Our "TEAM" changed history! William Henry Long is Harry Alonzo Longabaugh, also known as, "The Sundance Kid."

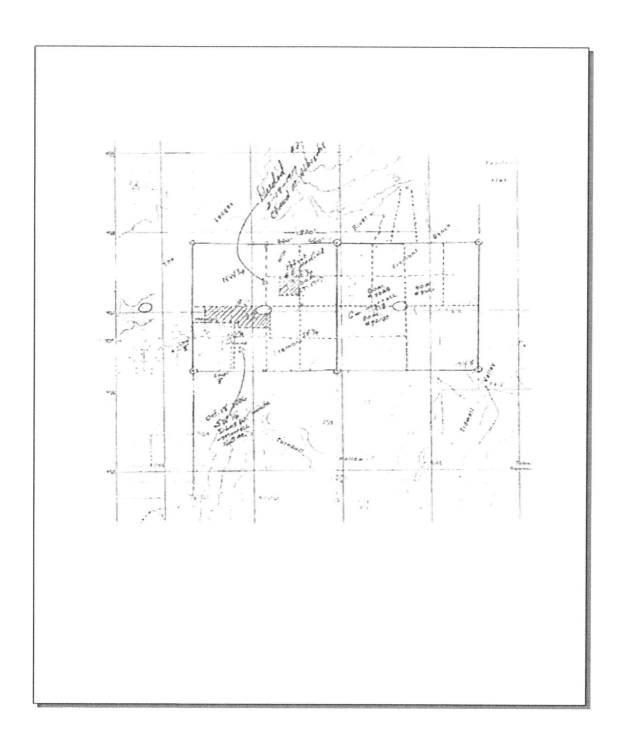

# Plat A.

"Patent of Silas W Morrell Recorded in Book A page 2 transfer page

## Record of Freimont Townsite plat A.

Consists of 12 Blocks - 48 Corner Lots Each Lot is twelve Rods square, Each street is 4 rods wide Each Lot's area is $\frac{144}{160}$ of an acre. With 2 street running though the Town from North to south and three streets running from east to West, With a street running on each side of the Town, their parallel lines being East to North 12° 30' and situated in South West corner of Section seventeen (17) Township twenty Seven south of Range three (3) East. Scale of Plat is one Eighth of an inch to the Rod. Said survey was made April the 28th. A.D. 1887. and certified to as follows

I Certify that this plat is correct as surveyed by me April 28th A.D 1887.

L. G. Long, Kossharem

County surveyor of Piute County Utah.

Approved by me this 20th day of March A.D 1894.

Alvin L. Robinson, Probate Judge

Wayne County Utah

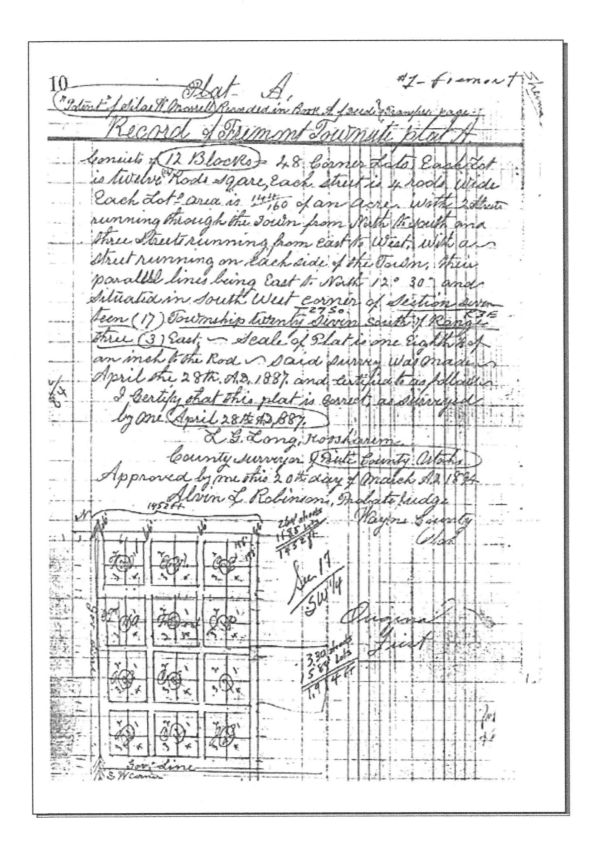

No. 30 The People of the Territory of Utah, }
County of Wayne.

# MARRIAGE LICENSE.

TO ANY PERSON LEGALLY AUTHORIZED TO SOLEMNIZE MARRIAGE, GREETING:

You are hereby Authorized to Join in Holy Matrimony, Mr. _William H Long_ of _Fremont_, in the County of _Wayne_, and Territory of _Utah_, of the age of _twenty seven_ years, and Mrs. _Luzenia Morrell_, of _Fremont_, in the County of _Wayne_, and Territory of _Utah_, of the age of _thirty six_ years.

Witness my hand as clerk of the Probate Court and the seal of said Court hereto affixed at my office in Loa, in said County, this _fourteenth_ day of _November_ A. D. 1894.

_John T Lazenby_ Clerk of Probate Court.

By _____ Deputy.

TERRITORY OF UTAH. }
County of Wayne. }

I Hereby Certify that on the _fifteenth_ day of _November_ in the year of our Lord one thousand eight hundred and ninety-_four_ at _Fremont_ in said County, I, the undersigned, a _Minister of the Gospel_ did join in the Holy Bonds of Matrimony, according to law, _William H Long_ of the County of _Wayne_ Territory of _Utah_, and Mrs _Luzenia Morrell_ of the County of _Wayne_, Territory of _Utah_. The nature of the ceremony was according to _the Laws of Utah_, and was a present mutual agreement of marriage between the parties for all time.

We were married, as stated in this certificate, and are now husband and wife.

Signed, _William Henry Long_ Groom.

Signed, _Luzenia Long_ Wife.

In the Presence of _Hyrum Morrell_ Witness.

_Henry A Maxfield_ Witness.

_Eliott E Maxfield_
Minister of the Gospel.

31

## Note:
### Marilyn Grace Journal Entry - April 19, 2008
*Mrs. Jerry Morrell (Georgia) told me a family story about Luzernia Allred Morrell Long, (Bill Long's wife). Georgia Morrell said, "When Grandma Long became really mad, she would sit on the porch and rock, then pull her apron up over her head and mumble to herself... you knew Grandma Long's mad! When anyone in the Morrell family is pouting, or fuming mad, the saying in the family is, 'Stop Grandma Long'ing'!"*

Etta Forsyth (93), of Duchesne, Utah, William Henry Long's step-great grand-daughter, gave me this information. It is in her handwriting. She shared this with me after I showed her the photo transparencies of William Henry Long and Harry Alonzo Longabaugh.

**Note:** *She filled in "Sundance Kid" above William Long.*

said it was like the cancer she and father had years before. Whatever it was, Brother Blackburn did cure.

While I was growing up everyone talked of the miraculous cures Brother Blackburn could do, and he was held in great respect. I have never, in my lifetime, known anyone who was so beloved and trusted.[29]

The George Chappell family is often mentioned in Elias's journals. They had their share of typhoid, diphtheria, and other diseases and childhood afflictions. In one case recorded July 19, 1903, Elias administered "to Sist Chappel for 'Cancer' on Nose. I have adm to Sist Chappel 12 times. A bad Case of cancer." He also blessed her again on June 21, 1904, nearly a year later. A brief statement from a granddaughter tells the results of this treatment: "My Grandmother, Arilla Chappell (George Armstrong Chappell's wife) she had a cancer on the top of her nose. P[atriarch] Blackburn gave [her a] Blessing and Olive oil on her nose. Her cancer was cured. She had a hole in the top of her nose the size of a match, the rest of her life but her life was saved."[30]

In Teasdale, Elias often treated the Williams families, and they had confidence in him. In the fall of 1897, "young Sister Williams" came to him with a cancer, and he began administration. On September 18, he wrote, "The young Sister Williams Came again with her 'Cancer.' It is now well. She is greatly thankfull to the Lord that she is well from the 'Cancer.' I have administered to her 8 times. I gave her, her Patriarchal Blessing. She is a good girl." The girl was Cora Williams King. Her daughter adds some extra details. When Cora discovered the breast cancer, she went to a doctor in Salt Lake who wanted to cut it out immediately. She wanted time to consider the decision and returned home. She consulted Patriarch Blackburn, and he told her not to let them touch her body with the knife. He then administered to her and cured the cancer. Mrs. King lived eighty-two years and never had surgery.[31]

Nor did he limit his attention to Church members only. In December 1907, he treated sick "Billy Hay for wart near Eye." Billy Hay was a non-Mormon Irishman who had moved into Wayne County. He was quoted as saying that when he died he wanted to be buried in a Mormon cemetery because "that was the last place on earth that the devil would look for a good Irishman."[32] Billy was buried in Hanksville as he wished.

Bill Long, who appeared in Wayne County about the time the Robber's Roost gang disbanded, was another non-Mormon. Long married Luzernia Morrell, the widow of Silas Morrell. Elias recorded that on January 19, 1900, William Long came to him with a cancer on his lip. He administered to Long that day and three other days, but gave no further details. In a story passed down through Luzernia's descendants, Elias asked Long, "Do you have the faith Bill?" The reply came, "Hell Elias, do you think I'd have come if I didn't have faith you could help me?" Bill was healed.[33]

Elias's journal is actually a who's who of Wayne County families. At times there were other doctors in the county, and many people were administered to by bishops of various wards, by Presidents Robison, Bastian, Eckersley, Hanson, or by E. K. Hanks, Patriarch Coleman, or Benjamin Brown. However, most families, at one time or another, came to Elias.

But Elias H. Blackburn became known as a healer in areas far beyond Loa. His journal and other accounts tell of many people who came from California, Nevada, Arizona, Colorado, Wyoming, Oregon, Idaho, Kansas, Nebraska, and even Canada and Mexico.

On July 25, 1895, "Bro. Edward Bunker and wife Came to my house with their Son 22 years of age with a bad Cancer on his arm. Came all the way from Bunkerville [Nevada] 275 miles. . . . I administered Anointing with Oil. Also ministered to Bro. & Sister Bunker, they being feeble and Enjoyed the Spirit."

Elias administered to the Bunkers on the twenty-sixth. The next day, "Administered to Bro. Bunker. . . . His 'Cancer' is much better. Gave him, Geo. S. Bunker his Patriarchal Blessing. Bro. Bunker before leaving felt very thankful to the Lord and me. Gave me a Small present in money."

Later, August 27, 1904, Elias recorded another visit of "Bro. & Sister Bunker," who came from Bunkerville "very sick." When they started home four days later, she was well enough to walk to the wagon. They gave $20.00 and thereby "proved their thankfulness."

While Elias was in Salt Lake City for conference in October 1897, he recorded the visit of a "Bishop Sevie of Mexico," who brought his sick wife with a stone cancer. With her was a Sister Baker, who had a tumor. They followed Elias to Loa, arriving October 12 and lodging at the hotel. Elias recorded administering to them daily from the twelfth through the eighteenth. October 19, he wrote, "Last night Mrs. Sevie Died from Lungs & Cancer at hotel.

## Bill Long
## Helping in the Community

Putting up ice on the Duchesne River about 50 years ago, to have a supply to make that pitcher of cold lemonade for the July 4th community celebration was quite a process. On the wagon is Bill Long, standing at left, Joe Danner and at right, Fred Oldstrum. Point of harvest is near the junction of the Duchesne and Strawberry Rivers, directly east of Duchesne. They were not treading on thin ice; it was 20 inches thick in the block. Mr. Long was the father of Mrs. Evinda (nicknamed Vinda or Vinde) Merkley, Duchesne, Utah. She contributed this picture for publication in the local paper.

(The picture is taken some time after 1917 - See Photo Album.)

# CHAPTER FOUR
## Fingers Curled Under

I rushed to the Sun Glow Café (Famous for their Pickle and Pinto Bean Pie) in Bicknell, Utah outside of Fremont, Utah. Our TEAM had arranged to meet and began planning the filming schedule for our documentary. I could not wait to show everyone what I had discovered. My heart is racing with anticipation! We were about to capture William Henry Long's life story on film. I had been up half the night looking over, and over again at photos of William Henry Long and "The Sundance Kid."

Jerry Nickle, our executive producer, arrived from Gilbert, Arizona. Mike Karr, our director, came into the restaurant from Lehi, Utah. His car loaded with cameramen, equipment and an assistant. Kelly Taylor, who lives in Fremont, arrived next to be our location scout and guide. We were all excited to get together. Before everyone had a chance to catch their breath, I announced that I had something really-important to show everyone. Filled with anticipation, everyone settled into a large circular booth and I passed around a picture of William Henry Long and his wife Luzernia when they were in their late sixties. I showed them the picture of "The Sundance Kid" in the famous "Fort Worth Five" photograph. "Look at the fingers," I said, as I held up the two photos for all to see. "The fingers are curled under in the exact same manner in both photos." Jerry is sitting next to me. He saw the fingers and said, "Yes, they are exactly, the same." The photos were passed all the way down the table and everyone agreed that both men had their fingers curled under in the exact same way. The right hands in both pictures look exactly alike.

We all visited and chatted all through dinner at what an incredible piece of evidence this is for our project. Everyone felt the magic! We had just found an important clue for our film to prove our case. We were hot on the trail of "The Sundance Kid." This is not a dream... we are here where "Sundance" hid out and lived a double life! He escaped the law with the help of his family and friends.

Although there were several other important pieces of evidence that we planned on including in our documentary, for some reason, this one jumped out at me and screamed! "Yes! You are on the right track! This has to be in the documentary!"

(See Photo Album for comparison pictures.)

# CHAPTER FIVE
## Bill Lost His Right Thumb

On Aunt Mary and Cussin' Charley's ranch in Fremont, Utah sometime after 1910, Long lost his right thumb. We don't know the exact date. On January 29, 2010 Sherma Payton, a step great-grand-daughter, told me a story about her parents. Sherma's great grand-parents are Silas Morrell and Luzernia Allred Morrell. Her grandfather is Hiette. Sherma's father is Silas Morrell, (named after grandpa Silas) and her mother is Hilda Bragger. Hilda said Bill had always been so kind to them!

Sherma stated that, "Daddy knew Cussin' Charley personally and Cussin' Charley became heavily involved with Bill Long and the outlaws." The whole family knew he is a member of "The Wild Bunch," but Bill Long kept it a secret as to what name he used as a member of the gang.

Diann Peck, (Etta Forsyth's daughter) remembers her grandmother, (Clara Morrell) saying that Luzernia had a hard life. She lost a young son and caring for an invalid husband and six children for three years, had been hard on her; then her husband died. The family all knew about his outlaw life and other women, but Grandma Long put up with it. If she didn't go along with whatever Bill did, she would have been penniless, just like when she first met Bill."

Bill went to help Charley with the round-up in Fremont. Like many a cowboy in his time, he had an accident. While throwing out the rope to lasso a cow, the rope wrapped around his right thumb and the force of the rope pulled his thumb off. You must remember, these were times of hardship! You just were not able to run to the doctor or hospital the way we do today. His thumb is pulled off and that is that. You patched yourself up and got on with it... survival of the fittest.

Bill stayed in a room with a fireplace and he put the thumb on the mantle. The mice were eating the thumb in the night, so in the morning he asked that it be buried. While recovering from his wound, he still had phantom pain that his thumb is still on his hand. It felt like it's still there! The following day, Bill asked for help in digging up the thumb and wanted the thumb buried six feet under. As soon as the thumb went down in the ground six feet, Bill Long said, "The pains gone."

Gaylen Robison, the great grandson of Bill Long, sent us a picture of Bill and Luzernia with a prized pumpkin that they raised. It is so big that Etta Forsyth, his step grand-daughter said they had to get a machine, (sometime after 1917 and before 1936) to bring it closer to the house so they could cut it up and cat the "GIANT PUMPKIN!" Etta remembers all the grandkids playing on it.

We did not know which thumb he lost when we exhumed Bill Long's body in Duchesne. There were no thumbs; they had decayed over time. When I first saw the picture, I saw that the right thumb is missing. Here is another little mystery as to which thumb he had lost. We receive a picture of Bill and Luzernia in their older years and there you go; we know it is his right thumb!

To us this may seem like a grizzly story, but it is what happened when Bill lost his right thumb.

(See Photo Album)

# CHAPTER SIX
## A Wink and a Haircut

In 1894, William Henry Long (Bill) traveled on horseback from the Hogan Ranch in Loa, Utah to the Morrell Family Homestead. It takes two-and-a-half-hours to visit the widow of Silas Morrell. Bill would stay for two-to three-hours and would get his hair cut. "Wink! Wink!" Everyone in this small town of only a handful of people knew Bill had been getting more than a haircut! When Bill and Luzernia married, Luzernia is close to seven weeks pregnant.

Luzernia Allred's first husband is Silas Morrell and they are the parents of seven children. One of their children, Silas Warren Morrell, drowned as a young boy behind their house in their stream. Luzernia had six living children and is in a bad way financially. Her husband had passed away September 26, 1893 having suffered with a back injury for three years. Silas had been injured in a sawmill accident. Silas worked with a black man that he hired to help in the saw mill. People in the town referred to him as, "The Speckled Nigger." The Utah Historical Society has a picture of a man called, "The Speckled Nigger." We have two photographs; they may be the same person but we do not know for sure. It is not our intention to offend anyone, and we now know that his real name is Albert Welhouse, nicknamed SPECK. He really looks WILD when he's young! As a hired hand, he is supposed to hold heavy logs while Silas used the saw. Because he did not have a firm hold on the logs, they fell, and Silas broke his back. Luzernia grabbed her rifle and took aim. She is so furious at this man and blamed him for her husband's broken back; she chased him out of town with a rifle and he never returned to Fremont or Wayne County ever again. For three years, she had to take care of six children and an invalid husband. A widow without money and mouths to feed, she gratefully accepted the help of William Henry Long. He helped her save the ranch and provided for her family. Women did not own property in the 1900's, so she paid for the ranch or her family would have been homeless.

Bill and Luzernia first met in Cortez, Colorado where Luzernia and Silas Morrell were with a group of Mormon pioneers heading for Mexico. Bill came riding into the camp yelling; "Circle the wagons! The outlaws are shooting up the town!" Bill had just robbed the bank and Bill "IS" the outlaw. He had received a bullet wound to the leg. Luzernia and her 12-year-old daughter Clara helped to dress his wound and took care of him. Silas could not make the trip to Mexico; the decision is made to return to Fremont and the family ranch. Bill traveled with them and found a job as a "horse breaker" at the Hogan Ranch in Loa, Utah. He is known for breaking the unbreakable horses. He would start by whacking them between the eyes with a wagon spoke until they submitted. Not exactly a "Horse Whisperer!"

The whole family knew how much Bill loved Luzernia's home cooking. After courting her, he married Luzernia Allred Morrell on November 13, 1894 in Fremont, Utah. The step-children called him "Uncle Billy." They just lost their father and it seemed friendlier to call this strange man who married their mother, "Uncle Billy Long." Etta Forsyth, (Bill Long's 93-year-old step grand-daughter) told us a story of one hot sultry day out in the fields, Bill came home to Luzernia who is baking in their kitchen. She always wore an apron and had hot bread cooling on the kitchen table under a white cloth. He took one look at the bread and immediately went over and tore off a piece with his bare hands, not bothering to use a knife to cut off a slice. He devoured the homemade bread and everyone knew how much he loved her turkey roasts, beef roasts, with simmering carrots, onions, potatoes and homemade gravy. The old saying, "The way to a man's heart is through his stomach," is true. Luzernia had Bill's heart.

Bill went from robbing a bank in Cortez, Colorado with just the clothes on his back, to being introduced to the Morrell family. With a bullet in his leg, Clara (Luzernia's daughter) and Luzernia, helped remove the bullet and wrapped the wound. The Morrell family decided to return to Fremont because of Silas's poor health and Bill joined them. Bill took a job at the Hogan Ranch in Loa, as a "horse breaker," for two dollars a day. After Silas passed away, Bill then courted and married Luzernia. Luzernia did not own her own property and women were not even allowed to vote until 1919. She still had to pay the mortgage or she would have become homeless with six young children to care for. Etta Forsyth (step grand-daughter) stated, "My Grandma needed help, and Uncle Billy offered, so she took it." The Silas Morrell homestead and home he built with the logs from his sawmill, were now the property of William Henry Long.

What a great cover for an outlaw with a $6,500.00 price on his head. "WANTED: 'Dead or Alive'!" Who would suspect a married man with six step-children, with two more children of his own, is really "The Sundance Kid?" A double life, indeed!

There is absolutely no record of Bill Long's signature anywhere. He claimed to be illiterate and unable to write his name so he would sign with an "X" or have someone else sign for him. This is of course a lie to hide his identity. Bill never learned to drive or owned a car. He is still riding a horse into town in 1936. Bill and Luzernia's first child, Florence Viola, is born on June 30, 1895 in Fremont, Utah. Their second child is Evinda Ann, (Vinda) Long, born March 29, 1898, also in Fremont. On the 1900 census, Luzernia is listed as the head of household and Bill has been gone from the family for eight to ten years. Bill and Luzernia's homestead is a show place, and in his absence, the family always had plenty of money. Luzernia bought land in Bill's name twice, once in 1903, and then again in 1907. They never worked and always had money. Diann Peck who owns the "Floating Feather Ranch" in Duchesne, (Etta Forsyth's daughter) remembers stories of how Grandpa Long had been missing for all those years. Diann asked, "How could a man leave a wife and all of those children and be gone for such a long time?" Bill Long is listed as head of household in 1910. He returned after an estimated ten-year absence and no one dared to ask where he had been or why he could speak fluent "French," or they would be in trouble.

The Long Family stayed in Fremont until 1917. Bill bought a ranch in Duchesne, Utah to be closer to family. Bill went on a trip to Fish Lake, Utah and he returned with enough cash, (gold coins) to pay for the ranch in Duchesne. Family members agree that they were all oblivious to what is really going on. Now that time has passed and they are older, it makes sense that Grandpa Long had been an outlaw with a stash of "gold" coins buried at Fish Lake. There is no other explanation for paying cash for the Duchesne Ranch. Etta Forsyth said, "As a young child, I saw bags of 'gold' coins on the kitchen table." She stated, "Who has bags of gold on their kitchen table?" Now that she is older, it makes sense that her step-grandfather is an outlaw! They were all so close to the situation, that they could not see the truth at the time.

Bill and Luzernia lived in Duchesne and helped with their grandchildren. Then the banks failed and they lost all their money; that is in 1929 during "The Great Depression." Bill Long had a joint bank account, according to Etta Forsyth, with Matt Warner, a former member of the "Wild Bunch." After the money vanished, and from that time on, Bill and Luzernia had to live off the land; they had a hard life. When I interviewed Etta, she had no idea that Matt Warner had been a member of the "Wild Bunch." She is genuinely shocked when I explained Matt Warner became a member of "The Wild Bunch." She just knew Matt Warner as Grandpa Billy's friend and business partner. They kept money in the Price Bank where Matt Warner lived, to do business transactions together.

On November 27, 1936 Bill Long died.  Betty Bird, a great granddaughter, had been told twice by her mother Eva, (Eva's mother, Evinda Ann) that Matt Warner had murdered Bill.  The family knew that Bill became upset with Warner for writing a book on his life as a former member of the "Wild Bunch."  Bill had heated arguments with Matt not to write the book.  Bill worried that he could be found out as "The Sundance Kid."

Dr. McCullough's forensic examination of Bill Long's bullet wound to the head shows that someone murdered him with a 22 rifle from two to three feet away.  The bullet hole showed that the rifle had been fired from an upward angle.  Near impossible to inflict on one's self.  His death certificate states that he committed suicide and family members reported that he had taken his own life.  The family covered up his murder so the authorities would not look closer into his death and his "secret life" as "The Sundance Kid."

What a tragic ending for a man that had escaped the law and lived a quiet life with his family in the remote wilderness area of Duchesne, Utah.  Bill stopped robbing and he is no longer an outlaw and became a contributing member of society.

He is born into a family of "poor farmers" and died a "poor farmer" living off the land.


## Note:
### Journal Entry of Marilyn Grace - December 24, 2010 "Christmas Eve"

*I went to Cedar City, Utah on Christmas Eve.  I spent time with my son Sterling, his wife Mindy, and my four grandchildren.  I showed Sterling our book and he looked at the pictures of "The Speckled Nigger."  He said, "Mom, you can't call him 'The Speckled Nigger' you are going to be on 'Oprah'!"  He's just horrified! I had to laugh and explain that I do not have any other name for this man, but I am thrilled that he just knew that we were going to be on "Oprah!"*

*Eddie Fast, one of our TEAM MEMBERS, found Albert Welhouse's name from a photo in Salt Lake City, Utah.  Now we can call him "SPECK!"  Thanks Eddie Fast for hunting down that information… you and Chris are THE BEST!*

*(See Photo Album for "Speckled Nigger" Photos.  We now know his real name is Albert Welhouse.)*

# CHAPTER SEVEN
## Treasures in Tremonton

In January 11, 2008, our film crew met with Sherma Payton, along with her sister, Ray McDonald. Their brother, Jerry Morrell, his wife, Georgia and their son Rod, all met at Ray's home in Tremonton, Utah. Unfortunately, Ray McDonald passed away shortly after our visit. We were glad to capture her lovely personality and story gems before her passing.

Sherma also shared with us a letter written in the hand of Bill Long's oldest daughter, Florence Viola. In that letter, she writes to her half-brother, Hiett Morrell, that she seeks information about her father and "his people." She wonders if his real name is "Long." She had been unable to trace any family genealogy, either through the LDS Genealogical Library or public records. She says that her father would never talk about his "past" with the family.

According to Sherma, Viola, (as she is known) had tried to obtain her father's birth records in Wyoming, using the limited information her father had revealed about his origins. Her father had claimed he had been born in the Big Horn Basin Territory of Wyoming. Viola found out that there were no white settlers or birth records for that time, in The Big Horn area of the Indian Territories.

When Viola could not obtain any birth records or verify any of the family history that her father had given her, she began to write to others in search of clues as to her father's identity. Viola wrote to Hiett (Silas Morrell and Luzernia's son) asking him if he had any information about her father. Viola had also written letters to her father's best friend, Irwin G. Robison, to learn more about her father's mysterious past. Irwin married Clara Morrell, Luzernia's second daughter and Clara is Florence Viola's half-sister.

Irwin became Wayne County Sheriff from 1915 to 1917. Bill Long had taught Irwin how to shoot so he could become Sheriff of Wayne County. The outlaw teaches the sheriff how to shoot by going down to the shed and shooting the heads off nails. Bill could shoot equally well with both hands and taught Irwin how to do the same. Sherma believes that Irwin knew William Henry Long is a wanted man, but is protecting him from being exposed and captured by other lawmen. Irwin wanted to go off with Bill and join "THE WILD BUNCH," but his family would not allow it. Getting involved with the outlaws is just too dangerous. Irwin kept Bill's identity hidden out of regard for his wife Clara, as well as for her mother's family. The whole family knew he's an outlaw. Irwin and Bill became genuinely good friends.

When Sherma's father is dying, he entrusted Sherma with the Viola letter, William Henry Long's photo and the sister's pictures. Sherma remembers what a serious tone her father had when he surrendered the items— "Take good care of them Sherma!"

Josie and her sister Ann Bassett dated both, "Butch Cassidy and The Sundance Kid." They knew the two outlaws who worked for their parents in Brown's Park when the Bassett girls were young.

Curiosity got to Sherma, so she and her brother Jerry, along with Jerry's young son Rod Morrell, visited an elderly Josie Bassett in the early 1960's. As a young boy, Rod remembers an 80-year-old Josie, with dirty and torn overalls. Josie lived in a small log cabin with dirt floors that she had built with her own hands in the foothills of Vernal. She lived off the land and had no running water or electricity. She's a known bootlegger and made her own whiskey. It is rumored that you better not let your cows drift over to Josie's spread; or they will vanish. According to Rod Morrell, her neighbors knew she butchered at least one of their cows a year, but they just let it go. Josie could kill and butcher a cow, as well as a deer, all on her own. She did help her neighbors survive during the 1929 Great Depression by butchering deer. The law looked the other way during the depression, families were hungry. She would also grow food in her garden to share with her neighbors.

Sherma and Jerry showed Josie the original photograph of their step-great grandfather, William Henry Long, and asked Josie if she recognized the man in the picture. They both recounted how, "her eyes lit up and she started to say, 'yes, why that's...' and then she became silent and said that she didn't know him."

Jerry and Sherma were determined to find out from Josie Bassett who Bill Long really is, so they returned to Josie's home a few months later. They had the exact same response; Josie would not tell! She died a few years after their visit and her secret died with her.

"Dad used to tell me that 'Grandpa Bill' always had a horse saddled and ready to go in the barn at all times," reports Sherma. Etta Forsyth, (93) and Bill Long's step grand-daughter verified that story as well and told us about a flag on the porch that the family would wave if they could see trouble coming. Bill also had a disc or bell on the porch that is so loud, it would summon or warn him when he's out in the fields.

Sherma told me a story, "Her father Silas Morrell, at 6 years old, is sent to Boulder Mountain in Fremont to herd sheep. All he had is a lard sandwich. He had breakfast and no lunch, and saved his lard sandwich for dinner or he would have felt hunger pangs all night." She also explained how rough living in Wayne County is, and how very poor her father's family were. "A lot of the men were not famous, but they were outlaws just the same," Sherma stated.

Rod Morrell shared one more treasure with us before we left—a 45-70 Winchester rifle that belonged to Silas Morrell, Luzernia's first husband. Bill Long later used the same rifle on hunting trips. It is the same rifle that Luzernia threatened the black man with. ("Speckled Nigger" Albert Welhouse, nick named,"Speck!") She chased him out of the county, blaming him for her husband's back injury.

These treasures in Tremonton, which had thankfully been carefully preserved by the Morrell side of the family, yield some interesting clues as to the true identity of William Henry Long. The original photograph of Bill, the original photograph of his sisters and the original letter from Florence Viola, questioning her father's true identity - these are important pieces of the puzzle, swinging wide open the door to the possibility that William Henry Long is an alias for Harry Alonzo Longabaugh, "The Sundance Kid."

Bill Long's original picture as a cowboy, (age 25) his sisters picture that match "The Sundance Kid's" sisters picture and the Florence Viola letter asking, "Who is my Father?" are included for you to review and to compare for yourself! WHAT FUN!

(See Photo Album)

The record of my father
as near as I know
my Grandfather James Gay
        father Ann

Grandfather Adrian killed by Indians
and his horse brought half home
    Charlie
    Brant
    William Henry my father
    Adam
    Lucy married Jim Moore
    Sarah Selina
    Missey Mahala
These names are not in
order of age but I don't
know which is the oldest

but the picture
was taken at Sun City, Arizona
J. W. Riga photographer

Viola with great grandson
Robbie Vincent Robison
April 1962

# CHAPTER EIGHT
## Family Name Comparison

In 1978, the Sundance Film Festival with Chairperson Robert Redford and Utah's Governor Scott Matheson, set out to showcase American Independent Films to increase visibility of film-making in Utah. The Sundance Film Festival has grown to be the largest film festival in the world and is hosted every year by the town of Park City, Utah. My favorite show ever to premier at the Film Festival is "Whale Rider." I highly recommend viewing this beautifully crafted and spiritual movie, filmed exclusively in New Zealand.

The instant you enter Park City, the scent of pine from pinion and ponderosa trees welcomes you with an intoxicating blast of fresh mountain air. The forest grows thick over the entire mountain. Stands of shimmering quaking aspen dance, while the fire-red Indian paint brush, crown-leaf evening primrose, blue bells and other wild flowers and wild grasses surround the ancient trees. Friendly locals welcome you to this beautiful mountain playground.

Park City is a "World-Class" Ski Resort Community! The population is over 7,000 with an elevation of 7,000 feet above sea level. The famous slogan, "The Greatest Snow On Earth!" is why Park City is thriving. Deer Valley, Park West, The Canyons, Park City Mountain Resort, Westgate, and the Dakota Mountain Lodge, and Golden Door Spa, are part of the affluent lifestyle that can be found just 32 miles southeast of downtown Salt Lake City, Utah. Once a busy mining town with the first claim being the Young American Lode in 1869, acted as a catalyst for the Pinion, Walker, Webster, Flagstaff, McHenry, Buckeye, and the most famous, Silver King Mines. The gold, lead, and silver came out of the mountain a shovel at a time and 400 million dollars later, there were 23 millionaires. Park City, Utah is one of the richest towns in the United States. Settled by non-Mormons, there were social halls, saloons and theaters, contrasting the Park City lifestyle from the rest of the state. Victorian, "turn-of-the-century" architecture gives the town an old-world atmosphere.

Olympic Park is a major tourist attraction. The spotlight shined on Park City as the world watched the "2002 Winter Olympics" from Utah's most beautiful and pristine mountain tops, located in Wasatch and Summit Counties.

The mines were getting close to being tapped out by the 1920's; then came the 1930's "Great Depression" and development halted. By the 1950's the towns almost dead. Due to the increase in winter activities, especially skiing, the town experienced a rebirth.

While attending the "Sundance Film Festival 2008," I am "lucky" enough to get snowed in. Park City is beautiful in winter, with a blanket of white covering everything for as far as the eye can see. My car had been buried in the night, so I decided to spend my time studying my copy of the "Longabaugh Genealogy Book." At the LDS Genealogy Library, across from Temple Square in Salt Lake City, I purchased a copy of the Longabaugh Genealogy book. The genealogy book had been compiled by author, Donna Ernst, whose husband is the great-nephew of Harry Alonzo Longabaugh, a.k.a., "The Sundance Kid." Donna wrote another book called, "Sundance, My Uncle," which is based on Paul's, (her husband) family stories about his "infamous" great uncle.

With a cup of warm cocoa, I settled in with my one hundred plus pages of the Longabaugh Genealogy. The task of reading slowly and mindfully through the pages of names, dates of birth, marriages, deaths, notations and comments, ended up being a wonderful way to pass the time, while being surrounded with drifts of snow. I am stuck, not going anywhere until the streets were cleared, so this became a wonderful time to look through the genealogy book. Family history is my first love and as I studied, it became apparent that the Long and Longabaugh family shared many similar family names.

In deep thought, wondering about the possible meaning of this discovery, even as the falling snow deepened the drifts imprisoned my car. According to several sources, it used to be fairly common at the "turn of the century" to name children after relatives, especially those who had died as a means of carrying on the family heritage. Given this reality, it is truly remarkable how many family members share the same names between Harry Alonzo Longabaugh's family and William Henry Long's family. It would be hard to imagine all the similarities as being coincidences. Just think about it! William Henry Long first appeared on the scene in Loa, Utah the same month that Harry Alonzo Longabaugh's brother, Harvey Sylvester Longabaugh, had a son that he named William Henry Longabaugh. William Henry Long - William Henry Longabaugh. Harvey also had a daughter named Florence Ann and William Henry Long had two daughters he named Florence Viola and Evinda Ann. Also, Harry Alonzo Longabaugh's mother's name is Ann (nickname Annie) and William Henry Long's mother's name is also listed as "Ann" on his death certificate. Harry Alonzo Longabaugh's beloved sister Samanna had two daughters who both died in infancy. She named her girl's Bertha Viola and Emma Elva. William Henry Long named his first daughter Florence Viola and his first grand-daughter is named Elva. "Etta Place" is the famous alias given to Harry Alonzo Longabaugh's (a.k.a., Sundance Kid) girlfriend or "wife." No marriage license has ever been found. Irwin G. Robison (Sheriff of Wayne County 1915-1917) married Long's step-daughter Clara Morrell, and they named their daughter, "Etta." Family members relate how Etta is teased that she had been named after "Etta Place," and Bill Long is doing the teasing. Etta told me in a two-hour interview that her step-Grandpa Billy, would tease her that she's been named after "The Sundance Kid's" girlfriend, "Etta Place."

As a young child, Bill taught Etta how to ride a pacer pony for the first time. While he's teaching her how to ride, Bill said, "You know, The Sundance Kid's girlfriend's name is Etta; you must have been named after her?" Etta is old enough to know he is teasing her about being named after the famous lady outlaw, "Etta Place."

## Note:

*Look at the document I have included of Pinkerton Detective Rupert J.T.C. from Pennsylvania, 3 April 1902, showing "Harry Longabaugh as 32, German descent, a wanderer, a cowboy, a wild fellow, wrote two years ago to his sister Samanna, who is Mrs. Oliver F. Hallman, Montclaire, (Mont Clare) PA., may be writing him now." There are notations where Rupert intercepted letters that were written by "Sundance" to his sister Samanna, visited his brother Elwood in San Francisco, and a cousin Seth Longabaugh, a miner, in Eureka, Nevada. "Sundance" received news of the family names, dates, and births.*

*Study the Family Name Comparison Chart and the Pinkerton File of 1902 included in this chapter. Coincidence or clues?*

Samanna Longabaugh married Oliver F. Hallman in 1878
Children:

| | |
|---|---|
| A. Adelle Hallman | 18 Oct 1879 — 24 Sept 1902 |
| Furman 'Bud' A. Hallman | 25 Oct 1880 — 9 Jun 1969 |
| Bertha Viola Hallman | 13 Dec 1881 — 5 Jan 1882 |
| (Bertha Viola lived 23 days) | |
| Granville L. Hallman | 2 Apr 1885 — 18 Aug 1963 |
| Emma Elva Hallman | 19 July 1887 — 26 Jan 1888 |
| (Emma Elva lived six months) | |

**Note:**

## Marilyn Grace - Journal Entry

*I didn't have the dates of the girls who died in infancy. Sue Balsamo, a relative of the Longabaugh's from Pennsylvania, just told the dates to me. Harry Alonzo Longabaugh is there when Bertha Viola died. Samanna kept a journal entry for her husband, Oliver F. Hallman. Samanna said, "Harry left with Cousin George and Mary for the West." "Sundance" loved Samanna's children. He loved to play with them. He and Samanna were very close.*

*The Pinkerton File explains that they found out that Samanna and "Sundance" were writing letters. That Pinkerton letter is dated 1902 and said that for two years previously, they knew that Samanna and "Sundance" had been writing; they wanted to remain close even though the letters were used as a way of tracking Harry.*

*I just now pieced this together! "Sundance" knew Samanna's baby that died and Bill Long, (Sundance) named "Florence Viola" after "Bertha Viola." He knew Bertha Viola before he left for Cortez, Colorado with Cousin George Longenbaugh (different spelling, still related) and his wife Mary.*

Harry left home in October 1882 to go West with Cousin George Longenbaugh and his wife Mary. Samanna, "Sundance's" sister, wrote in a business journal that Harry Longabaugh left for the West to help Cousin George and family. Harry would have been 14 or 15 years old when he traveled West with family. Mary is pregnant and had a small child, a son, Walter. George handled horses and Harry worked alongside him. Their destination is Durango, Colorado where George homesteaded with his family. Later the Longenbaugh family moved to Cortez.

At age 17, Harry joined "The Wild Bunch" and became the first of "Butch Cassidy's Gang." He served 18 month's hard labor for horse theft. He served his time and had a full pardon when he is released from the Sundance, Wyoming Jail. He is pardoned and released because he's under the age of 21.

William Henry Long married Luzernia Allred Morrell, in 1894 in Fremont, Utah. Their first daughter Florence Viola, is born in 1895. He wanted strong family ties, so Bill named his firstborn after Bertha Viola, an infant of Samanna's who died shortly after birth. Harry saw her come into the world, held her, and in less than a month she's gone.

Harry visited the family in Pennsylvania in 1901 with girlfriend, (wife?) "Etta Place," and would have known about the death of Emma "Elva." A generation later, Bill Long's grand-daughter is named "Elva." Bill Long's second child is named Evinda "Ann" and "Sundance's" brother Harvey, has a child by the name of Florence "Ann." "Sundance's" mother's name is Ann "Place." "Sundance's" female companions name is "Etta Place." Bill Long's step grand-daughter is named "Etta."

Elva and Bill Long were very close. He would hold her on his lap and rock her on the porch. He would hum the tune, "In The Good Old Summer Time." Elva at the time of this interview is 93. She has loving memories of "Grandpa Billy." She knew she's loved by him and felt she's his "favorite" grandchild. His step-children called him "Uncle Billy." They had just lost their father, Silas Morrell, so calling him "Uncle Billy" seemed more appropriate at the time. Etta said the same thing that "Uncle Billy" is the only grandfather she ever knew. Her real grandfather Silas Morrell, had died before her birth. Etta and Elva both said that he would rock them on the porch and quietly hum the tune, "In The Good Old Summer Time."

Elva told us the true story of how "Grandpa Billy" saved her from certain death.  She fell off a plow horse while in the field and suddenly the horse would not move.  The horse had his giant hoof on her tiny head; Bill did not know that Elva is underneath and in danger.  When the horse would not move, he went to investigate and found Elva lifeless on the ground.  She had the wind knocked out of her and he revived her.  She is five or six when this happened.  Elva told us, "Grandpa Billy saved my life!"

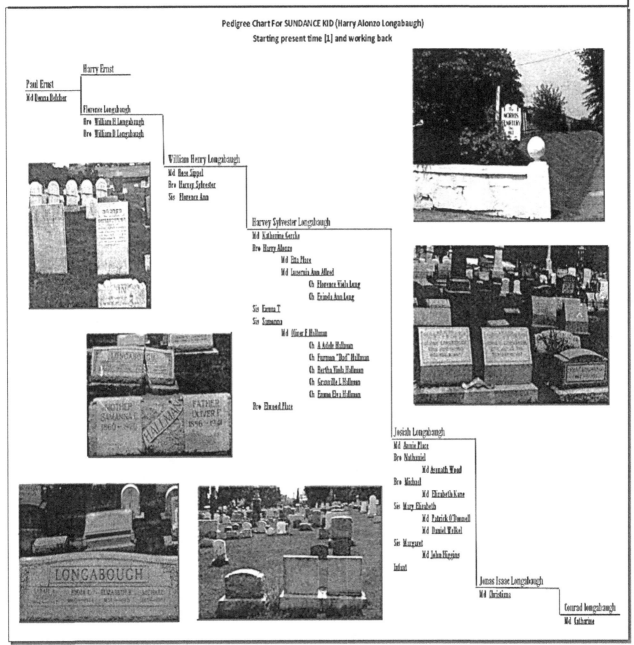

Pedigree Chart For SUNDANCE KID (Harry Alonzo Longabaugh)

Starting present time [1] and working back

Paul Ernst
Md Donna Belcher

Harry Ernst

Florence Longabaugh
Bro William H Longabaugh
Bro William B Longabaugh

William Henry Longabaugh
Md Rose Sippel
Bro Harvey Sylvester
Sis Florence Ann

Harvey Sylvester Longabaugh
Md Katherine Gercke
Bro Harry Alonzo
   Md Etta Place
   Md Lucernia Ann Allred
      Ch Florence Viola Long
      Ch Erinda Ann Long
Sis Emma T
Sis Samanna
   Md Oliver F Hallman
      Ch A Adele Hallman
      Ch Furman "Bud" Hallman
      Ch Bertha Viola Hallman
      Ch Granville L Hallman
      Ch Emma Elva Hallman
Bro Elwood Place

Josiah Longabaugh
Md Annie Place
Bro Nathaniel
   Md Asenath Wood
Bro Michael
   Md Elizabeth Kane
Sis Mary Elizabeth
   Md Patrick O'Donnell
   Md Daniel Welkel
Sis Margaret
   Md John Higgins
Infant

Jonas Isaac Longabaugh
Md Christina

Conrad longabaugh
Md Catharine

Etta's 20 and had her first child when Bill died. She attended the funeral in Duchesne in 1936. Etta also attended the exhumation of her "Uncle Billy Long," in December of 2008. Etta and Elva both dearly loved their "Grandpa Billy Long!" Etta and Elva have recently passed away, but their stories have helped to put all the pieces together and they will never be forgotten. Such precious souls!

There are so many names that match the "Longabaugh" family names with the "Long" family names! This had to be deliberate on the part of William Henry Long. His girls had the same names as his family back in Pennsylvania. He created a connection to his past that could not be severed in time, but would last "forever!"

Robert ... ...

... Harry Longbaugh is 32

German descent

a Wanderer, a ... ...

with fellows.

Left Pa. ... years

wrote ... ... to his sister

Samanna ... ...

O. J. Halleman, Montclair

may be writing him now

... ... ... in ... last

Summer (190) in Buffalo, N.Y.

... ... ... he got an

... ... of rifle ...

... relatives in Montclair, Pa.

Longbaugh is from Montclair

Pa. Parents both dead.

Bro. Edward P. 192 Julian Ave.

San Francisco

Harry — Phila.

Samanna, Sister, m. to Oliver P. Halleman

Montclair Pa. —

Emma — at Wanamaker's

Harry visited his bro. Edward P. 2

years ago, i.e. 1900, ...

think Edward P. & Harry ...

... with Mrs. Halleman in

Montclair & Emma in Phila.

Harry has a Cousin Seth Longbaugh

a miner, in Nevada

probably at Eureka.

See San Francisco papers J.M.L.

March 4 & 6/1902

...

...

...

...

...

...

...

Harry ... ... boy

... ...

by 3 men to ... ... Matta ...

... Longbaugh ...

Harry Bass ...

Bill Madden 14

... ... ... ...

... rather hastily

C. S. Gardiner, ... Matta ...

... with Robert, boys, ... ago, ... San

Longbaugh, George

June 18 ... ...

Crook Co., Wyo.

# CHAPTER NINE

## Timeline Comparison

### Timeline Comparison of the Lives of
### Harry Alonzo Longabaugh and William Henry Long

As you review the following chart which compares documented events in the lives of "both" men, you will see another piece of the puzzle coming together. Notice how the mysterious ten year absence of William Henry Long coincides with the travels of the infamous Sundance Kid and his companion Etta Place, and how only after the alleged death of the Sundance Kid does William Henry Long reappear and remain with his family in Utah.

| Harry Alonzo Longabaugh | William Henry Long |
|---|---|
| Spring 1867 - HAL is born to Josiah and Ann (Annie) Place Longabaugh in Mont Clare, Pennsylvania. He is their fifth and last child. No birth certificate available. | February 1860 - According to WHL's obituary, written by his second daughter Evinda Ann, he was born in February 1860 in Wyoming's Big Horn Basin Territory. On his death certificate it gave his mother's name as "Ann". No birth certificate available.<br><br>However, WHL married Luzernia Morrell in November 1894. On their marriage license he put his age as 27 years old. This would mean he was born in 1867.<br><br>WHL's step-granddaughter recalls that the family celebrated his birthday on March 13 each year. |
| August 1882 - HAL travels west with his cousin George Longabaugh's family. They homestead in Cortez, Colorado. | |
| 1885 - HAL (age 17) and Robert LeRoy Parker (aka Butch Cassidy) become outlaws with half a dozen other partners. The "Wild Bunch" is formed. | |
| 1887 - HAL steals a horse in Sundance, Wyoming and is later caught, convicted and sentenced to eighteen months in the Sundance, WY jail, earning him the moniker, "Sundance Kid." | |

| | |
|---|---|
| June 24, 1889 - Telluride Bank Robbery by the Wild Bunch. It is believed Sundance Kid participates in the robbery having escaped from jail in Wyoming. | |
| December 1892 - Sundance Kid, Bill Madden and Harry Bass hold up the Great Northern Train at Malta, Montana. Bass and Madden were tried and convicted to 10 and 14 years respectively. Sundance Kid escaped and is a wanted fugitive. There is a $1000 reward for him, dead or alive. He goes into hiding and disappears. | |
| | 1893 - Silas Morrell and his family are traveling west when they first meet WHL in Cortez, Colorado. WHL rode into their camp of Mormon settlers yelling, "Circle the wagons. There are outlaws shooting up the town!" He had a bullet wound to his leg and Silas's wife, Luzernia and her oldest daughter, Clara, tended to his wound. It is believed he was one of the outlaws "shooting up the town" and entered the camp to avoid getting caught. |
| | September 1893 - Silas Morrell dies of a back injury leaving his widowed wife, Luzernia, and six children. |
| | October 1893 - WHL is recorded on the books as a cowhand receiving $2.00 a day and living at the Hogan Ranch in Loa, Utah. |
| | November 1894 - WHL courts and marries Luzernia Morrell. |
| | June 1895 - WHL and Luzernia have a daughter, Florence Viola Long. |
| 1897 - HAL's brother, Harvey Sylvester Longabaugh, has a daughter and names her Florence Ann. She dies at the age of 12. | |

| | |
|---|---|
| | March 29, 1898 - WHL and Luzernia have a second daughter and name her Evinda Ann Long. |
| | June 1900 - Luzernia Morrell Long is listed as the Head of Household on the US Census Bureau Records. |
| November 1900 - HAL (aka Sundance Kid), Butch Cassidy, Ben Kilpatrick, Will Carver and Harvey Logan pose for the Famous Fort Worth Five Photograph in Ft. Worth, Texas. | |
| January 1901 - HAL (aka Sundance Kid) and his girlfriend, "Etta Place", visit his family in Pennsylvania. They had their picture taken at DeYoung Studios in NYC. | |
| February 1, 1901 - Sundance and Etta Place register as Mr. and Mrs. Harry Place at Mrs. Taylor's Boarding House in NYC. Butch joins them and registers as Etta's brother, James Ryan. Etta purchases a lapel watch stick pin at Tiffany's. | |
| April 2, 1902 - Sundance and Etta Place register at Mrs. Thomson's Rooming House in NYC and they tour Coney Island together and visit his family in Atlantic City, New Jersey. | |
| July 1902 - Sundance and Etta Place board the ship, "Honorius" and set sail from New York to Buenos Aires, posing as stewards. | |
| August 9, 1902 - Sundance and Etta register at a hotel in Buenos Aires, Argentina. | |

| | |
|---|---|
| August 15, 1902 - Sundance and Etta travel aboard the steamship, SS Chubut and return to their ranch in Cholila, Argentina. | |
| | 1903 - Luzernia Long purchases land in WHL's name. He is not present for the transaction. |
| Summer 1904 - Sundance and Etta return to the U.S. to visit her family. The Pinkertons track them at the World Fair in Ft. Worth Texas but they head back to Argentina before getting caught. | |
| June 30, 1905 - A letter dated June 30, 1905 from Sundance Kid saying that he and Etta are leaving Valparaiso, Chili for San Francisco. Sundance says in the letter that he never wants to see Argentina again. | |
| May 1, 1906 - Sundance, Butch and Etta sell their ranch in Argentina to avoid the law. | |
| 1907 - Etta (Ethel) Place is living in San Francisco where, it is believed, Sundance set her up with a place to live, two years previously. | 1907 - Luzernia Long purchases land in WHL's name. He is not present for this transaction in Loa, Utah. Family members and neighbors knew of WHL's long absence and were puzzled over how Luzernia and the children were so wealthy and had a "show place". |
| 1908 - Sundance Kid and Butch Cassidy are reported by newspapers to have been shot and killed in San Vincente, Bolivia. | |
| July 31, 1909 - Etta (Ethel) Place tried to obtain death certificates for Butch and Sundance but is unsuccessful. Etta disappears from all records after this. | |

| | |
|---|---|
| | **1910** - WHL reappears as Head of Household in the 1910 US Census Bureau Records in Fremont, Utah. Elva O'Neal the granddaughter of WHL, daughter of Florence Viola Long, states that he came home from a ten year absence and could speak French fluently. Elva's son, Gaylen Robison, said that according to family stories no one was allowed to ask him where he had been all those years or how he had come to learn French. |
| | **November 1917** - WHL and Luzernia relocate from Loa, Utah in Wayne County to a ranch in Duchesne, Utah. According to WHL's step-grand daughter, Etta Forsyth (92), who still lives on a nearby ranch in Duchesne, WHL (whom she called "Uncle Billy") went on a two day trip to Fish Lake and came back with enough money to pay cash for the ranch in Duchesne. |

| | |
|---|---|
| | **1925 - 1928** - Family stories reveal that WHL would leave home for several days at a time. Everyone knew it had to do with another woman and Luzernia said that it was okay with her but she would pull her apron over her head and pout while he was away. No one was allowed to question him or ask about his frequent absences. Despite this odd arrangement, WHL genuinely loved and cared for Luzernia, his children, step-children and grandchildren. |
| - ı | **October 29, 1929** - Stock market crashed leaving WHL penniless. According to Etta Forsyth, the step-great granddaughter of WHL, he had a joint bank account with former Wild Bunch member, Matt Warner. They lost all of their money in the Duchesne bank. Genealogist, James Petty is searching for documentation to verify this family story. |

| | |
|---|---|
| | **November 1936** - WHL is found dead with a bullet wound to his head at his ranch in Duchesne, Utah. On his death certificate it says cause of death is "suicide". Dr. John McCullough, however, has exciting new evidence that indicates WHL may have been murdered. According to Betty Bird her grandmother, Evinda Ann Long, WHL's second daughter, has always suspected that WHL was killed by Matt Warner. It is believed family members put suicide as cause of death on the death certificate to avoid an investigation which could possibly have uncovered WHL's true identity. |

# CHAPTER TEN

| Physical Description Comparison Between Harry Alonzo Longabaugh and William Henry Long | | |
|---|---|---|
| Physical Characteristics | Harry Alonzo Longabaugh | William Henry Long |
| Height | 5'9" or 5'10" (wanted posters) | 5'8" (forensic examination) |
| Weight | described as being 185 to 190 pounds in wanted posters | undetermined |
| Eye Color | blue / grey | grey |
| Hair Color | dark hair w/light brown or sandy colored mustache | dark hair w/reddish mustache |
| Complexion | described as smooth faced, face much tanned by sun, medium complexion in wanted posters | dark complexion, weathered |
| Build | strong, muscular build<br><br>described as having feet turned in, bow legged and not bow legged in various wanted posters<br><br>described as having a shuffle to his walk | strong, muscular build<br><br>not bow legged according to forensic examination<br><br>Had a left hip and ankle injury according to forensic examination |
| | unusually long fingers | unusually long fingers |
| | bullet wound to leg | bullet wound to leg |
| | broken nose, sinus problems | broken nose, sinus problems |
| | notch in ear | notch in ear |
| | dimple in chin | dimple in chin |
| | could shoot pistol equally well with left and right hands | could shoot pistol equally well with left and right hands |

# Sundance Kid's Birthday

Luzernia Allred Long, born on April 27, 1857 in Spring City, Utah. Luzernia passed away four months after her husband's death. William Henry Long said he had been born in the "Big Horn Basin" of Wyoming when there were no white settlers. Etta Forsyth, Bill Long's step grand-daughter, said that the family celebrated his birthday on March 13. When Bill Long married Luzernia, his license stated he is born in 1867. "The Sundance Kid" had, (about spring of 1867) as his birth year. The Long Family said he had been born February 1st or 2nd, 1860? They were not sure where or when he had been born? William Henry Long died on November 27, 1936. Age 69.

William Henry Long

# CHAPTER ELEVEN
## Getting Scientific

Sometime in 2006 some of William Henry Long's descendants exhumed his body to find out if Bill could be William Henry McCarty (Bill). Tim Kupherschmid, the head of Sorenson Forensics in Salt Lake City, reported DNA tests proved that William Henry Long is not Bill McCarty.

Dr. John McCullough did a preliminary forensic examination of the bones and skull before the remains were re-interred in the Duchesne Cemetery. In November 2007, around that same time, Dr. McCullough completed a scientific photo analysis with photographs of William Henry Long and Harry Alonzo Longabaugh, "The Sundance Kid." William Henry Long's photo matched Harry A. Longabaugh's photo, they are one in the same.

In November 2008, using Dr. McCullough's photo analysis results and the preliminary forensic report, our TEAM obtained a court order allowing us to exhume the skeletal remains and do our own DNA testing. Our TEAM exhumed the remains of William Henry Long a second time in December of 2008. It's now January of 2009 and Tim Kupferschmid successfully extract a DNA samples from the exhumed remains. Tim sent the sample to an undisclosed DNA lab back east. The entire TEAM anxiously awaited the results!

The ideal outcome of the DNA testing would reveal that the DNA extracted from the remains of William Henry Long, matches the DNA of a known living descendant of Ann, (Annie) Place Longabaugh, the mother of Harry Alonzo Longabaugh, Carl Schuch. Carl and his wife Delia live in California. This would prove beyond any doubt that William Henry Long really is Harry Alonzo Longabaugh. This would be a definitive answer to the mystery.

We have the results from the DNA. The good news is that the lab back east successfully obtained a full DNA sample, according to Tim Kupherschmid. The relatives only had a partial sample to work with that did not match Bill McCarty. We can say that we have the DNA, but we are now looking for living Longabaugh's so we can match Bill Long's DNA profile to Josiah Longabaugh. More samples, more lab tests, and more time! We are sorry folks, the DNA is still not conclusive, but we are working on it!

What if the DNA results are not the conclusive match that we are hoping for? Will that discredit all the other pieces of the puzzle that have gone into identifying William Henry Long as Harry Alonzo Longabaugh? Will it mean that we were wrong and that William Henry Long is not "The Sundance Kid?" ABSOLUTELY NOT!

There is always the remote possibility that the body buried in Duchesne, in 1936, and later exhumed, may not have been the body of William Henry Long. Etta Forsyth, the step grand-daughter of William Henry Long, is the only remaining person alive who attended his funeral. She reported that its a closed casket funeral, no viewing, and no one saw the body that the family buried on that day.

Our TEAM is fully convinced that this is not a possibility that they have to worry about, considering the forensic evidence. There were several characteristics of the exhumed remains that were shared by William Henry Long and Harry Alonzo Longabaugh.

The size, height, stature and build of the skeletal remains match the physical descriptions and photographs of both William Henry Long and Harry Alonzo Longabaugh. Also of significance, the nose of the exhumed body is broken, as were the noses of William Henry Long and Harry Alonzo Longabaugh. The skull shows evidence of sinus problems. Hospital records indicated that "The Sundance Kid" sought treatment at a hospital for a sinus condition. The remains also revealed a bullet wound to the leg. William Henry Long had a bullet wound to the leg when he rode into the Morrell camp outside of Cortez, Colorado where he first met Luzernia and her family. History documents that "The Sundance Kid" sustained a bullet wound to his leg. He's an outlaw, so there is even the possibility of wounds to both legs. The X-rays our TEAM took of William Henry Long's leg, show the bone damage of a possible bullet wound to his leg. The X-ray needs further examination by a specialist.

Dr. John McCullough came to the conclusion that the deceased had lost all of his teeth about two to four years prior to his death. Etta Forsyth, step grand-daughter of William Henry Long reported, "Uncle Billy didn't like to wear his teeth so he kept them in the sugar jar in the cupboard."

As would be expected, with both the rugged "Sundance Kid" and William Henry Long, Dr. McCullough's forensic examination revealed that the skeletal remains showed extensive wear and tear, including many fractures, indicating an extremely rough and active lifestyle.

There is also evidence of extensive arthritis throughout the remains. A living relative of William Henry Long who lives in a nursing home in Salt Lake City, Elva O'Neal, reports that her grandfather, William Henry Long, suffered terribly with "Lumbago," which today we call arthritis.

Our TEAM feels confident that the remains are those of William Henry Long of Duchesne, Utah. We are back to work searching for Longabaugh family members back east for more DNA tests.

Dr. McCullough shared with us another reason why the DNA may not match. He told me the true story of his own birth. He related how his parents left the hospital after his birth and when they got home and unbundled him, his father exclaimed, "This is not my son!" and went right back to the hospital. His father inquired as to anyone else who had a baby that same day. He learned that a Jewish family who lived nearby, had also given birth to a baby boy. So, he went to their home with baby in hand, to discuss his dilemma. They looked at the two babies and agreed a mistake had been made and swapped the babies right then. "I was almost raised by a Jewish family," laughed Dr. McCullough. "I sure would have loved to have had a Bar Mitzvah!" "So, do you think Harry Alonzo Longabaugh may have been switched at birth?" I asked John. "No, I don't think that happened," Dr. McCullough chuckled, "but you did ask for any possibilities, right?"

His story started me thinking about another possibility. I had learned that William Henry Long did not have a birth certificate. He supplied none of the information about his birth or family of origin to his daughter Florence Viola and his birth could not be verified by any church, genealogy, or public records.

It said that the State of Pennsylvania did not require birth certificates at the time of Harry Longabaugh's birth. Interestingly, all of Harry Alonzo Longabaugh's siblings' dates of birth are known and are recorded in the family bible, but the exact date of birth for Harry has not been recorded. In the genealogy records it states his date of birth, "about spring of 1867." The possibility exists that perhaps Harry Alonzo Longabaugh is not Ann (Annie) Place and Josiah Longabaugh's child, but had been unofficially adopted. If adopted, Harry would not share the same DNA as descendants of the Place family. We are still considering doing Josiah's DNA. James Petty, our professional genealogist also suggested that Harry had been adopted in his report dated July 10, 2008. "The Sundance Kid" is once described on a wanted poster as, "Looks like quarter breed Indian."

Could it be that Ann (Annie) Place Longabaugh took in a baby that is part Indian because he would most likely be unwanted by a white family during that time?  Strong prejudice existed against Indians back then.  Long told his daughter Florence Viola, that he had been born in the "Big Horn Basin" of Wyoming in 1860.  The Big Horn Basin is "Indian Territory," with no white settlers, adding to the mystery of his origins.

William Henry Long recorded his age as twenty-seven on his marriage certificate to Luzernia in 1894; this would make his date of birth 1867, the same year as "The Sundance Kid" birth.  These could just be interesting pieces of information, or they could be clues pointing to the possibility that Harry Alonzo Longabaugh, a.k.a., "The Sundance Kid," a.k.a., William Henry Long, is actually part Indian.  Harry may not have been a natural born Longabaugh?  His mother Ann, (Annie) Place Longabaugh would have been older at the time of Harry's birth.  Although not impossible, it is improbable that a woman would give birth so late in life during that period of history when nutrition is very poor.

Josiah is 45 at Harry's birth.  Dr. John McCullough can see a family resemblance in Josiah and Harry.  Josiah's hand looks very much like Harry's hand as an adult.  Harry and Josiah both have unusually long fingers.  The possibility exists that Harry Alonzo Longabaugh is related to Josiah, but Ann is not his natural mother.  We still need Josiah's DNA profile to match to Bill Long.

Remember, we are talking about possibilities that exist as to why the DNA extracted from the remains of William Henry Long may not match the DNA of a descendant of the Place and Longabaugh families.  Even if the DNA results are inconclusive, it will in no way invalidate all the other research and scientific evidence that has led to the discovery of William Henry Long's identity as the real "Sundance Kid."

# CURRICULUM VITAE

## JOHN M. McCULLOUGH

Department of Anthropology
University of Utah
Salt Lake City, Utah 84112
Phone: (801) 581-8539

## PERSONAL INFORMATION

| | |
|---|---|
| Date of birth: | March 9, 1940 |
| Citizenship: | U.S.A. |

## EDUCATION

1964-1969
University of Illinois
Ph.D., 1972 - Anthropology
Dissertation: *A Physiological Test of the Bergmann and Allen Rules Among the Yucatec Maya.*

1958-1964
Pennsylvania State University
B.A., 1962 - Anthropology

## ACADEMIC POSITIONS

2000-2001
Visiting Fellow
Cambridge University, England

1995-2000
Associate Vice-President for Academic Affairs, University of Utah

1993-1994
Chair, Academic Senate, University of Utah

1991-present
Professor
University of Utah, Department of Anthropology

1975-1991
Associate Professor
University of Utah, Department of Anthropology

1984-1985
Visiting Fellow
University of Newcastle-Upon-Tyne, England
Department of Human Genetics

1978-1984
Chairman
University of Utah, Department of Anthropology

1969-1975
Assistant Professor
University of Utah, Department of Anthropology

1986-present
Forensic Anthropologist

1976-1980
Office of the Medical Examiner

1969-1975
Utah State Division of Health

| 1966-1969 | NIMH Fellow |
|---|---|
| | University of Illinois, Department of Anthropology |
| 1965-1966 | University Fellow |
| | University of Illinois, Department of Anthropology |
| 1965-1966 | Assistant and Grader |
| | University of Ilinois, Department of Anthropology |
| 1962-1964 | Graduate Assistant |
| | Pennsylvania State University, Department of Anthropology |
| 1961-1962 | Special Senior Assistant |
| | Pennsylvania State University, Department of Anthropology |

## PROFESSIONAL AFFILIATIONS

### REFEREE

Human Biology
Current Anthropology

### PROFESSIONAL AND HONORARY ORGANIZATIONS:

Society for the Study of Social Biology, 1971
Sigma Xi, 1991

### OFFICES HELD:

American Association of Physical Anthropologists, Nominations Committee, 1990-1992
Human Biology Council, Nominations Committee, 1989-1990 (Chairman)
Human Biology Council, Nominations Committee, 1988-1990
Human Biology Council, Nominations Committee, 1984 (Chairman)
Human Biology Council, Nominations Committee, 1982-1984
Human Biology Council, Nominations Committee, 1974-1975
Human Biology Association, Ad Hoc Public and Scientific Affairs
        and Information Committee, 1995-present

### EXTERNAL DEPARTMENT REVIEWS:

Department of Anthropology (Graduate Program), University of Colorado, Denver, March 1990
Department of Sociology and Anthropology (Undergraduate Anthropology Program),
        Weber State College, May 1990
Department of Sociology and Anthropology (Undergraduate Anthropology Program),
        Weber State College, January 2007

## FIELD EXPERIENCE

### ARCHAEOLOGY

| | |
|---|---|
| 1962-1963 | Valley of Teotihuacan, Mexico<br>Excavation Director and intensive survey (under William T. Sanders) |
| 1961 | Sheep Rock Shelter Site, Huntington, Pennsylvania<br>Excavation worker (under John Witthoft) |

### PHYSICAL ANTHROPOLOGY

| | |
|---|---|
| 1987-present | Demography of Colonizing Populations. |
| 1987-present | Historical Demography of Native Americans, with special emphasis upon the Puebloan groups of the Southwest (1690 to 1956). |
| 1986-present | Nevada. Diabetes and Demography among the western Shoshone of Nevada. |
| 1983-present | Salt Lake City, Utah and Pátzcuaro, Michoacán.<br>Demographic and family linkage studies from 1900 to 1930. |
| 1981-1984 | Ft. Duchesne, Utah. Growth assessment of Ute and other children participating in the Head Start Program (with Dr. B. Josea Kramer, Director, Head Start, Fort Duchesne, Utah). |
| 1976 | Merida and Ticul, Yucatan. Cross-sectional anthropometric study of upper-class and rural children in a sub-tropical climate (self and Drs. Renan Gorgora Biachi, Eduarda A. Lavlada Arrigunaga, and A.H. Puga Navarrete of the School of Medicine, University of Yucatan). |
| 1976-present | Salt Lake City, Utah. Demographic and family linkage studies of rural Yucatecans from 1866 to the present (student and self, with the cooperation of the Genealogical Society, Church of Jesus Christ of Latter-Day Saints) (in progress). |
| 1971 | Salt Lake City, Utah. Cerumen studies (assistants and self) (in progress). |
| 1967-1968 | Ticul, Yucatan, Mexico. Adaptive physiology, anthropometry, genetics, demography, cultural anthropology, and meteorology (self). |
| 1966 | Ticul, Yucatan, Mexico. Anthropometry and meteorology (self). |
| 1965 | Ticul, Yucatan, Mexico. Genetics (under Eugene Giles). |

# PRELIMINARY REPORT

## EXAMINATION OF WILLIAM HENRY LONG OF DUCHESNE, UTAH

### 15 November 2007

In mid-October I received a telephone call from Ms. Marilyn Grace concerning the possibility of a forensic examination of an interred decedent who may have been buried under a pseudonym. The decedent, Mr. William Henry Long, died in 1936 and was interred in the city cemetery, Duchesne, Utah. Ms. Grace suggested that Mr. Long might have been born a Mr. Harry Longabaugh, of Montclaire Pennsylvania, better known in the western United States as the Sundance Kid, a wanted criminal originally thought to have died in South America.

On 26 October 2007 I attended the disinterment of Mr. Long. Already exhumed had been major portion of his skull, a portion of the hyoid bone, a calcified section of the larynx, a humerus and a femur, a large section of which had been sectioned for DNA analysis by Sorensen Genomics. After exhumation of all recoverable parts the skeleton was laid out in anatomical order to discern any osteological lesions or anomalies.

The skull had been significantly damaged by an apparent self-inflicted 22-calibre GSW to the left temple about 3 centimeters superior and 2 cm posterior to the external auditory meatus. The inferior portion of the temporal bone was shattered and dislocated from the upper portion. The rebound effect of the blast was to disassociate the lower half of the face and skull base from the remainder of the skull. In field circumstances' facial reconstruction was impossible. An additional complication was the edentulous state of the decedent, with complete and apparently simultaneous tooth loss only some 2 to 5 years before death, as the alveolar borders had completely healed, but not significantly retreated from their earlier positions. Rapid examination of the skull revealed classic Caucasian features - a sharp nasal spine, a sharp inferior nasal border, and a small, narrow palatal surface.

Examination of the postcranial skeleton revealed significant arthritic development along the borders of the lumbar centra 3-5 and to a lesser degree, thoracic 10-12 and lumbar 1-3; accompanying this were arthritic outgrowths along the superior and lateral borders of the sacrum. The fifth lumbar veliebra also showed signs of fracture of the posterior portion of the veliebra, a condition known as spondylolysis; this is caused by a series of micro-fractures from frequent pressure on the vertebra by activities such as heavy athletic activity. The result would be very painful. The acetabula and femoral heads were also deeply involved in arthritic growths along the articular surfaces, probably maldng walking very painful directly in the hip, but also along the lower spine and possibly legs with restriction of nerves from the vertebral arthritis.

An exostosis on the anterior medial surface of the proximal end of the tibia was noted. A radiograph was obtained and examined by a local doctor who stated that the origin of the exostosis was unclear. A metal detector was applied to the surface with a completely negative reading; the radiograph likewise showed an absence of dense material consistent with the presence of metal.

As a general observation, the long bones had exceptionally well-developed ridging along the muscle lines, indicating that the individual had highly developed musculature and undoubtedly lead a very active life. Stature was estimated from all long bones but the right fibula which had broken with non-matching ends, making measurement impossible. Results are found in Appendix A. The stature suggested for this individual would be approximately 5' 8" tall. The Sundance Kid was reported to be either 5' 10" or 5' 9" in stature. Our estimate is quite close to these early reports if one considers the general inaccuracy of casual observations, and the use of high-heeled Western boots by many in the region.

Photo examination was carried out on the following pictures:

Longabaugh with the "Wild Bunch"
Longabaugh with Etta Place in New York
William Long in 1892
William Long in old age with his wife
McCarty, Pere
McCarty, Fille
Longabaugh Sisters in Pennsylvania
Two women found in a photo purportedly taken in Idaho.

Measurement were made of the individuals along the facial midline, as the faces in different photographs were posed at different angles, making accurate lateral measurements impossible. Because the faces are at unknown scales, ratios of various facial measurements were the only fair means of comparison. The ratios represent facial proportions. Results of the examination are found in Appendix B as charts. Each chart is a one-on-one comparison of two individuals; a straight line indicates identity while dots which deviate from a straight line indicate differences in the facial proportions; the greater the deviation the less likely the individuals portrayed are identical. The photos were generally dark and unclear, making measurements extremely difficult. In future, the application of photo enhancement techniques would make the photos much easier to read.

It is absolutely clear that the photo of Mr. William Long taken in 1892 and the photo of Mr. Harry Longabaugh taken with the "Wild Bunch" are of the same person. Comparison of photos of Mr. Long in 1892 and with his wife many years later yield very different results. I believe that the results are changed because of tooth loss in the latter photo that dramatically alters Mr. Long's facial proportions. The pictures of Mr. Long are not consistent with the photos of either of the McCartys.

It is slightly less clear that the women in both photos are his sisters, although the lines of concordance are very strong. Certainly it is not unreasonable to think that the woman standing in one photo is the woman sitting in the other (A1 to A2 and B1 to B2). As with most of the other photos, photo enhancement techniques would yield more accurate results.

A last type of inspection was visual. Transparencies were prepared for comparing faces posed at similar (but unfortunately not identical) angles. These are placed at the end of the report as Appendix C. It will be immediately apparent that the photo of Mr. Long in 1892 and Mr. Longabaugh as one of the "Wild Bunch" are two photos of the same person. Although the pose angles are somewhat different, the points of similarity along the nose, the Mitchell's Notch on the chin and the peculiar shape of the ear pinnae are all absolutely identical. Comparing the late photo of Mr. Long and the New York photo of Mr. Longabaugh with Etta Place is less successful, in part because these photos were taken many years apart, the faces are oriented differently along the horizontal plane, and, I suspect, after Mr. Long had his teeth removed.

Comparison of the two sisters with the women Mr. Long claimed to be sisters is difficult because of the different angles for the two women in the two photos. Nonetheless, comparison of the women on the midline – the one sitting in one photo with the woman standing in the other – suggests a strong resemblance. As in other photos, I suspect the photos were taken many years apart so some amount of aging will have occurred, including possible tooth loss.

Conclusion.

It seems clear that all evidence – osteological, anthropometric and visual - is consistent with the hypothesis that Mr. William Henry Long of Duchesne, Utah, was a pseudonym for Mr. Harry Longabaugh, also known as the Sundance Kid. Photo of the Longabaugh sisters is consistent with Mr. Long's claim that these are his sisters – the Longabaugh sisters. Equally clear is that Mr. Long is not a pseudonym for either of the McCarty's.

Suggested further work on identification would include DNA comparisons of known family members of Mr. Longabaugh with the samples extracted from Mr. Long, and facial reconstruction of the skull of Mr. Long. The usual practice of dentally-based identification is impossible.

Submitted by:

John M. McCullough, Ph. D.
Professor of Anthropology
University of Utah

**Regression Summary**
HL92 vs. SDWB

| | |
|---|---|
| Count | 8 |
| Num. Missing | 0 |
| R | 1.000 |
| R Squared | .999 |
| Adjusted R Squared | .999 |
| RMS Residual | 2.057 |

William Henry Long

Sundance Kid

**ANOVA Table**
HL92 vs. SDWB

| | DF | Sum of Squares | Mean Square | F-Value | P-Value |
|---|---|---|---|---|---|
| Regression | 1 | 27571.470 | 27571.470 | 6516.793 | <.0001 |
| Residual | 6 | 25.385 | 4.231 | | |
| Total | 7 | 27596.855 | | | |

**Regression Coefficients**
HL92 vs. SDWB

| | Coefficient | Std. Error | Std. Coeff. | t-Value | P-Value |
|---|---|---|---|---|---|
| Intercept | -4.335 | 1.425 | -4.335 | -3.042 | .0227 |
| SDWB | 1.067 | .013 | 1.000 | 80.727 | <.0001 |

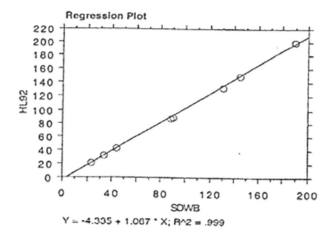

Regression Plot

$Y = -4.335 + 1.067 * X; R^2 = .999$

*i)ᵗʰ H Long (1892) vs. Sundance k
( Wild B*

**Regression Summary**
A1 vs. A2

| | |
|---|---|
| Count | 8 |
| Num. Missing | 0 |
| R | .978 |
| R Squared | .957 |
| Adjusted R Squared | .950 |
| RMS Residual | 14.152 |

William Henry Longs sisters

William Henry Longs sisters

**ANOVA Table**
A1 vs. A2

| | DF | Sum of Squares | Mean Square | F-Value | P-Value |
|---|---|---|---|---|---|
| Regression | 1 | 26695.911 | 26695.911 | 133.294 | <.0001 |
| Residual | 6 | 1201.670 | 200.278 | | |
| Total | 7 | 27897.581 | | | |

**Regression Coefficients**
A1 vs. A2

| | Coefficient | Std. Error | Std. Coeff. | t-Value | P-Value |
|---|---|---|---|---|---|
| Intercept | -16.982 | 9.943 | -16.982 | -1.708 | .1385 |
| A2 | 1.365 | .118 | .978 | 11.545 | <.0001 |

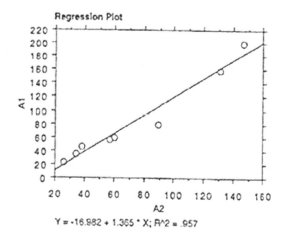

Regression Plot

$Y = -16.982 + 1.365 * X; R^2 = .957$

Sister A1 vs. Sister A2

# Suicide

While examining the bones of William Henry Long, Dr. John McCullough proved with forensic science that Bill Long did not commit suicide, he is murdered. It would be close to impossible with the angle of the bullet wound, fired by a 22 rifle from an upward position and two to three feet away, to inflict this type of wound.

Bill Long has been murdered in cold blood and Matt Warner is suspected of being the murderer. Matt Warner had been Bill Long's best friend. They even had a joint bank account. The money however vanished in 1929, during the depression.

Bill Long strongly opposed Matt in his writing a book on his outlaw life. Surprisingly enough, Bill Long is found dead after Matt Warner went on a four-day hunting trip. Bill's body, found on the ranch with a rifle by his side and he's slumped over a pile of wood. We believe that the family made up the "suicide" story to close the case and not have the authorities probe into his past as an "outlaw."

# CHAPTER TWELVE
## In the "News"

New movie on Sundance Kid may delay DNA results
June 1, 2009
By John Hollenhorst

SALT LAKE CITY, UTAH

Ever since some bones were dug up in Eastern Utah a few months ago, DNA test are underway. It's a story that captured a lot of interest because, some say, they're the remains of the notorious outlaw: the Sundance Kid.

http://www.ksl.com/sid=6679624&autostart=v

# John Hollenhorst of KSL 5 News Story, Salt Lake City, Utah... 2009

## WILLIAM HENRY LONG ~ "THE SUNDANCE KID"

### JOHN HOLLENHORST

John explained that our TEAM has been exploring the theory that rancher William Henry Long is really "The Sundance Kid." He said that Long's bones were dug up in the Duchesne City Cemetery a few months ago, but DNA evidence failed to link him to "The Sundance Kid."

The DNA did not match that of the Sundance Kid's mother, Annie Place, but he explained that we are not giving up.

Our investigation began last year. OLD FAMILY STORIES tied Long to the outlaw gang known as "The Wild Bunch." The leaders, "Butch Cassidy and the Sundance Kid," supposedly died in a shootout in South America in 1908, but Long lived to a ripe old age and died in Utah in 1936 at the age of 69.

### DR. JOHN MCCULLOUGH

Anthropologist John McCullough said months ago, that Long's photo is an astounding match with Harry Longabaugh, a.k.a., "The Sundance Kid." But new DNA findings from Long's bones do not support the theory that Long and Longabaugh were one and the same person.

"The material we got from Bill Long, it does not match the material we got from a distant relative of the Sundance Kid," McCullough said. "The TEAM hopes to get a fresh DNA sample from Long's bones and do the tests again to be sure."

"We know that the cemetery is flooded nearly every year, so we might have DNA material washed in from some other individual," McCullough said.

### MARILYN GRACE

Documentary Producer, Marilyn Grace, is also exploring alternative theories to explain the disappointing DNA evidence. For example, "Sundance's" family, the Longabaugh's, had no birth certificates or baptismal records.

"It's not conclusive that he was a member of their family," Grace said. "He could have been adopted."

### JOHN HOLLENHORST

John said, "The DNA findings likely will lead many to close the book on the Bill Long theory, but not everyone. They are writing books and continuing their research."

### MARILYN GRACE

"We'd love to just say, 'Hey, world! We found the Sundance Kid!' The reality of the situation is it's an ongoing investigation."

### JOHN HOLLENHORST

They claim they've found lots of supporting evidence in the family histories of the Long's and Longabaugh's, but the DNA setback comes at a tough time when Grace would like to fund another documentary.

Below appear the photographs, descriptions and histories of GEORGE PARKER, alias "BUTCH" CASSIDY, alias GEORGE CASSIDY, alias INGERFIELD and HARRY LONGBAUGH alias HARRY ALONZO

GEORGE PARKER.

*Name*....George Parker, alias "Butch" Cassidy, alias George Cassidy, alias Ingerfield
*Nationality*.....................American
*Occupation*................Cowboy; rustler
*Criminal Occupation*.......Bank robber and highwayman, cattle and horse thief
*Age*...years high.. *Height*....5 feet 9 in
*Weight*...170 lbs.....*Build*......Medium
*Complexion*..Light..*Color of Hair*..Flaxen
*Eyes*....Blue.......*Mustache*.Sandy if any
*Remarks*:—Two cut scars back of head, small scar under left eye, small brown mole calf of leg. "Butch" Cassidy is known as a criminal principally in Wyoming, Utah, Idaho, Colorado and Nevada and has served time in Wyoming State penitentiary at Laramie for grand larceny, but was pardoned January 19th, 1896.

GEORGE PARKER.

HARRY LONGBAUGH.

*Name*............Harry Longbaugh, alias "Kid" Longbaugh, alias Harry Alonzo, alias Frank Jones, alias Frank Boyd, alias the "Sundance Kid"
*Nationality*.........Swedish American...*Occupation*............Cowboy; rustler
*Criminal Occupation*..........Highwayman, bank burglar, cattle and horse thief
*Age*...........35 years.............*Height*..........................5 feet 9 in
*Weight*......165 to 170 lbs.........*Build*............................Good
*Eyes*.......Blue or gray.............*Complexion*.......................Medium
*Mustache or Beard*................(if any), natural color brown, reddish tinge
*Features*.....Grecian type..........*Nose*............................Rather long
*Color of Hair*.........Natural color brown, may be dyed; combs it pompadour
**IS BOW LEGGED AND HIS FEET FAR APART.**
*Remarks*:—Harry Longbaugh served 18 months in jail at Sundance, Crook Co., Wyoming, when a boy, for horse stealing. In December 1892, Harry Longbaugh, Bill Madden and Henry Bass "held up" a Great Northern train at Malta, Montana. Bass and Madden were tried for this crime, convicted and sentenced to 10 and 14 years respectively; Longbaugh escaped and since has been a fugitive. June 28, 1897, under the name of Frank Jones, Longbaugh participated with Harvey Logan, alias Curry, Tom Day and Walter Putney, in the Belle Fourche, South Dakota, bank robbery. All were arrested, but Longbaugh and Harvey Logan escaped from jail at Deadwood October 31, the same year. Longbaugh has not since been arrested.

☞ Officers are warned to have sufficient assistance and be fully armed, when attempting to arrest either of these outlaws, as they are always heavily armed, and will make a determined resistance before submitting to arrest, not hesitating to kill, if necessary.

☞ This circular cancels circulars No. 1 and 2, issued by us from Denver, Colo., May 15th, 1901 and February 3rd, 1902, respectively.

IN CASE OF AN ARREST immediately notify PINKERTON'S NATIONAL DETECTIVE AGENCY at the nearest of the above listed offices.

Or

JOHN C. FRAZER,
Resident Sup't., DENVER, COLO.

# Pinkerton's National Detective Agency,
Opera House Block, Denver, Colo.

# CHAPTER THIRTEEN
## That "Darn" DNA

**Marilyn Grace - Journal Entry - August 23, 2010**

I talked to Brent Ashworth in Provo, Utah and he has read what I have so far. Our book is, "Finding 'Butch Cassidy & The Sundance Kid' ~ Solving the 'Wild Bunch' Mystery," by Marilyn Grace and Dr. John McCullough. I mailed a copy of completed research for Brent to review. He said the most wonderful things! I have not shared our book with a lot of folks because I wanted to wait until we were finished. Bill Betenson, (Lula Parker Betenson's great grandson) introduced me to Brent Ashworth. We began talking about our project. I cannot thank Bill Betenson enough for introducing me to Brent Ashworth. Brent has been collecting "Wild Bunch" photos and documents for 30+ years. He purchased a photo of a young "Sundance Kid" when Harry is about 14.

The photo is taken in Pennsylvania. Brent purchased the photo from Matt Warner's family. The Warner family had many valuable items that they were willing to sell to Brent 30 years ago. Matt Warner, a former member of the "Wild Bunch." Although he had been imprisoned, he eventually became sheriff of Price, Utah. Matt always played both sides of the law. When he acts as sheriff, Matt Warner is known for boot-legging whiskey and the town of Price had "Ladies of the Night." He would look the other way and favored the side of the ladies!

I believe the young "Sundance Kid" photo had been taken before Harry left Pennsylvania and went to help cousin George and Mary Longenbough, (different spelling but still related) homestead in Cortez, Colorado. Matt Warner wrote "Longenau" on the back of the photo, probably because Matt Warner is not sure how "Sundance" spelled his last name, Longabaugh. We are working on finding the Pennsylvania photography studio where the photo is taken. We will do more research when we travel back to Pennsylvania. We want to know everything about this rare, never-before-seen photo of "Sundance."

Anyhoo... back to the ranch- I mailed off a copy of the book to Brent Ashworth and his response delighted me! Remember, not many people have even read our book. He said, "I started reading last night and I could not stop, I read it all the way through. I loved the time-lines and how you made the name-comparison, body-analysis charts, and all of your research. I love all the stories! My favorite story is how Bill Long lost his right thumb and asked to have it buried six feet under, and then the pain vanished." Brent also said, "You have found 'The Sundance Kid!' BUT THAT 'DARN' DNA!" I just loved what he said so much that I decided to write this chapter, "That 'Darn' DNA!"

I explained to Brent that the birthplace of "The Sundance Kid" is 122 Jacobs Street in Mont Clare, Pennsylvania. The place where he is born... a 10-room boarding house in Mont Clare, by the Schuylkill Canal. There were 10 rooms and only one large suite. While traveling up and down the canal, the boarding house became a place where weary travelers could eat and spend the night. I also talked about the 1870 Census record when Harry is 3 years old. Harry is listed as living with the Longabaugh family. The Longabaugh's were living about a mile or so down the canal in Port Providence, from where "Sundance" came into the world.

We are talking to Kurt and Joan Callow who own the property at 122 Jacobs Street in Mont Clare, Pennsylvania. Joan and Kurt sent us pictures of the boarding house that burned down in 2004. They are also helping us search back in the year 1867 when "The Sundance Kid" is born on Jacobs Street. Who owned the boarding house in the spring of 1867? Who owned the property where the Longabaugh's lived? We are hoping to find tax records for the Longabaugh's so we can find exactly where they lived. They never owned property and rented land to farm. What years did they live there? Why is Harry born in a boarding house when the Longabaugh's lived a mile away? These are questions that can only be answered by going back to Pennsylvania and getting documentation that will help us piece all the evidence together. Kurt and Joan Callow have invited me to come and stay with them in Pennsylvania. We will go to all the places where the Longabaugh Family lived and worked. I just know we will be able to gather all the information and find the missing pieces.

I so look forward to meeting Kurt and Joan Callow, George Longabaugh Senior and Junior, along with family members. I will be meeting ALL the Longabaugh's in Pennsylvania. We will hunt down more clues and look for more descendants of Josiah Longabaugh, "The Sundance Kid's" father, for DNA testing!

# CHAPTER FOURTEEN
## Lula's Interview

Circleville, Utah
November 29, 1979
9:48, 9 minutes, 48 seconds
Dee Bitton and Lula Parker Betenson

**Interview:**

**Dee:** "Let's see, you are a sister to Butch Cassidy?"

**Lula:** "Yes, I am. I've written a book about him and it is called 'Butch Cassidy, My Brother.' He was a kind, loving boy. He worshiped his mother if ever anyone did. I think about when he was a boy. She was a small woman and he would dance her around the room and then he'd set her up on the table and he'd say, 'Come on kids, bring on the crown, here's the queen.' Now I can't remember that ... but I have been told this... because I was just a tiny baby when he left home."

**Dee:** "Yes."

**Lula:** "But he was a man who never killed a person in his life. If he's like the rest of my folks, he couldn't kill a dog save nothing of a person."

**Dee:** "Sure."

**Lula:** "And ah, he was a, he was so kind and good to the family and to the kids. He went away and found work and was so happy in Colorado, and then he was arrested for stealing his own horse. And, ah, my father went out, and it was at Montrose, Colorado. And my father went out to the jail and there he sat, reading with the door open and he looked up and he saw my father and said, 'Dad, what in hell are you doing here?' That's just what I would like to ask you, young man?"

**Dee:** {Laugh} "Uh-huh."

**Lula:** "My father has told me about this. And he stayed and found out it was his own horse he had taken out to pasture."

**Dee:** "Oh my goodness."

**Lula:** "Course, that didn't help any. He was a little upset and furious over it, you know, but, he says, 'I am not leaving until I get my horse.' And they had a trial, a short trial, and had too many witnesses against the other fella, at the law. But when he first left home he worked in the mines and different places. He was so good to send money home to my folks. And but after he started after he got in trouble in Telluride, that was the first bank robbery was in Telluride, {To Hell You Ride}. He and two men were there and they robbed the bank. I have been all through that country where they camped and so on... of course the posse went after then... and they never did catch up to them."

**Dee:** "Uh-huh."

**Lula:** "And then this is what I wanted to tell you... then when they stayed there several days in hiding and they divided the money and the other two men wanted to go to Denver and rob another bank, and, uh, my brother said, 'No, I'm through. I'm going home'."

**Dee:** "Going home."

**Lula:** "And he started home and I cry when I think how he rolled along, trying to make up his mind. He couldn't face it, see... he come, started home, and he stopped... and he told us that he just prayed to know what to do; but he just couldn't face it. So he started the wrong way, but he lived a good life a long time after he come home from South America; but he was so kind to other people. He didn't keep money. He gave it."

**Dee:** "That's right. That's right. He passed away in this country, then, didn't he?"

**Lula:** "Yes, Yes! He went to South America but he came back here; after that he came home."

**Dee:** "He visited with you, did he?"

**Lula:** "He came and stayed with us - Oh, I guess two or three weeks; went out in the hills and camped... with the Boys... and uh, we lived, ya know, one house on the lot. Nobody knew."

**Dee:** "Did he die in this vicinity?" {Circleville, Utah}

**Lula:** "No. No. He died in the 'North West,' but that is our secret."

**Dee:** That's right.

**Lula:** "My father said, when we got the word, he has now... he has been chased a good deal of his life. Now he is going to rest in peace and that's what we've done, and I have had a lot of compliments about it and I have some who would dig into your heart to find the place and the Pinkerton's are some." {laugh}

**Dee:** "Yeah, that's really nice. I'll just stop."

**Dee:** "Would you relate about your parents, the ones that came across with the hand cart company?"

**Lula:** "Oh, yes. Yes. My mother was Ann B. Gillis and her father and mother was Robert Gillis and Jane Gillis, Jane Ann Gillis, and they lived in Scotland. My mother was born in Scotland, but they moved to England later. And they sailed from England to America, and as I remember them telling, I believe nine weeks on the water. And ah, they cooked for themselves and done for themselves and I told this story about my Grandfather Gillis—he went to drain the potatoes, and the wind came up and he had to either lose his hat, or lose the potatoes, so he lost the hat and saved the potatoes." {Laugh}

**Lula:** "I thought that was quite a story."

**Dee:** "Really." {laugh}

**Lula:** "Anyway, they came across the plains with, ah, Martin Company. They landed in Salt Lake City and later lived near Bountiful. What's the name of that place?"

**Dee:** "Centerville, right in there?"

**Lula:** "But anyway, my grandfather, they moved to Beaver (Utah) and he was a carpenter and he had plenty of work to do. They lived there in a little two roomed house, and, uh, he went back to this place, I can't think, on business, and he took 'phenonia harmony' and died and he's buried there and they have one little boy buried there. My grandmother lived in Beaver and she had three children. She had my mother, Annie, and Christina - Christine, my aunt, and Dan, a boy, and then she adopted a little girl, 'Little Liddy.' Liddy, her name was Liddy LeBaron... Liddie LaBaron. And she married...? Ah, you know I'm 95, will be 96 in April, so I'm not very smart." {laugh}

**Dee:** "Oh, yes you are."

**Lula** and **Dee:** {laughing}

{---Tape was cut off---a bit confusing as to whom she is talking about---}

**Lula:** "She was a very thrifty woman, if there ever was one. My father used to say that she could sell milk, make butter and have all the cream she wanted out of a gallon of milk."
{---Tape cut off—restarted}

**Lula:** "I have really enjoyed visiting with you Mr. Bitton and I hope I have given you something worthwhile on the Martin Company and, ah, I do hope you come and see us again sometime. I am always glad to see people. I have lots of company and I love them. My name is Lula Parker Betenson and I live in Circleville, Utah, and I have written a book, 'Butch Cassidy, My Brother.' How's that?"

Tape ends--- 9:48---Interview

## Note:

*Dee Bitton loved Western History and especially books on the "Wild Bunch." He deserves credit for capturing this interview with Lula and helping with the major clue that, "Butch died in the NORTH WEST, but this is our family secret," said Lula. Thank you so much Deanne and Michael Phillips. You hunted me down through John Hollenhorst, with KSL 5 News, and allowing me to include the interview in our research. Your help has been invaluable in solving the "Wild Bunch Mystery."*

*Three years ago, Deanne and Michael Phillips found this tape of Lula's interview when Dee Bitton, (Deanne's father) passed away and they were going through his personal belongings.*

*"Lula's Interview" is invaluable to our research on William Thadeus Phillips, of Spokane, Washington. Spokane is in the NORTH WEST and Chapter 16, "Solving the 'Wild Bunch' Mystery," helps to tie in the "Bandit Invincible" manuscript that Phillips wrote during the depression when Phillips needed money desperately. He tried to sell his 200 page document to "Hollywood," but he was unsuccessful. On the right column in paragraph 8, of "Bandit Invincible," read the description Phillips gives of "Butch" going to Paris, France. "Butch" had surgery to disguise his appearance. Then go to the end of the book and look at Dr. John McCullough's photo comparison of "Butch Cassidy" and William Thadeus Phillips. Phillips is "Butch Cassidy!" We need to also keep in mind that William Henry Long came home to his family in Fremont, Utah. Bill returned after a 10 year absence, speaking fluent "French." Bill Long said that no one was to ask why he could speak French, or ask where he had been, or they would be in trouble!*

*It all comes together! "Butch and Sundance" left Bolivia and went to Paris, France. "Butch" had plastic surgery to change his appearance.*

# Side Story

In Matt Warner's book, he tells how Robert LeRoy Parker came to be known as "Butch Cassidy." In "Last of the Bandit Riders," Matt told of an incident at Thompson Springs.

"In the rough country in eastern Utah we came to a shallow lake with a rock in the middle of it. Roy was standing on a sloping rock that stuck out into the mud and water on the edge of the lake, holding a needle gun in his hands. That gun used such long shells and kicked so hard when we fired it, it nearly took us apart and we called it "Butch."

I saw what the gun would do to Roy if he fired it while he was standing there on that sloping rock... "Bet you can't hit that rock out there in the middle of the lake, says I," to egg him on. "Gimme something hard, he jeers," and throws the rifle to his shoulder and fires."

It knocked him flat on his back in the mud and water alongside of that rock. He flopped and floundered like a fish and by the time he was out, he was smeared with mud from his head to his feet... we named him 'Butch' after that kicking needle gun. After that, he took the name 'Cassidy' to hide his identity, and Tom and I called him 'Butch Cassidy'."

# WILLIAM HENRY LONG

## DNA RESEARCH

"Sundance's" fathers DNA will need to be compared to Bill Long's DNA in order to leave no stone unturned. George Senior and George Longabaugh Junior from Browns Town, Pennsylvania, are helping by giving us their DNA samples. They live 20 minutes away from where "Sundance" was born. Jim Petty, is our professional genealogist and it was Jim's idea to test Josiah Longabaugh's DNA. We need more Longabaugh DNA from Jonas and Samuel Longabaugh. We will also test Robert Longenbaugh's DNA.

**DNA RESULTS**

| MITO | Y-STR |
|------|-------|
| 16126 T-C | DYS456 17 |
| 16294 C-T | DYS389 I 13 |
| 16296 C-T | DYS390 23 |
| 16304 C-T | DYS389 II 28 |
| 16519 T-C | DYS458 17 |
| 73 A-G | DYS19 15 |
| 263 A-G | DYS385 11, 14 |
| 309 1C | DYS393 13 |
| 315 1C | DYS391 12 |
| | DYS439 12 |
| | DYS635 23 |
| | DYS392 13 |
| | GATAH4 12 |
| | DYS437 14 |
| | DYS438 13 |
| | DYS448 19 |

# CHAPTER FIFTEEN
## "The New Wild Bunch Gang"

I know that almost everyone I have talked to about finding "Butch and Sundance" has said the day Dr. John McCullough called and told me that the photo of William Henry Long is "The Sundance Kid," must have been the happiest day of my life!

A cameraman from KSL 5 News said the exact same thing; as well as friends of mine. I decided to look up in my journal the day that Dr. John called me and told me the news that William Henry Long is "Sundance." I think everyone should have a great memory to remind them how joyful life is!

I think I will stay in JOY for the rest of MY HAPPY LIFE!

## Note:

*Dear Journal,*

*I just received a call from Dr. John McCullough and he said, "It's him! It's 'Sundance'!" I screamed and almost peed my pants! I said, "It's 'Sundance'?" John said, "Yes! It's 'Sundance' – the overlays are perfect!" We talked this morning about his background, and he said that he has been an anthropologist on many high-profile Utah murder cases where they exhumed bodies.*

*He said that he worked on the "Ted Bundy" case and they found the body of two girls, but were unable to prove him guilty. He also said that he had worked on the "Gary Arthur Bishop" case; he killed six boys. They exhumed three remains and proved Gary murdered the boys. "Gary Arthur Bishop" subsequently asked to be executed. "The LeBaron Polygamy Murders" is another case he had been involved with. Dr. McCullough said, "I am so excited and elated, I can hardly stand it!"*

*I called Mindy my daughter-in-law and told her. She said she would tell my son Sterling. Mindy said, "Oh my hell, it's really him! This is so amazing!"*

*I called Jerry Nickle and he is so excited! REALLY EXCITED! William Henry Long is his step great-grandfather and he has suspected he could be "Sundance" for five and a half years. I have been looking for "Sundance" since May of 1997... eleven years. Michael Karr, our director, did not pick up, so I e-mailed him. I said that I would be there Friday at 2 p.m., in the Anthropology Department at the University of Utah. We filmed Dr. John's photo analysis... WOW! What a day! I feel itchy all over – Thank You Dear Lord! You have answered my question – if they didn't die in Bolivia, where did they go? Harry Longabaugh went to Loa, and Fremont, Utah! "Sundance" became William Henry Long, (Bill or Billy Long) and he died in Duchesne.*

*He married the widow of Silas Morrell, Luzernia Allred Morrell. She had six children (she had 7 children, one child drowned as a small boy) from her first marriage and then Bill and Luzernia had two girls, Florence Viola and Evinda Ann. Now their family has roots! Florence Viola now has an answer to the letter she wrote in 1937 asking; "Who is my father?" WHAT GREAT NEWS!*

*Well Gang! That is what I wrote the day Dr. John called me with the news that William Henry Long's photo matched Harry Alonzo Longabaugh's, "The Sundance Kid."*

# Gaylen Robison,
## Great Grandson of The Sundance Kid

"It is evident that the outlaws were charitable in sharing the booty with the common lot. Robbing the trains seemed to be like acts of patriotism on their part.

Part of the history of the Church of Jesus Christ of Latter Day Saints, is an account of when the railroad needed men to work on building the railroad tracks across the territory. President Brigham Young provided the men for the work. Men came from hundreds of miles in every direction to work as they were 'called' by the Prophet. The Church was supposed to get compensated, and the workers were also to be compensated. They completed their work as scheduled, and President Young waited for the money—which never came. President Young, (allegedly) pleaded to the railroad company to keep their appointment. He was ignored.

All those good men had to work for nothing and returned home to their hungry families, 'broke.' It's almost like the outlaws collected the money.

As my Uncle Thomas Jackson told me back in 1961, 'Gaylen, your grandma's dad was an outlaw. He run with the outlaw gang in Montana, he run with the gang in Wyoming, and ran with the bunch at Robber's Roost. When the marshal came into Wayne County showing his picture and asked folks if they had ever seen him before, they always denied ever seeing him. They liked your great grandpa.' It is a well-known fact that everybody in Wayne County, Duchesne County, and Uintah County, either knew him personally or knew of him. They could have had him arrested at any time, but they didn't.

I want to tell you the story of what happened to me in 1969 or 1970 up at Crowheart, Wyoming. There was a real neat couple we became good friends with while we lived at Riverton, Wyoming. They are Ray and Leona Weber. Earlier in 1961, I had been informed by Uncle Thomas Jackson that my great grandfather Bill Long, was once an outlaw who associated with a gang of outlaws in Wyoming. My Grandmother Viola, who raised me, never knew that fact or rejected the idea that her father was an outlaw. All she knew about her father was that his name was 'William Henry Long' and that he was gone for long periods of time and was in association with Kit Carson, which we believe is a cover story that is not true. Once I moved to Wyoming in 1966, I began asking everybody I met if they knew anything about the outlaws there.

The Weber's related to me an account told by a rancher friend in Fremont County who knew Butch Cassidy and the gang. The story the rancher told was about meeting some of the gang as they were traveling toward the Northwest. It was right after the train robbery down by Wamsutter, Wyoming where they blew up the box car and made off with a fortune. The outlaws had bags of gold which were so heavy that their hands were bleeding; there was blood on their clothes and saddles from the chafing caused by holding the heavy bags of gold draped across the front of their saddles. Their secret was safe with many of the ranchers around Fremont County. At that time they traveled to... only the Lord and the outlaws knew, where.

Then Mrs. Weber asked me what my great grandpa's name was. I answered thus: 'His last name was Long.' She then said, 'Harry Longabaugh?' I said, 'No it couldn't have been him.' I learned a hard lesson from jumping to conclusions.

That was a real serious mistake on my part. I found out that at that time there were people still alive in Fremont County that knew Butch Cassidy and the outlaws personally. Ray Weber and Leona knew many of those old timers, but I was stuck on 'Bill Long' as being his real name and I pursued no further. For years I searched for Bill Long, only to discover that he was Harry Alonzo Longabaugh. My Weber friends gave me the answer forty years ago."

# CHAPTER SIXTEEN
## "Lone Tree Dance"

## Jail Record, of

| No. 1889 | NAME OF PRISONER | Of Whom Received. | Nature of Offense. | Date of Receiving (March / Day) | | Amount of Fine and Costs (Dollars / Cts.) | | Jailer's Fee (Dollars / Cts.) | | Amount Received |
|---|---|---|---|---|---|---|---|---|---|---|
| 266 | Robt Wild | Sheriff | Larceny | Jan | 6 | | | | | |
| 267 | John Crandell | " | Shooting | " | 25 | 17 | 00 | | | |
| 268 | Chas H Smith | " | Larceny | Feby | 1 | | | | | |
| 269 | Joseph Jackson | J A Holmes S.D. | Disturbing the Peace | " | 18 | 6 | 00 | | | |
| 270 | Harry Long | Dep Sheriff Newell | assault with a deadly weapon | " | 18 | 100 | 00 | | | |
| 271 | William Henry | Sheriff | for witness | " | 21 | | | | | |
| 272 | C.A. Bell | O. Gugell | Larceny | " | 22 | | | | | |
| 273 | Sol Sheffield | S W. Smith | Burglary | " | 22 | | | | | |
| 274 | Wm Benton | " | " | " | 22 | | | | | |
| 275 | David Ker | " | " | " | 22 | | | | | |
| 276 | John Smith | Sheriff | Drunk | " | 23 | | | | | |
| 277 | Chas Hudleston | Deputy Newell | Larceny | " | 25 | | | | | |
| 278 | Wm Riley | S W. Smith S.D.S. | Drunk selling liquor | March | 1 | 8 | 00 | | | |
| 279 | Wm Newsnyder | Sheriff LeCain | with out license | " | 11 | 100 | 00 | | | |
| 280 | S. Beck | " | " | " | 11 | 100 | 00 | | | |
| 281 | Rosina Fisher | " | " | " | 11 | 100 | 00 | | | |
| 282 | Thos. Carson | J N Newell D.S. | Vagrant | " | 12 | 10 | 00 | | | |
| 283 | Harmon Stohr | Sheriff LeCain | Forgery | " | 20 | | | | | |
| 284 | David Scott | " | using long hand truck | " | 23 | 10 | 00 | | | |
| 285 | James Peterson | " | Assault Battery | " | 23 | 15 | 00 | | | |
| 286 | Ling Lee | Const Pepper | using Opium | " | 25 | 75 | 00 | | | |
| 287 | Quong Seong | " | " | " | 25 | 75 | 00 | | | |
| 288 | Ah Ock | " | " | " | 25 | 75 | 00 | | | |
| 289 | Lee Won | " | " | " | 25 | 75 | 00 | | | |
| 290 | Ah Foo | " | " | " | 26 | 75 | 00 | | | |

# THE LONE TREE DANCE

## WRITTEN BY

## ART DAVIDSON

*Aprox 1912*

Up in the Idaho area where Dad's Uncle Lorenzo lived, four outlaws had stolen a herd of horses and driven them out onto the Lost River Desert . The posse chasing them shot two of the outlaws but the other two escaped and appeared to be making their way back to Wyoming . It was expected that the two men would go up the Bear River and then cross the divide in an effort to get to Browns Park . From what Dad wrote, it appears the sheriffs in Uinta County and in Sweetwater County were not at all interested in apprehending the two fugitives.

However, during the afternoon before the scheduled Thanksgiving Dance, a Pinkerton Detective came to the R. J. Gregory store in Lone Tree and organized a posse to go out and capture the outlaws at Hole-in-the-Rock Springs. I only know two of the posse members, Josh Gregory who ran the store, and a cowboy working for Eugene Hickey who ordinarily played the fiddle for the dances. The posse, led by the Pinkerton, went up to Hole-in-the-Rock to ambush the two horse thief's, one of whom the Pinkerton man said was also a train robber, wanted far and wide under the name of Harry Longabough.

Not very long after the posse rode out, families from up and down the Henry's Fork of the Green River began to arrive for the Thanksgiving Dance, unaware that the fiddler had gone with the posse. The women and children went into the school house, but some of the men went across the road to the Gregory store, which Mr. Greggory left in charge of Bill Donahue who had a crippled arm

The two outlaws hadn't done what the Pinkerton man expected them to do. They hadn't gone by the upper trail past the springs, but instead had followed the main road from Robertson to Lone Tree.

Bill Donohue was the only man that looked up when the two outlaws entered the Lone Tree store, and he found himself face to face with the man who had murdered *July 6th 1909* John Jarvie at Browns Park only three years before. The next moment one outlaw lay dead on the store floor and Harry Alonzo was in custody. Meanwhile, across the road, the dance could not begin because there was no fiddler. Time passed and people wandered back and forth between the store and the school house. In the meantime, the women had learned that Mrs. Luckey (whom no one thought could do anything) was able to chord the piano, but she couldn't play a tune.

After a time the uninjured outlaw, Harry Alonzo, offered to fiddle for the dance if they would turn him loose. No one trusted him that far, but it was finally decided to carry the dead outlaw over to the school house and put him on top of the piano. One of his wrists was then chained to the wrist of Harry Alonzo, who was then able to fiddle for the dance, only slightly hampered by the upheld wrist. Mrs. Luckey chorded the piano for accompaniment, missing a beat now and then.

When the dance was finally over, Harry Alonzo demanded he be paid for fiddling. When he was told it was a school dance and the school board had no money to pay fiddlers, he said he would consider he had been fully paid off if he be permitted to dance one dance with the woman of his choice in the school house. At last, it was decided the men could keep him from escaping, so he was released from the dead outlaw.

When Harry Alonzo was released, he strolled twice around the room, looking each woman over, as if he were trying to pick out a house he would like to purchase. On the second trip around the room, he stopped and asked Grandma Stoll to dance, but she said she was too old. Next he asked the wife of Corey Hanks to dance, but she replied that she never danced because her crippled and blinded husband was unable to dance. Then Harry Alonzo stopped in front of Mother, bowed like a Frenchman, and asked if she would dance with him. Mother refused, but just then Mrs. Luckey announced that while she could chord passable well and did not know any other dance tunes, she could play La Varsuvvienne. At this all the people in the school house began to clap, and urge Mother to dance. Reluctantly she agreed, while Dad looked like black thunder and shook his head.

As Mother began to dance with Harry Alonzo to the faltering strains of La arsuvvienne, the other people began to sing the words of the tune: "Do you see my, do you see my, do you see my new shoes? With Buckle and bow, and the hole in the toe?" Dad was about to begin "weeping and waillin and gnashing his teeth" and there would have been "Hell to Pay", except...except...]

When the dancing couple was down near the outside door, and while the crowd was still singing, the door was pushed open and the Pinkerton Detective entered the school house. Harry Alonzo abandoned Mother there on the dance floor, grabbed the detective's gun and out the door. He shot at two members of the returning posse, mounted a horse and disappeared into the night. The posse members remounted and chased him up on top of Cedar Mountain (once called Phil Mass Mountain) Riding east, two of the posse saw a rider go by in the half light of the coming dawn. They riddled the rider with bullets, and then found the downed man was the Pinkerton Detective. This appeared to be a ticklish situation for several people. So, for the good of all, it was decided to bury the Pinkerton man as Harry Alonzo. His grave, covered with rocks, can still be seen on top of Cedar Mountain . No one expected to ever see Harry Alonzo again..

# JUST FOR FUN!

Gaylen Robison is the great grandson of William Henry Long and Idonna is his side-kick and wife. They found this true story of THE LONE TREE DANCE. I love this story so much! They also found the Uinta County Jail documents. The documents show that Harry Long is arrested for "assault with a deadly weapon" in 1886. Harry Long is a known alias for Harry Longabaugh, "The Sundance Kid."

Gaylen and Idonna are working on the date of the LONE TREE DANCE story. They think that the event took place on Thanksgiving Day, 1912; four years after they were supposed to have been killed in Bolivia! Coincidence or clue? You decide!

## HISTORY OF UINTA COUNTY, WYOMING, JAIL

J. J. LaCain is elected sheriff in 1886. He spends his time keeping white miners from killing the "Chinese miners" about that time. William Richard Lowman is re-elected twice. "His name has become 'a menace to evildoers' and conveys a feeling of safety to law abiding citizens." Sheriff from 1886-1912.

Evanston and Lone Tree are in Uinta County, Wyoming. Study the Jail documents. Read the list of crimes, some are pretty humorous: assault with a deadly weapon, larceny, disturbing the peace, drunk, selling liquor without a license, vagrant, using opium, and stealing clothes off the clothes line. "George Cassidy," a known alias for "Butch Cassidy."

Deputy David Welling of the Uinta County Sheriff's Department helped Idonna and Gaylen obtain this information. Thank You Deputy Welling!

## UINTA COUNTY JAIL
## Evanston, Wyoming

Idonna and Gaylen Robison of Woodruff, Utah, (Gaylen is the great grandson of "The Sundance Kid," alias, William Henry Long) arranged for me to go to the Uinta County Jail in Evanston, Wyoming. We had an appointment to meet with the Sheriff and his Deputies concerning {1886 document} Harry Long, a known alias for Harry Alonzo Longabaugh, "The Sundance Kid" and George Cassidy, {document from 1891} when he is in the Uinta County Jail. "George Cassidy" is a known alias for "Butch Cassidy" and a copy of the original documents are included in this chapter for you to review.

The Uinta County Jail is also the source of the "LONE TREE DANCE" story that is just so FUN! We Love It! "The Lone Tree Dance" is the true story of Harry Alonzo's escape from jail. A Pinkerton Report is included in the book and states that "The Sundance Kid," also known as, "Harry Alonzo." Harry is arrested and ended up playing the fiddle for the Thanksgiving Dance.

When Deputy Welling mailed Gaylen the story of the "LONE TREE DANCE." "1912" is in the top left hand corner on the front page, written by hand, in ink. It is now my mission to find out why Deputy Welling wrote that date on the front page?

I dressed up for our meeting along with Idonna and Gaylen. We were excited to meet with the sheriff and his deputies. The Uinta County Jail has a lobby full of historical pictures with photos of the sheriffs from the past, displayed on the walls in the waiting area as you come into the building. I wanted to meet the folks that had given us such wonderful historical documents for our book. Their documents seemed to have been "hidden" away for a very long time and very few had EVER seen them before!

We went to the office window where the receptionist greeted us. Crystal Thompson is the lovely young lady who arranged for us to meet with everyone when we dropped in last week. She said to come back on Monday and we could meet with everyone; they would open the safe and show us the original jail documents for "Butch Cassidy and The Sundance Kid."

Deputy Welling had been paged, he came in and talked with us. We shook his hand and we showed him our beautiful full color coffee table book. He is in awe as he turned the pages; he saw for himself the evidence that we have gathered since May of 1997. We can now tell the story of William Henry Long, alias, Harry Alonzo Longabaugh, "The Sundance Kid." Then in a matter of minutes, we had four deputies surrounding us and telling us all the stories they knew about the documents and the "Lone Tree Dance" story. They let us know that the Sheriff is on his way and would be there shortly.

How exciting to be in the same town where "Butch and Sundance" were arrested and spent time in jail.

We were escorted to the interior of the building to a meeting room that had an overhead projector. We could see the documents on a full screen right in front of us. Deputy David Welling and Deputy Steve Cheney were two of the deputies that showed us to the meeting room. They opened the safe and started to bring out thick, oversized, turn of the century books. Some of the books were three inches thick with torn brown leather and gold letters on the books. They were OLD Historical Documents! Deputies Dave Evins and Jamie Schmidt were also with our group and were most helpful.

Book after book came out of the safe and I saw Harry Long/William Henry document from 1886. Then in the same book, we looked at the 1891 document of George Cassidy, a known alias for "Butch Cassidy." The outside of the books and edges were worn and torn, but the inside pages were pristine, as if they had been written yesterday.

We went through all four or five books looking for more clues but we did not find anything else on "Butch and Sundance."

Then the Sheriff came into the room and I gladly shook his hand. I am overjoyed to see the man that had made it possible for us to show the documents in our research and book. Sheriff Lou Napoli, the Sheriff of the Uinta County Jail, wanted the documents to stay in the safe and not be turned over to Cheyenne, Wyoming. He felt that the documents belong to the citizens of Evanston. He locked them up for safe keeping.

When everyone came in the room, I wanted to know why the date "1912" is written on the "Lone Tree Dance" story. They explained to me that a Scottish store keeper by the name of John Jarvie, from Browns Park, had been murdered June or July 6, 1909 and the "Lone Tree Dance" story took place three years later, around Thanksgiving time. That is how they knew that the "Lone Tree Dance" story took place in 1912.

I did some research on John Jarvie of Browns Park, in the Vernal area of Utah. He had a career as a successful store keeper who searched for a location for a store on the Green River. He also ran the ferry that would take horses, wagons, and supplies to the other side for a fee.

John Jarvie and his wife built a dug out before they built their living quarters and store. There is a replica of what it looked like then and you can tour the John Jarvie Museum in Vernal. He's a poet and a story teller and would recite poetry to entertain the folks when they would gather for parties or events. He and his wife were well loved and liked in their little community. The "Lone Tree Dance" story and the John Jarvie murder tie in together; they give us the date of the Thanksgiving Dance, 1912.

June or July 6, 1909 (the exact month is not known) Bill McKinley and a Mr. George Hood robbed and killed poor John Jarvie. He is shot in the back and in the temple. They took him down to the river and placed him in his own boat, lashed him to the boat, and sent him floating down the river.

Everyone in town knew that John would keep 100 dollars in bills and change to give to people that he would trade with. Let's say that someone brought in a beaver skin and some eggs to trade, and he's not there. They knew that they could leave their goods and come back later and collect the money, or take items in trade. He let people know he had money in the safe, along with a pearl handled revolver, so they would know that he is good to pay up.

After the two men sent him off down the river, they went back and cleaned out the safe and robbed the store. They only had one horse, so the horse, so loaded down with goods that eye witnesses said that the horse became wobbly with the load of items strapped on his back.

They needed another horse and set out to steal one. Ranchers identified them as the two men who murdered John Jarvie.

When you read the "Lone Tree Dance" story, the man who is killed... who is with Harry Alonzo, had been identified as one of the men that killed John Jarvie three years earlier. The man is either Bill McKinley or Mr. George Hood. No one knows for sure. There were citizen that recognized him as the man that killed John Jarvie; he shot him dead and did a citizen's arrest placing Harry Alonzo in jail, along with the dead outlaw.

Deputy Welling made copies of a story of Josie Bassett Morris; the story tells how she knew "Sundance." Josie Bassett's ranch is right next to the John Jarvie ranch. You can tour both sites in Vernal. He also made a copy of a newspaper story on "Butch and Sundance." They furnished us with a map and said that we really should go out to the Bassett and Jarvie ranch for more stories and research.

The 1912 date is now verified and I had my answer! Harry Alonzo's companion is dead; he is the known murderer of John Jarvie. He committed the murder in June or July 6, 1909, and three years later, he is shot dead and handcuffed to Harry Alonzo on top of the piano. Harry played the fiddle for the Thanksgiving Dance, 1912.

This is such an important and historical find! There have been sightings and stories about "Butch and Sundance" coming back to the United States after they were supposed to have been killed in Bolivia, November 7, 1908. Here you have Harry Alonzo, "The Sundance Kid," being captured and playing the fiddle for the dance, 1912. This is an eye witness account and great detective work on the part of the Sheriff and Deputies of the Uinta County Jail in Evanston, Wyoming.

After we went over all the books and they explained the connection between John Jarvie's death and the date on the document; we just relaxed and visited. I explain to the officers all of my research on "Butch, Sundance, and Etta," and how their documents help our case. I let them know that I am writing another book and we would get them a copy later on. They were excited because they had one copy in their hands, and I promised copies for them in the future.

Deputy Welling said that he had to go and feed the prisoners. We all laughed and wondered who is running the jail? I had the Sheriff and his Deputies visiting with me, Idonna, and Gaylen. Deputy Welling said that they had 36 prisoners this week and last week they had 50. I said that I would be happy to come and talk to the prisoners and explain what an awful life it had been for "The Sundance Kid." He lived a double life and is always on the run. He had a horse saddled at all times. The family put a disc on the front porch that would ring loud enough to warn him when he is out in the fields in Duchesne, Utah. They also had a flag that they would wave to warn him if the law came after him. I explained that this is no way to live. In the end, he lost ALL of his money in the Great Depression and died a "poor farmer." In 1936, Matt Warner, (Sheriff of Price, Utah, and a former member of the Wild Bunch) shot and killed "Sundance," because Bill Long, (Sundance Kid) opposed Matt Warner writing a book about his outlaw life. Bill wanted his secret to be a kept "secret." All that time he hid out, and he ended up being murdered by a member of his own gang. There is no honor among thieves!

Everyone went back to work; the Sheriff said that he had a cold so he didn't want to get us sick. I said that if he didn't have a cold, I would kiss him! He looked rather embarrassed, so I just bowed and blew him a kiss. I told him how grateful I am that he stood his ground and kept the documents at the Uinta County Jail, or who knows, we would never have known that they existed!

We all went our way, but one Deputy stayed and helped us get a photo of the Jail where "Butch and Sundance" were arrested in 1886 and 1891. We also had other pictures taken of all of us looking at the documents.

I made sure to thank the lovely secretary, Crystal Thompson. I also wanted her to see the transparencies of William Henry Long and "The Sundance Kid," so she could put them together for herself, as well as look at the entire book. Also wanted Crystal to see the "Lone Tree Dance" and jail documents in our book.

Never in history has anyone found documentation that "Butch and Sundance" didn't die in Bolivia! What an important and historical day in our time to finally have these stories come together. They didn't die in Boliva, but came back to the United States, and Harry Alonzo, "The Sundance Kid," played the fiddle for the Thanksgiving Dance in 1912. He is hand-cuffed to the dead man who had killed John Jarvie, three years before. The date is "1912" by golly, and we've got the story!

John Jarvie had lived a good life and is a very good man; he is missed by his wife Nellie, and all of the folks that worked and traded with him. His death made it possible to document the fact that "Sundance" did not die in Bolivia!

We are so grateful to the Uinta County Jail for their participation in this historical discovery. Sheriff Lou Napoli has even contacted the Pinkerton Detective Agency to see if they could find out who is missing from their group in "1912." It has been suggested that the grave of the deceased Pinkerton Man at "Lone Tree" be exhumed and obtain some DNA testing on the body. It would prove that the man in the grave is a Pinkerton, not Harry Alonzo, "The Sundance Kid."

34

## Uinta County, Wyoming.

## Jail Record, of

1891

# CHAPTER SEVENTEEN
## Solving the Wild Bunch Mystery

Years and years of reading all the books, filming the Bill Long Story, interviewing relatives and working with our TEAM, all came down to one moment in time. The clue of all clues, "Grandpa Long came back from a ten-year absence speaking fluent French," said Gaylen Robison, (Great grand-son of William Henry Long.) Gaylen's mother Elva, (Story in book, "Remembering Grandpa Long") told Gaylen that Grandpa Long left home for a long time. He always sends money home to the family in Fremont, but he is missing. We are not sure if he came home in 1908 or 1910, but the 1910 census records show that Luzernia Long, Bill Long's wife, is no longer head of household; Bill Long is now home. It must be 1908 when he returned. William T. Phillips arrived in Spokane, Washington in 1908.

Gaylen said, "My mother told me that Grandpa Long came home from a ten-year absence speaking fluent French. No one dared ask why he could speak French, or where he had been, or they would be in trouble."

My mind flashed to "The Bandit Invincible" document. Author Larry Pointer wrote, "In Search of Butch Cassidy." I read Larry's book and in the text, he made reference to a manuscript written by William Thadeus Phillips. Phillips had been a successful business man but now broke in 1929 because of "The Great Depression." Bill is so desperate to make some money, he wrote a manuscript called, "The Bandit Invincible." He tried to sell the script to "Hollywood." Phillips did not have any success. He could not reveal he is indeed, Butch Cassidy. The producers did not understand the story. Phillips story seemed to the producers, a fantastic tale of the life and times of '"Butch Cassidy." Phillips died in the "poor house" of stomach cancer and the script ended up with his family.

In the 200 typewritten pages about the exploits of "Butch Cassidy," at the very end, Bill states: "Finding the three dead men, the world would feel that Cassidy and his band had been killed. He would let it be that way. From Pernambuco [he went] to Liverpool and to England and Paris. At Paris, he entered a private hospital where he submitted to several minor operations. In three weeks, [he] left the hospital [and] he could see very little trace of his old self in the mirror, so cleaver had the transformation been worked out. He retired for the night defying anyone to identify him." "Butch Cassidy" left Valparaiso, Chili, boarded a ship and went to Paris, France; and had surgery so no one would recognize him. BINGO! – They didn't die in Bolivia and I finally had my proof.

Can you even imagine my excitement? I am ecstatic! No words can explain how elated and happy I am on January 11, 2010, to have finally solved "The Wild Bunch Mystery." This is a story that has eluded everyone from "The Pinkerton's" to "Wild Bunch" enthusiasts the world over.

Paul Newman thought that they "bought it" in Bolivia. Robert Redford visited Lula Parker Betenson every year for twenty or so years, at her home in Circleville. Lula wrote the book, "Butch Cassidy, My Brother." Lula said, "He came back and visited the family in 1925."

We have Lula's voice on tape (that we just found a few years ago) stating that her brother, Robert LeRoy Parker, alias "Butch Cassidy, "died in the North West," (whole interview has been transcribed and is included in this book) "but that is our family secret," said Lula. William Thadeus Phillips lived in Spokane, Washington, the "North West."

I had always suspected that Ann Bassett could be, "Etta Place." I asked Dr. John McCullough to do the photo transparencies and compare "Ann" and "Etta." They came back a "yes!" Ann Bassett is the "Etta Place" in the (so called) wedding picture taken in New York... a match!

I asked Dr. John to compare "Butch Cassidy" with William Thadeus Phillips...a match... all three are an exact match!

### Janet Taylor, Forensic Scientist with the Texas Rangers and
### Teacher at the "FBI Lab" at Quantico, Virginia

**Janet:** "The eyes match, the measurements match, but the ears and nose don't match. So I compared these elements of both faces and looked at them as a gestalt, the overall of those faces and then I had a look at the minutia of the individual traits and elements of each face. I can see why people would think they were one in the same individual. One striking thing is that the layout of each face was very, very similar. The spacing between the features was very similar. Another thing that is very similar about the faces of Phillips and "Cassidy" in the earlier photo's, is the look in the eyes, and that struck me right away. It would be easy to imagine those piercing blue eyes of "Butch Cassidy" growing older to look like those of the eyes in the photos of Mr. Phillips. In addition to comparing the facial features of Mr. Phillips, I wanted to have a look at the hands. Similar things that were notable had to do with the gesture of the hand. The nail shapes are very similar."

**Announcer:** "But the similarities do not hold up under the trained eye of a forensic artist."

**Janet:** "What I have done here is had a look at the left ears for comparison. It becomes obvious that this helix form is structured differently in Cassidy's ear. It runs all the way around the edge. The anti-helix is more pushed back, in contrast in Phillips ear, 1930. The helix pushes in, in this area and this anti-helix projects out more. This bridge is not of the same shape as this one. This one is far more pinched in and depressed in further. Cassidy had this very flat plane, (nose) that the flare of the nostril itself is very straight and then going down to the photo of Phillips it would not be obvious for it to have suddenly started to flare up like this. "Butch Cassidy" had a very distinctive wide mandible, (jaw line). This could not have changed while he could have gotten thinner. Things could have sagged with age. The actual bony width could have gone to this bony width, (moving to Phillips' photo) over time. It has become ever so clear that we are dealing with two different individuals in "Butch" and Phillips. In my opinion, as a facial identification specialist, they do not appear to be the same individual. My conclusions are not definitive, but my conclusions are that I don't think they're the same person?"

**Announcer:** "That is not a surprise to "Butch's" family. Phillips has always been seen as an impostor, and they still hold fast to their story."

**L. Paul Applegate:** "We know that Butch did come back. And uh, he came back to the house. My grandmother went up and cooked for him. The other members of the family knew it was common knowledge that he came back, and there's been a lot of people, probably most of the authors have still maintained that he was killed in South America, but he wasn't. He came home then he left home and stayed in the United States. Where he went and what he did, my grandmother would never say."

**--end of interview—**

**Note:**

I have contacted the Texas Rangers Anthropology Crime Lab in Austin, Texas, and Janet Taylor has since retired. I will continue to contact Janet to see if I could interview her concerning her 2004 forensic examination of William Thadeus Phillips and "Butch Cassidy" for the History Channel special on "Butch and Sundance." She said that the blue eyes looked the same, the measurements were the same, but the ears and nose were not similar. The jaw line could have changed with age and her findings were inconclusive. She even said the hands and posture of the hands, and the thumbnail are similar.

If she had the information from "The Bandit Invincible" manuscript by William Thadeus Phillips stating that "Butch" (talking about where he went after Bolivia) went to Paris, France, to a private hospital and underwent plastic surgery, would her findings have changed?

# From "The Bandit Invincible" by William T. Phillips

Billings was wounded in the first attack but the bandits killed eleven soldiers and wounded seven. Billings was finally killed and at that point Cassidy and Maxwell blew teh heads practically off of two soldiers. Where Cassidy and Maxwell were hiding they could get good aim and were much protected from the firing of the soldiers.

After fifteen or more soldiers were killed and several wounded, the firing ceased for a while as the soldiers knew it was instant death to come out in open fire. Such deadly fire had never been seen before. Later on in the evening, Haines was wounded and with what care Maxwell and Cassidy could give him helped for a while but finally, he was weakened from loss of blood and slumped in an expanded position and was shot by the soldiers.

That left Maxwell and Cassidy to fight their way out. Later on, Maxwell received a shot through the body and a scalp wound. Butch managed to get to Maxwell's side and began to give him what aid he could. But Maxwell had been hard hit and Butch saw at once the best he could do was to make him as comfortable as possible as they lay there behind the rocks. Maxwell gave Butch a letter from [for?] Betty and requested him to notify her of his death in case he [Butch] got away. He also informed Butch that Betty was his legal wife and had been for many years.

Butch brought down two more soldiers who were working around the upper edge of the canyon to get a better shot at he and Maxwell. It finally grew dark and Maxwell [gave] a long sigh and said, "Good-bye, Butch, my old pal. Don't forget Betty. Take my belt with you if you can get away and send it to little Betty and she will know I died fighting and thinking of her."

And with these last words he quietly passed on.

Butch had seen many people die but never did anything affect him as did the passing of his old friend, Maxwell.

Forgetting himself for the moment, he had forgotten he was surrounded by soldiers. Hearing a sudden voice not far, he listened carefully for the direction from where it came. [He] took dead aim and got his man. He heard the thud of the body as it hit the ground.

Waiting silently and watching carefully for some time after everything had become silent in the darkness, he removed Maxwell's money belt and buckled it about his own body and then began to think of a plan by which he might gain the summit of the canyon wall. And once on top he might evade the troops which he knew were somewhere up there among the rocks.

He fired a couple of shots in the direction of the troopers' barricades to let them know he was still there and to alert them. He made his way carefully. He headed in the direction where they had hid and tied their horses. For an hour he crawled on his hands and knees so he could not be seen or heard so easily and every now and then he would stop and listen carefully for any possible sound. After going three or four hundred yards, he lay quietly for some time to rest and listen again. Hearing no sound, he got to his feet. The horses could not get out of the gorge on either side but Butch was afraid they might have broken their tie ropes and worked their way out of the head of the gorge two miles from where they were tied and so he too was worried that the soldiers might have found them and made away with them.

He was relieved by hearing one of the horses move some distance ahead and stopped to listen and reasoned if the troops had discovered the horses they would have undoubtedly have followed them on down the gorge and attacked them in the rear instead of remaining with the horses. He listened again and hearing no noise except the horses, he made his way to the first one.

Being dark, he could not tell at first which one was his. Locating his own horse, he removed all the food from the saddle bags and filling his own, and rolling the remainder in his coat, he tied it with the bag and water bottles on the back of his saddle.

-57-

Then he and [his] horse made their way slowly to the head of the gorge.  Gaining the summit of the canyon wall, he continued on toward the Plateau of Cacaaca. From the plateau, he set his course east as near as he could due to darkness and continued on to daybreak the next morning.

Allowing his horse to rest a while, he continued on eastward where he knew he would reach one of the streams flowing to the north, to the Beni River.  That evening he was at the headwaters of a stream that flowed into La Paz River which was twenty miles from where the La Paz emptied into the Beni.

Feeling no pursuit, he made camp for the night, then [he] would continue on down the Beni River to some point in Brazil. [After] rest [and] breakfast, he went down the La Paz to [the] Beni.  Day after day alone he went and he reached the Madeira River near Villa Bella. [He went] from this Villa Bella to Santo Antonio and on down the Madeira River to Para and stopped for a week.  The trip down the Madeira was made by foot and the scenery was beautiful.  Both banks were covered with heavy timber and tropical vegetation.

Had it not been for the recent loss of his pal Maxwell, he could have enjoyed the trip very much.  He finally concluded since he was all alone now and no one to indentify him, he would settle down to a normal life.

He went to Para, spent two weeks waiting for a boat down the coast to Pernambuco. At Pernambuco, he had to wait a month for a boat to Europe.  Before leaving for Europe, he wrote a letter to his "one girl in the world" [in] which he explained everything for their future and [that he] would write her as soon as he arrived there.

At Pernambuco, he sent by express Maxwell's belt to Betty Price in Buenos Aires.  He knew that Betty would understand and he did not write her.  Betty would never know who sent the belt and no one would ever know except the one he loved that he alone survived the terrible battle.

The troopers had seen but three bandits and there were three left behind.  In his haste to take the belt from Maxwell's body he -- Butch -- had lost a small folder which he had carried for several years with some clippings and a letter and a little gold chain and cross.  Finding the folder with the three dead men, the world would feel that Cassidy and his band had been killed.  He would let it be that way.

From Pernambuco [he went] to Liverpool and to England and Paris.  At Paris, he entered a private hospital where he submitted to several minor operations.  In three weeks, [he] left the hospital [and] he could see very little trace of his old self in the mirror, so clever had the transformation been worked out.

He got a room in a comfortable hotel, wrote a letter to his sweetheart in California telling of his intentions and where to meet him in the United States. He retired for the night defying anyone to identify him.

Reports from the troopers with Cassidy and his bandits in La Paz in Bolivia [were given to] the various governments of North and South America [which] accepted their story as authentic [--thus] the name of Butch Cassidy became only as a memory. All of the members of the original Wild Bunch of the Hole-in-the-Wall gang, as they were usually spoken of, except two, had been wiped out.

The one who had been most sought and now became a man of mystery and the man who he first met upon the day he entered the Hole-in-the-Wall, Tom O'Day.  O'Day is yet living and at the same place where he welcomed Cassidy on his first visit to the Hole-in-the-Wall.*

*Interestingly, Phillips reports Cassidy's denouement in a battle similar to the one reported by James D. Horan, the Pinkertons and others, except that of course Cassidy survives and Sundance dies.  Unlikely as it is, it may at least be possible for a person to leave Bolivia as Phillips writes, down the Beni River, then the Madeira and finally the Amazon.  At least he has his geography correct.  Lula Parker Betenson in her book, Butch Cassidy My Brother, quotes Butch himself as scoffing at this tale because "the Amazon is only about a thousand miles from Bolivia."  Perhaps true, but you can still reach the Amazon from Bolivia!

- 58 -

---

104

# Marilyn Grace
## Journal Entry-January 12, 2009
## Janet Taylor Interview

When Janet did her analysis she said, "The eyes of "Butch Cassidy" match the eyes of William Thadeus Phillips. The ears and nose do not match, so her report is inconclusive. Even William Thadeus Phillips' fingernails matched Butch Cassidy.

A hand writing test comparing William Thaddeus Phillips handwriting to Butch Cassidy's handwriting proved that they are the same person.

We finally have the science to prove that:

- "Butch Cassidy" (Robert LeRoy Parker, from Circleville, Utah) is an alias for William Thadeus Phillips. [Nicknamed Bill]
- "The Sundance Kid" (Harry Alonzo Longabaugh, of Mont Clare, Pennsylvania) is "William Henry Long." [Nicknamed Bill]
- Ann Bassett, of Browns Park, "The Sundance Kid's" first love, is really "Etta Place."
- "Ann" is both, "Butch Cassidy's" mother's name, and "The Sundance Kid's mother's name- "Ann" Place, and "Ann" Parker.

What an adventure I have been on for all these years! What wonderful places I have traveled too and people I have met in order to be able to pull this together, and we're not done. We still have more research and filming to do.

I highly recommend that you watch the History Channel Special on DVD, "Butch Cassidy and The Sundance Kid." You can order a copy on-line or your local library can help you obtain a copy for you to view. You will see for yourself the interview of Janet Taylor, the forensic scientist who did the William Thadeus Phillips and "Butch Cassidy" analysis. She has worked for the "Texas Rangers" and the "FBI Labs" at Quantico, Virginia. If she had the knowledge that William Thadeus Phillips had a face lift, would her report have been conclusive?

I have attempted to contact Janet Taylor in Austin, Texas, and left a message at the Texas Ranger's crime lab. I have not had the time to follow through. We will save this information for our next book. It will be exciting to interview her and get her response.

Bill Long is the missing piece that solved the mystery. It took over 100 years to solve the mystery of the "Wild Bunch." Did they die in Bolivia or did they return to the United States under different names? Now you know the truth. They didn't die in Bolivia and this is just the beginning.

I have tromped all around Loa, Fremont, and Duchesne, Utah. Our TEAM has gathered all the clues! The folks who own the property where "Sundance" was born, Kurt and Joan Callow, have invited me to come and stay with them at 122 Jacobs Street in Mont Clare, Pennsylvania. We will be able to gather more clues regarding, "That 'Darn' DNA." The boarding house burned down in 2004 but Joan sent pictures that are included in Chapter 17, "What's Next?"

How amazing it is for the Long family descendants of Florence Viola Long and Evinda Ann Long, to finally have Bill Long's, (Harry Alonzo Longabaugh's) DNA genealogy. Now they have a family tree that says, "I belong." They have roots that can be traced back to even more family.

My colleagues, family members, and friends, have made "Solving the 'Wild Bunch' Mystery" possible. I am so grateful to everyone involved. Stay tuned, and thank you everyone for your participation with this historical and exciting project. I will continue to keep you informed and I promise there are more adventures coming up in the future!

### Your Friend and Detective ~ One Lucky Gal!

# Tom Fares Story
## "Sheriff Without His Pants"

### Journal Entry - Marilyn Grace - January 13, 2011

*While researching information for our book, I came across this really fun story about how the outlaws really lived. I also thought you would enjoy a photo we found of Sundance, Butch, Matt Warner and Sheriff Tom Fares. We don't know when this photo was taken? They must have kissed and made-up because they became good enough friends to have a photo taken together, or it could have been before they took his pants. Enjoy!*

*(See Photo Album)*

### The Last of the Bandit Riders - Matt Warner and Murray E. King

In the extreme heat of the summer, Matt Warner referred to Robber's Roost as a "lonesome, godforsaken country." Butch Cassidy had left the Roost and made a fifty-mile trek into town for supplies. Because he was a well-known outlaw, someone in the town of Green River recognized him. Dan Gillis rode to warn those at Robber's Roost telling them that men were tracking Butch. Matt Warner thought that probably Sheriff Tom Fares and his deputies would be coming. Matt Warner said that Fares was "one of the stubborn'ist, fightin'est old mules in the West." The outlaws skirted their camp looking for a trace of the sheriff.

One day Matt found tracks of steady-moving shod horses. It was blistering, deathly hot, and too hot to be chasing anyone. When Matt Warner, Tom McCarty and Butch Cassidy saw that the men were heading away from water, they decided to save them. They knew if the sheriff and his men lost their way, they would suffer a horrible death from thirst and heat. So, Matt fired his rifle and waved his hat. Sure enough, Fares and his two deputies came back down the south fork and headed up a steep twisting trail toward the rim of the canyon. Matt made the comment, "No one but Fares would be so foolhardy as to take such a risk of running into a trap." Matt left a message on the trail. "You are headed for death if you go south. Foller me if you want water."

At the water hole, Matt, Butch Cassidy and Tom McCarty hid behind some rocks; they heard the sheriff and his deputies say that they guessed 'we was right' to show them the water and save their lives. The deputies wanted to head back and say Cassidy couldn't be found but Tom Fares told them, "I'm the sheriff and you'll do bloody well just what I say. Tom Fares never goes back without his man."

When Matt Warner heard what Tom Fares said, "After the risk we took to save his life, he went plumb loco." Matt jumped out and surprised them. All three raised their hands. "If you'd been decent," says Matt, "we never would have bothered you, but now, you low-down coyote, you'll get yours." He turned them around and threw their guns out of reach. When Matt was taking Fares' gun he couldn't resist the temptation of shooting close to his back to give him a scare. That bullheaded hombre never moved a muscle or changed color. Matt later said, "I'll hand it to him for being one of the nerviest men I ever met."

The shot brought Butch and Tom right down on top of them. When Matt explained the situation, "they was so mad I thought for a minute they was going to shoot him." "Let's teach the skunk a lesson," Tom roars. "Let's make him ride back without his pants."

Matt tells: "We took his guns and stars and Fares' saddle.  Then we took Fares' pants off and put him on his horse bareback and herded the three of 'em into the canyon and started 'em back the way they had come.  Fares was a tall, thin man with spindling legs and the funniest sight I ever saw. His shirttail flapped in the wind.  His drawers was too big and bagged behind and hung over his spindling legs like a couple of flour sacks.  As he rode, his thin ankles and big feet hung out of 'em like bell clappers.  But he didn't bat an eye, and the way he cut loose and cussed us beat anything I ever heard."

"Tom Fares always gets his man," Butch Cassidy jeers.

"You're bloody right I do," says Fares, "and your bally turn will come next."  "That makes us laugh fit to kill ourselves, but while we are laughing we can't help admiring that fighting, bullheaded old mule.  We take the sheriff's pants and hang 'em on a pinion by a trail that is frequently used miles below our camp.  We fasten a note on 'em that says: 'Tom Fares never goes back without his man, but he sometimes goes back without his pants!'  We signed it, 'The High-Riding Three.'  We heard afterwards Tom cussed a blue streak all the way to Hanksville, the nearest settlement.  He got so sore riding horse-back without breeches that he had to walk and lead his horse the biggest part of the way.

When the deputies offered him one of their saddles he said: 'No, they are your saddles, and any sheriff that lets a bunch of cheap outlaws get 'im in this fix ought to be made to walk this way clear into 'ell'.  When they was near Hanksville a deputy offered to go ahead into the town and get him a pair of overalls.  'To 'ell with the hoveralls,' says Tom.  'It won't do them natives a bit of 'arm to see a man without pants.'  He walks right into Hanksville with his shirttail flapping in the breeze, leading his horse, cussing hisself and everything in general and paying no attention to anybody.  For a while the natives thought it was a couple of officers herding a lunatic in off the range."

# Betty Ann Bird & Yvonne Martinez

I'm Betty Ann Adams Bird. I was born 4/18/40. I married Llewellyn L. Bird 8/23/57 and currently we live in Lacey, Washington. My mother was Eva Merkley Adams, born 3/22/21, married William Ancel Adams 4/17/39. They had six children: Betty Ann, William A. Jr., Dennis R., Evinda, Chris D. and Yvonne.

My maternal grandmother was Evinda Ann Long Merkley. I'm not sure of her birth date. She married Jerry (Jeremiah Richard) Merkley. They had five children: William, Eva, Ercel, Roland and Mary Ilene. All are deceased except Ercel Merkley Nye (Mrs. Bud Nye) who lives in West Jordan, Utah.

My maternal great-grandparents were William Henry Long (Harry A. Longabaugh) and Luzernia Allred Morrell Long. Luzernia had children from her marriage to Silas Morrell and together her and Bill had two children. The girls were named Florence Viola and Evinda Ann. Both great grandparents lived the last days of their lives in Duchesene, Utah, and are buried in the Duchesne Cemetery.

Eva told me some stories about her grandfather, Bill Long. One of the stories she told me was about his death. She said that he was found dead in the corral, sitting up with a gun by his side. She felt that Matt Warner was responsible for Bill Long's death. She said Matt Warner, (who in his younger days had been an outlaw with "The Wild Bunch") had gone on a hunting trip alone for several days at the same time that Bill Long was murdered, and she felt that he was responsible for the death of her grandfather. If she elaborated on the story, I don't remember.

Excerpt from "In Pursuit of the McCartys" by Jon and Donna Skovlin: Charles Kelly interviewed Matt (Warner) in Price and was regaled with spellbinding stories, but Matt was reluctant to provide much specific biographical information. Although Matt was working on his life history, Kelly said he would not share the manuscript with him. In the late 1930s, collaborating with lawyer Murray E. King, Matt did write the story of his life, "The Last of the Bandit Riders," New York, Bonanza Books, 1940. A serialized version was printed in the Hearst's International-Cosmopolitan magazine beginning in 1938. Matt had a heated dispute with Kelly later in 1938, after Kelly published, "The Outlaw Trail," his epic account of western outlaws. Matt came to Kelly and violently objected to some of the material in it.

After this encounter, Matt, who had not been drinking for two years, began to drink heavily. He died December 12, 1938, after a ten-day drinking binge. Kelly said the Warner family felt he killed him. With Matt's death following so closely after his story was first printed, there was little chance for people to question and clarify his vivid tales. In December, 2009, Steve Lacy, with the help of Joyce Warner, republished Matt's book, along with memorabilia from his scrapbooks.

# Yvonne Martinez

"Hi, (Yvonne is talking to her sister, Betty) I looked through the Matt Warner book - cover to cover - today and it was strangely obvious that Sundance was not mentioned in the book. There is one picture from the late 1890's that shows Butch and Sundance, (along with some other outlaws) in front of Matt Warner's Saloon in Green River. The way it is printed, it's very difficult to tell if it really is Butch and Sundance. The others, you can tell... and by the way, the Sheriff was in the picture too... lol. There is one other mention in the book when they talk about whether Butch was killed in Bolivia or not. Matt Warner's daughter, Joyce, said that Butch visited them in 1939 after Matt Warner's death. They have letters he sent in 1930 with pictures. The reference to 'the notorious Sundance' was that he wanted to continue the outlaw life when Butch wanted to go straight.

You might want to check the library and see if they have the book. It has some interesting stories and gives you a perspective of how the outlaws thought and what they did. Matt Warner spent some time in Washington with the McCarty's, and it could be there that he got the cans of gold they found in his house after he died, if not from the Chinamen they shot, which he didn't talk about in the book.

If Bill Long was murdered, why consider Matt Warner? Since he doesn't mention Sundance in the book, it makes me wonder why. They had to know each other and had to have done some 'work' together. I need to go find 'The Outlaw Trail' and see if there are any dates that match up showing they were together sometime during the outlaw years. There was one guy in the book that he called, 'Bill Rose.' He said he ran around with this guy for 2 years and that this guy was a really bad guy - a true criminal, not just a cowboy outlaw like him. He was caught in the circumstances and did things that he had to do for fear this guy would kill him. He said he never knew the guy's real name. Could it be that he didn't want to name Sundance, or was this guy somebody else? I can't find any reference to anyone by that name as a Western outlaw on the Internet. Matt did say that they would use first names in their aliases so they wouldn't trip up when talking to each other. How's this for logic: Bill Long... Rose Warner... Bill Rose... Could something have happened between Bill Long and Rose Warner... hmmmmm...? Hehehe - Now I'm stretching it.

Something that Matt made a big deal about in the book was how he was pardoned for the two murders and crippling of the men over the mine shoot-out. How he shouldn't have been charged, how the jury had to convict him because of his past that Butch robbed the Montpelier Bank to get him a good lawyer, and how much the warden and governor helped him go straight. When he was the Justice of the Peace in Price, he spent much of his time working with kids to keep them from crime. Could Great Grandpa Long have known something he did after he went straight that Matt wanted to keep quiet? The other thing he was upset about was when people talked about him abusing Rose, his first wife. In fact, he drank himself to death over it - did Great Grandpa know if he did abuse her or what he did to her? They said when he was the JP, he was very tough on crimes against women. Could it be that he was making up for something he did that he wasn't proud of?

He talks about how you learn to shoot and how you learn to kill... he said that it became something you almost get addicted to the emotion of it and how it just becomes second nature. He could easily have shot someone, even after 36 years of "abstinence" I think. He really seemed to think a lot of Butch and told the Governor that he would look for Butch and see if he could get him to go straight. He doesn't even mention Sundance. When he talks about South America, he mentioned that Sundance went with him but nothing else... it's weird... something must have happened because I can't believe that he was that close to Butch and doesn't even talk about Sundance. Did he not want to bring any attention to any "disagreement" they might have had because he did go after him in later years? I don't know, just pure conjecture on my part, but it's interesting just the same. I'm probably not even close, but it's just weird that there is NO mention of "Sundance" in his stories, it just doesn't seem possible.

Oh ... one more thing... I remember Billy (our brother who lived in Price) telling stories about Price and how the law and the bad guys looked out for each other when the FBI or U.S. Marshalls came to try and... close up the whorehouses and the gambling halls. It's entirely possible that Matt might have done something after he was straight that Great Grandpa Long might have known about Matt and didn't want him talking to anyone about it... when did Charles Kelly start interviewing people for his book? Would Matt be worried that Great Grandpa Long might tell Kelly something that he didn't want anyone to know about... either during the outlaw times or not?

If they can get this forensic guy to look at the skull and get the rifle - it will be very interesting to find out what the conclusions are... along with the DNA. This would change history. Wow! Hopefully, it will be conclusive and none of this circumstantial stuff that leaves you wondering. We'll have to wait and see." Yvonne

## Note:

*Remember the explanation that Yvonne and Betty were working on concerning "Bill Rose" being an alias for "Sundance." As I continued my research in the Donna Ernst book, "Sundance My Uncle," I discovered the names William Henry Longabaugh, "Bill, and "married Rose -"Bill Rose." William Henry Longabaugh is "The Sundance Kid's" brother's child. Harvey Sylvester Longabaugh named his son William Henry Longabaugh. Our TEAM feels that William Henry Long took William Henry Longabaugh's name and then Bill's wife's name is Rose, and there you go... another alias for the "Sundance Kid," "Bill Rose."*

*Our TEAM believes that in Chapter 32 of Matt Warner's book, "The Last of the Bandit Riders," when Matt asks "Bill Rose" for money, he is actually asking the "Sundance Kid" for money. Matt states, "He (Sundance) showed me a belt chuck-full of gold and greenbacks." This supports Etta Forsyth's statement that Grandpa Billy Long always had bags of gold at the kitchen table and they "always" had money. Luzernia and Bill's home in Fremont, Utah, is a show place, and at that time no one worked. Etta said when I interviewed her that they were all rather "naive" about what's "really" going on in Grandpa Billy Long's life."*

# Bill Rose

Betty Bird and Yvonne Martinez are the great grandchildren of William Henry Long of Duchesne, Utah. Dr. John McCullough and I were examining Bill Long's remains at Sorenson Forensics in Salt Lake City, Utah. John discovered that the bullet wound to the head could not be a self-inflicted gunshot wound; Bill Long is actually, murdered. I started to call all the family members to find out what they might know. Betty Bird became so upset when I explained that Bill Long had been murdered! Betty said that twice her mother Eva, (Evinda Ann is Bill Long's youngest daughter - Evinda is Eva's mother) had always suspected Matt Warner of murdering Bill Long. She never did believe that Bill had committed suicide. Matt Warner just happened to be writing a book on his outlaw life and Bill Long vehemently opposed Matt writing his book. Matt Warner went on a four-day hunting trip and Bill Long ended up dead in Duchesne. November 26-27, 1936... Bill Long is found dead on that fateful day. The Long family had no idea that William Henry Long ran with the "Wild Bunch" and is called, "The Sundance Kid!"

In 1938, Matt Warner's book "The Last of the Bandit Riders" is out in print. The original book is so vile and Matt bragged about how many men he had killed. The language, so crude, the editor pulled it from the press and re-edited the book.

Betty and Yvonne went to work reading and studying the entire book, "Last of the Bandit Riders," by Matt Warner. They both came up with a very important discovery. There is absolutely no mention of "The Sundance Kid" anywhere in his book! There is an outlaw by the name of "Bill Rose" that helped Matt out when he needed money or help. I own a copy of Matt Warner's book so I joined in to see if we could figure out this side-mystery.

Not until about three months ago, did I figured out the "Bill Rose" mystery. In Donna Ernst's book, "Sundance, My Uncle," I noticed some information on William Henry Longabaugh. In 1903, "Sundance and Etta" were living law abiding lives on their ranch in Bolivia. They came back and visited Samanna and her family in Mont Clare, Pennsylvania. The couple also went to visit Harvey Sylvester Longabaugh, (Sundance's brother) in New Jersey. Harry (Sundance Kid) and ten-year-old William Henry Longabaugh went to the ocean to make a day of it; they collected sea shells.

William Henry Long and William Henry Longabaugh (remember the name analysis). William Henry Long appeared at the Hogan Ranch, October 1893. William Henry Longabaugh is born on October 28, 1893. Then it gets even better. In "Sundance, My Uncle," Donna states that William Henry Longabaugh "Bill" married Rose, "Bill Rose." How exciting to find the information on "Bill Rose." I immediately called and talked to Yvonne and Betty. We worked as a TEAM and we found out that "Bill Rose" is another alias for "The Sundance Kid." I even read that at the end of Matt Warner's life he had Cosmopolitan Magazine write a story on his outlaw life and lo and behold, Matt receives a letter from Robert LeRoy Parker, alias, "Butch Cassidy." Included in the letter are photos of days gone by of their outlaw years. Even Matt Warner thought that "Butch" had died in Bolivia until he received a letter and photos from his old pal. There were secrets that Sundance, Butch, and Matt Warner never shared.

Wow! They were living double lives and giving us a run for our money. What clever fellows with name changes, hidden families, and mistresses on the side. It never ended in Bolivia, November 7, 1908 but continued to be kept secret until January 11, 2010 when I put all the pieces together.

We still need to go back to Port Providence, Mont Clare, and Trappe, Pennsylvania for more research.

I am working on a new documentary where we can go back to Pennsylvania and visit all the places the Longabaugh family lived and worked. We want to physically go to the places where they attended church and worked their farms to see if we can find more clues. We need all the information to completely solve the mystery.

Bill Long did convince Matt Warner to not mention anything about "The Sundance Kid" in his book. Bill Long had to have been the one to tell Matt to use the alias, "Bill Rose." William Henry Long had many heated discussions with Matt Warner about not writing a book about their days as members of "The Wild Bunch." Matt had bragged in his book about killing twelve men and how he would get a rush from killing. Bill and Matt had a joint bank account until the crash in 1929 during the great depression. They did business deals together and were lifelong friends. In the end, there is no honor among thieves! Matt Warner murdered William Henry Long, alias, "The Sundance Kid."

(I am so AMAZED at Brent F. Ashworth of Provo, Utah. Brent is, THE WORLD'S LARGEST PRIVATE COLLECTOR. He owns the original hand written manuscript of Matt Warner's. I remember Betty Bird saying that maybe there are more clues in Matt's original manuscript. That is something we could follow through on in the future. Fun Research!)

# The Death of Bill Long
## Dr. John McCullough

Bill Long's death certificate reads "suicide," as the immediate cause of death. Bill was found by a seven-year-old grandchild, Rowland Merkley. He found Bill sitting down slumped against a pile of wood. There was a rifle or hand gun (?) lying by his side. On examination, a bullet had pierced his left temple and Bill Long was dead.

This scene is a common one for suicides, but at least three factors beg us to withhold judgment before agreeing with the common wisdom. These are the "un-charred" rim of the entrance wound, the apparent angle of the bullet upon entry, and a family story. There are also questions as to whether the weapon was a rifle or a pistol; this will be dealt with separately.

## The Un-Charred Wound

In cases of gunshot (GSW) suicide among males, especially, the gun is held flush with or close to the head. When discharged, the projectile crashes through the outer skin, the bone, the Dura matter, and enters the brain. The energy wave created by the bullet often fractures the skull; the more powerful the charge, the more likely the fracturing and extensive the damage. In Bill Long's case, the force detached the facial bone assemblage from the rest of the skull and blew out bones on the right side of the head upon exiting. Immediately following the bullet is the bursting of inflamed gunpowder at high temperature that burns the skin tissue and bone as it proceeds from the cartridge and gun barrel. All this assumes that the gun is held close to the skin or even touching the skin. The burst of energy created by the gunpowder is so great that a blank cartridge will kill if the gun is held sufficiently close to the body and, obviously, leave burn marks on the tissue and bone. While this sounds counter-intuitive, even preposterous, consider a powerful firecracker which is only allowed to explode in one direction, not only given full force to the explosion, but concentrated in only one direction. On the contrary, the further away the gun barrel, the less likely that burns will appear.

There are no burn marks on the left temporal bone at the entrance site. Only two reasons could be imagined for leaving no burn marks. First, Bill Long might have worn a thick cap which would have borne the brunt of the fire; second, the gun barrel might have been held at a distance of a foot or more from the head. If the death instrument was a rifle, suicide seems difficult to visualize geometrically. How can one commit suicide holding a rifle at a distance?

## Entrance Angle

Given the internal beveling of the entrance wound, the bullet seems to have entered at an angle of about 290 degrees, ("10 o'clock" in aviator parlance) and at an elevation of approximately 20 to 30 degrees from horizontal. In other words, from the left-front, from a slightly higher position William Henry Long was shot. This would have been an awkward angle of entry to inflict a wound to one's self, particularly with a rifle. It would be much easier to have the rifle at a much lower angle where the hand could more easily pull the trigger.

One caveat to this interpretation would be if he tilted his head, ("cocked his head") to one side, an awkward position, indeed. Suicide generally calls for a different geometry.

## Family Story

Lastly, one segment of the Long Family retains the story of his death which differs from the rest. In this version, Bill Long went hunting with a friend, Matt Warner, (known member of the "Wild Bunch" and once Sheriff of Price, Utah) and only Matt Warner came back alive. This variance with the story, as told by Etta Forsyth, who said that a grandson, Rowland Merkley, seven years-old who often brought food to Luzernia and Bill, came to the house one day. Luzernia noted that she had not seen Bill for a while and asked Rowland to find him, which he did, and Bill was slumped over a woodpile with a pistol, (rifle?) by his body.

The entrance wound in Bill Long's skull was clearly caused by a .22 caliber bullet. The question remains as to whether the bullet was discharged from a pistol or a rifle. The damage caused to the skull is great. The facial portion is detached from the remainder of the skull, (almost the whole right temporal bone was blown out) by the bullet and accompanying shock wave. This amount of damage is more consistent with a higher-powered bullet such as a .22 long rifle than a .22 hand gun.

I would therefore guess the damage was caused by a rifle. Of course, this begs the question of how do you commit suicide with a rifle and not leave burn marks on the bone.


# William Henry Long's Sisters Photo

There is a wonderful lady by the name of Sherma Gay Payton who lives in Tremonton, Utah. She is on the Silas Morrell and Luzernia Allred side of the family. William Henry Long is her step great grandfather.

Sherma has the original copy of Bill Long's sister's pictures, and a copy of the original William Henry Long picture when he was 25. She also owns the original letter that Bill Long's daughter wrote shortly after her father died. In the letter, Florence Viola Long wanted to know "who" her father was. She could not do any genealogy or temple work for her father, (Her mother, Luzernia, and Florence Viola, were active members of the Church of Jesus Christ of Latter Day Saints). Everything her father told her about where he was born, the names of his parents, etc., could not be traced.

On January 11, 2008, we met and interviewed Sherma Payton, Ray McDonald, Georgia and Jerry Morrell, and their son, Rod Morrell. Ray McDonald allowed us to come to her home and film for our documentary. Sherma, Ray and Jerry are brothers and sisters. Ray McDonald has since passed away and we will all miss her.

Rod Morrell owns a gun that Silas Morrell owned and was later used by William Henry Long for hunting trips. Another member of Bill Long's family, Elva O'Neal (Bill Long's grand-daughter, interviewed at age 93, and was living in Salt Lake City, Utah) said that her grandfather's sisters pictures were hanging in the living room in the Duchesne home of Bill and Luzernia Long. Bill Long's sister's pictures matched "The Sundance Kid's" sisters picture.

It is strange that pictures of Bill Long's sisters, the original Florence Viola letter, and the original picture of Bill Long, would end up with the step children. Sherma said that Luzernia gave her son Hiett, the family pictures and documents, and Hiett passed them down to her father Silas, (named after her grandfather, Silas Morrell). Her father gave the pictures and letter with family documents to Sherma Payton. Sherma's father gave her these treasures before he died and said with a serious tone, "Take good care of them Sherma."

(See Photo Album for The Sundance Kid's Sister's Picture.)

## NEW "WILD BUNCH" GANG!

*Hey guys! I wanted to know if any of you have seen a clip about Tom Cruz and John Travolta. They are going to do a remake of "Butch Cassidy and the Sundance Kid!" I saw it on YouTube. You never know what the date really is on YouTube. Tom Cruz will play "Sundance" and John Travolta will play "Butch." Paul Newman gave Tom Cruz his blessing for a re-make before he died. If any of you crazy "Wild Bunch" enthusiasts have any more information, please let me know! You can go to YouTube and see Tom Cruz and John Travolta in a big photo opportunity announcing the remake of the film.*

# Elva Remembers Her Grandfather

"I was told that my grandfather, William Henry Long, left home when a young boy. When he was about ten years old his brother was killed by Indian arrows in his back. His horse brought his body home and his father was so grateful to the horse that he put the horse out in the pasture and nobody could ever ride the horse again. One day when his father was away from home, grandfather rode the horse 'so hard' that the horse was covered with sweat and really tired. When grandfather saw his father coming, he ran away from home, knowing that he would get a really hard beating, and never returned. He went to a cowboy camp and the cowboys kept him until he grew up.

I must have been about two years old, maybe three, because my brother was a baby and we were visiting Grandma and Grandpa Long, and we were riding in a wagon with horses, of course, and I didn't want to go home. I wanted to stay at Grandma's and I wanted my parents to stay too. My dad would carry me out to the wagon and set me down in the wagon. I would climb out and go to the house crying and he would come and get me and we did this over and over. Finally he lost patience and gave me a spanking and took me to the house and set me down inside and went back to the wagon and drove off. I was just crying and crying and Grandma came and held me and sympathized with me. It was their dinner time and I remember sitting up to their table, eating bread and milk, and still just sobbing, and I think that is the earliest I remember my grandparents.

I was just a baby when we moved from Wayne County to Duchesne, so I don't remember that trip at all, but all the years and the time I spent with my grandparents, I think I loved them more than anyone, even my own parents. My grandfather was the kindest man I have ever known in my life. He used to hold me on his lap and hum, "In the Good Old Summer Time." He would rock me and hold me and I always felt so secure and loved. We would go for walks and he would hold my hand, and I loved that. That was the greatest thing that ever happened to me when he held my hand and walked with me.

He was a good neighbor, always helpful and I know that the neighbors always admired and trusted him because he was very honest with them. I remember hearing him say how he hated a liar. If anyone ever lied to him, that just finished them, as far as he was concerned.

He was always so good and so kind. I do remember a few occasions when I and my brother got in trouble; not that we did it on purpose. My Grandmother was a bad diabetic and she would go into these comas and so he hung this metal disk on the end of the granary and if she ever got sick and he was away from the house, she was supposed to go out or have someone else go out and hit on that disk, and he would be able to hear it anywhere on the farm. And he could come and take care of her. Well, we discovered what a nice sound that disk made, so we each took a hammer and just hammered that disk until it would just ring and practically deafen us.

Here we saw grandpa coming with a horse just running. He saw us beating on that disk and he asked us what we were doing. We said, "Nothing." He said, "Where is your grandma?" "I guess she is in the house," we said. So he went running in the house and found her and saw that she was okay. Then he came out of the house and just really gave us a scotch blessing. He told us that the disk was never to be touched and that it was there in case grandma got sick and needed help. Of course we didn't know that; he hadn't told us that before. He was really upset, but he was very forgiving and never held that against us. I am sure there were many other times that things went wrong, but he was always so sweet and nice.

I always felt that I was his favorite grandchild because he would hold and rock me. There were very few grandchildren that would sit on his lap and let him rock them like he did me. So of course, in my mind that made me special. Even when I was grown, I would sit on his lap and he would rock me and hum, "In the Good Old Summer Time." I don't know when he was born, but he was a few years younger than my grandmother.

When he went to Fremont, her first husband had passed away and left her with a family to care for and a farm to care for, so she was really having a struggle when Grandpa stopped and offered to help. I don't know whether he stayed there, but chances are he did because he took care of the farm for her and eventually they married. I don't know how long he was there before they married. They had two daughters, my mother and another girl, my aunt Evinda. Then my mother was married and I was a baby when they decided to go to Duchesne, which was quite a long trip and probably took several days because they traveled by horse and wagon. There were my parents and me as a baby; then my grandparents and my Aunt Evinda made the trip.

When they got to Duchesne, they cut down trees and built a one-room log cabin for shelter. There was nothing on the property until the house was built. It was there my brother was born. Later they built on two more rooms and lived in that for years.

Aunt Evinda married Jerry Merkley from Duchesne, and so they made their home there a couple of miles from Grandma and Grandpa Long. She started her family. We spent a lot of time with Aunt Vinda's children as we grew up. Then when we lived in Price, when I was 8 years old, Grandma would go into a diabetic coma and sometimes it would last for hours; Grandpa would call her on the telephone (Grandpa didn't have a telephone, so he would walk in to Duchesne and call her) he would call my mother and she would hurry and we would take the next stage and go take care of Grandma. I remember those trips. In the winter time we traveled in a big flatbed sleigh because of all the ice and snow, and we had to hang onto ropes to keep from sliding off the flat bed. We would stay with Grandma until she was well and was able to take care of herself again.

Even though Evinda's children lived so near Grandpa and Grandma Long, I spent more time with Grandpa than they did. He didn't pay nearly as much attention to them as he did to me. I was special.

He had a picture of his sisters hanging on the wall. One's name was Mary Mirilda, but I don't remember what the other's name was. My brother and I made up a little song about Mary Mirilda and sang it a lot. If I remember correctly, Ercel got that picture.

They had come to visit us in Price. Their lives were really hard in the winter time because Grandpa had to haul water in a barrel on a sled that he had made to fit the barrel. When the barrel was empty, he would have to go to the river and fill it again. In the winter time, that was really hard and Grandpa was getting old by then. So they used to come and stay with us in the winter in Price, and later in Salt Lake City.

One day he had to make a trip to Wellington, which was a few miles from Price, but he didn't want anyone to talk about it or question him because that was the only time he was ever going to mention it and he didn't want them to ever mention it, meaning my mother and Grandma Long. So he left and he was gone the whole day. When he came back, he didn't mention it except that there was someone there that he had to see, but they must not question it. My mother and Grandmother just accepted that and didn't ask anything about it. Nobody ever knew who it was but assumed that it was someone from his past life. There was a lot of mystery about my Grandfather. But I will never believe that he was a bad man. As I knew him, he was so good and so kind and I don't know of one bad thing that he ever did because he was honest and truthful."

# Interview of Elva Young Ehlers O'Neal
## November 8, 2007

**Gaylen:** "Did you ever remember or hear about a man coming to see Grandpa Long, and they talked out near the chicken coop for several hours? After he left, Grandpa had a leather article with the name "Lonie" (pronounced Low-nee) stamped on it. {See Curry Brothers photo} Did you know anything about that?"

**Elva:** "I have no idea.

(Lonie was a small-time outlaw, who ran with The Sundance Kid. They were very close when they were both arrested and jailed; they said they were brothers.)

**Gaylen:** "Grandma Ehlers used to tell me several times about the time Grandpa Long had a cancerous growth on his lip. He went to the Patriarch and asked him to give him a blessing. The Patriarch asked him why he had come to him, and Grandpa Long said that he believed that if he would give him a blessing, he would be healed." The Patriarch said, "Well, if you have the faith, you will be healed." "So he blessed Grandpa and put anointing oil on the growth. In a few days the growth was dried up and fell off."

**Elva:** "I don't know anything about that. I do know that he was asked several times about joining the church and he said that he believed the teachings and doctrines but he wasn't ready to join, so he never did join but lived it. Two boys and a girl were still at home when Grandpa married Grandma. The girl, Mary, was married around the same time. The two boys, Uncle Hyatt and Uncle Ernest, went to live with one of the older sisters. They didn't live with Grandma and Grandpa too long. I don't know why, but they didn't."

# The Candy Box
## NEW "WILD BUNCH" GANG!

Dianne Peck has a "Turn of the Century" candy box that had the copy of both William Henry Long's photo and the original "Fort Worth Five" photo. Included are letters from Etta's father, Irwin G. Robison, who became the sheriff of Wayne County. Also in the box were letters from her husband? Her father, Irwin G. Robison, one of the few people who knew that William Henry Long is, "The Sundance Kid." William Henry Long helped Irwin learn how to shoot. He is sheriff of Wayne County from 1915 to 1917.

The candy box has hand-written letters of Etta's father, but Diann has no idea the content of the letters. We may only get information on Etta's father, but it is sure strange that "Bill Long's" and the "Fort-Worth Five's" photos are both in that box. We would sure be remiss if we did not take the time to get this one last bit of information. I need to come and check out that candy box when I come up next week.

## Note:

*I went to Dianne and Etta's home in Duchesne the following week. We found a letter and story about Bill Long and also an untouched photo. The "eye" on "Sundance" is touched-up on all pictures of the FORT WORTH FIVE. The photo that Diann Peck has is not touched-up. That is the photo that Dr. John McCullough analyzed. This is an important and historical photo of the FORT WORTH FIVE along with the William Henry Long photo. All FORT WORTH FIVE photos are touched up. Someone decided that "Sundance's" eye needed a touch up. This is important because Irwin G. Robison left this "turn of the century" candy box with not one clue but with three clues in one candy box.*

*1---The famous FORT WORTH FIVE photo. (Not touched-up around "Sundance's" eye -- original photo)*

*2---William Henry Long's original photo.*

*3---A story written by Irwin G. Robison (Etta's father) about Bill Long helping in the cattle round-up. Pretty Cool Gang!*

*(See Candy Box in Photo Album)*

# William Henry Long ~ The Sundance Kid

Dr. John McCullough is our forensic scientist for our project on William Henry Long of Duchesne, Utah. John has a 40-year career, on staff, at the University of Utah. John has completed all the photo transparencies and examined the remains of William Henry Long.

The Longabaugh's are of German descent. There is a "Wanted" poster that states, "The Sundance Kid," "Looks like quarter breed Indian." Harry Alonzo Longabaugh is born at 122 Jacobs Street in Mont Clare, Pennsylvania, about "abt. spring" of 1867.

The Longabaugh Family lived in Port Providence, Pennsylvania from 1865 to 1870, according to census records. He is not born in the Longabaugh Family home. Mont Clare is a few miles north of Port Providence, Pennsylvania. The 1870 census record says he is living with Josiah and Ann (Annie) Longabaugh and is 3 years old. The Longabaugh Family Bible lists Elwood, Samanna, and Harvey Sylvester's day, month, and year of birth, but Emma only has the year. Harry's birthday says about "abt. spring" of 1867. Did Ann and Josiah not know Harry's date of birth? Why didn't they know Emma's birth date?

Civil War Records for Josiah Longabaugh show that he became deathly ill and is too sick to fight, so he's sent home. Is he too ill to have fathered a child in 1866? Josiah is 45 at "Sundance's" birth. He's at war when Emma would have been conceived. We really want to know if Emma is really their child.

Ann Longabaugh would have been older at the time of Harry's birth; born in 1828. In 1867, when Harry's born, nutrition is, very poor; giving birth at such an old age is possible, but we just don't have any birth certificates.

Also, at the turn of the century, disease would wipe out whole villages and children were left orphaned; typhoid, cholera, dysentery and yellow fever were common. The orphan trains would send children "West" to find homes. There were 150 thousand orphans that were adopted by families, in search of a better life.

Josiah and Ann Longabaugh lived across the street from a church on one farm that they worked. It is the custom to bring orphaned children to church and ask kind hearted folks to adopt these poor unfortunates. No one documented who took charge of the children.

The Longabaugh Family did not know his birthday and the Long Family had February 1st, 2nd, and March 13th, as Bill Long's birthday. They were just not sure when Bill Long had been born. The Longabaugh Family only had Harry A. in the family Bible. They didn't know what the "A" (Alonzo) stood for until his outlaw days. Alonso could have been an alias because his very first crime, "horse theft with a saddle and gun." The individual he robbed just happened to be Alonso Craven. Who knows if Alonzo is his real name? The Longabaugh Family only had abt. (about) spring of 1867, hand written in the Family Bible. Harry is born a few miles away from the Longabaugh family home?

## Sundance Kid Photo Analysis

Dr. McCullough's photo comparison using transparencies of William Henry Long of Duchesne, Utah and Harry Alonzo Longabaugh in the "Fort Worth Five" photo, is 99.9% that they are the same person. A photo comparison with the help of computers will prove 100%.

## Sundance Kid's Sister's Photo Compared to
## William Henry Long's Sister's Photo

Dr. McCullough states that they are the same individuals. What is William Henry Long doing with a picture of "The Sundance Kid's" sisters? The picture that William Henry Long had of his sisters shows that they were young; in their teens. The photo of Harry A. Longabaugh's sisters shows that they were much older, but they are the same people. Did "Sundance" bring the picture with him when he left his family in Pennsylvania at 14? Is the Brent Ashworth photo of a young "Sundance Kid" the photo he had taken before he left Pennsylvania?

## Family Name Analysis

Harry Alonzo Longabaugh's family names, compared to William Henry Long's family names. They are the same names as Harry's brother, Harvey Sylvester's children, and his sister Samanna's children. William Henry Long states on his marriage license that his mother's name is "Ann." Harry's mothers name is "Ann." "Etta" even shows up in Bill Long's family with Etta Robison Forsyth, the step grand-daughter of Bill Long; she was teased (by Bill) as a young child, that she was named after "The Sundance Kid's" girlfriend, "Etta Place." The only name that does not match is his father, Josiah. Bill said his father's name was James. James Ryan was an alias of "The Sundance Kid." Josiah and James begin with a "J." The outlaws would use familiar names to help them remember all their lies and not get tripped up under pressure. Using the name James, may have been an easy way to remember his father's name as "Josiah?" See the "Family Name Analysis" chart.

## Body Analysis

Dr. McCullough's examination is a match all the way down the list. William Henry Long's body matches Harry Alonzo Longabaugh's body. They both had sinus problems and they both had a broken nose, in the exact same way. They both had bullet wounds to the leg. Just from photos of the two men from young to older, they both have the same build. Dr. John did measurements and they are both the same height. Bill Long's body matches "The Sundance Kid's" body.

## Time Line

Bill Long's absence coincides with "The Sundance Kid's" adventures in South America. The Long Family had a showplace in Fremont, Utah. Bill Long's six step children and his two girls are well taken care of. Luzernia, (Bill Long's wife) purchased land in Bill Long's name while he is gone, once in 1903 and again in 1907. Bill Long came home from a ten-year absence speaking "Fluent French" and no one dared to ask why he could speak French or they would be in trouble.

## Family Stories

They all knew he was a member of the "Wild Bunch," they just didn't know which outlaw. He had a joint bank account with the former member of the "Wild Bunch," Matt Warner. Bill purchased the Duchesne Ranch with "gold coins" after he made a trip to Fish Lake, in 1917. He had gold coins in a bag when he paid for needed items and it was a common occurrence for Bill to pay for items with gold coins. Etta Forsyth looked at the famous photo of "Sundance and Etta," and said, "That's 'Uncle Billy!' I see the resemblance now!" Remember in the family name analysis, Etta was teased by Bill Long when he told her that she was named after "The Sundance Kid's" girlfriend, "Etta Place." Etta said, at age 93, that she was pretty naive as to what was really going on. Most families do not have bags of "gold coins" sitting on the kitchen table; he had to have been an outlaw. When I interviewed Etta, she had no idea who Matt Warner was. She didn't know that he was a former member of the "Wild Bunch," she just knew that Grandpa Billy Long and Matt Warner had a joint bank account and that Matt Warner did business deals with Bill. That is why Matt and Bill had a joint bank account in Price, Utah. Etta Forsyth, Bill Long's step granddaughter, was completely oblivious to the fact that Matt Warner was an outlaw with the "Wild Bunch." When Bill Long came back from Fish Lake with enough cash to completely pay for the ranch in Duchesne, Etta finally was clued in to the reality that Grandpa Long was an outlaw with a stash of "gold coins" hidden at Fish Lake.

## Adoption or Illegitimate

Was Harry born in the Longabaugh Family home? In a wanted poster for "The Sundance Kid," it states, "Looks like quarter breed Indian." His family did not know when he was born. The information they had been in the Family Bible gives his birth record, "abt. Spring" 1867." Illness and old age would have been less likely for Josiah and Ann Longabaugh to have been his parents. There is also the possibility that he was related but his family could not take care of him, so the Longabaugh's adopted him. We have two samples of male DNA. Another sample from Josiah's descendants is in the works. We are looking for Josiah's brother Nathaniel's male descendants. The hands of Josiah look like Harry's hands. "Sundance" had unusually long fingers and curled them under in photographs. Was Harry born at the boarding house at 122 Jacobs Street in Mont Clare, Pennsylvania and Josiah was the father but Ann is not the mother? The Longabaugh Family Farm was a mile down the canal in Port Providence. There are more clues and more questions that need answers.

## Concluding Thoughts

As we are explaining all the evidence that William Henry Long is really "The Sundance Kid," we have to take very seriously the importance of telling the truth. We have to back up our claims with documentation and scientific evidence.

While doing my research about "Sundance, Butch and Etta," I have read some stories that cannot be verified. "Etta" is more confusing than both "Butch and Sundance" put together! Stories of how so and so said he saw "Sundance" in Wyoming, or a story about how "Butch Cassidy" drove a 20-mule-team wagon train full of Borax through the California Desert in Death Valley at a death defying speed, are the stories I am referring too. Stories that are obviously over exaggerated with embellishments that tell a fantastic and exciting tale. I like dealing with the facts and I have really enjoyed working with such accredited and professional scientists that have given us documentation for all of our evidence.

**What a "Wild Ride" our TEAM has been on while solving the MYSTERY of**
**William Henry Long, "The Sundance Kid!"**

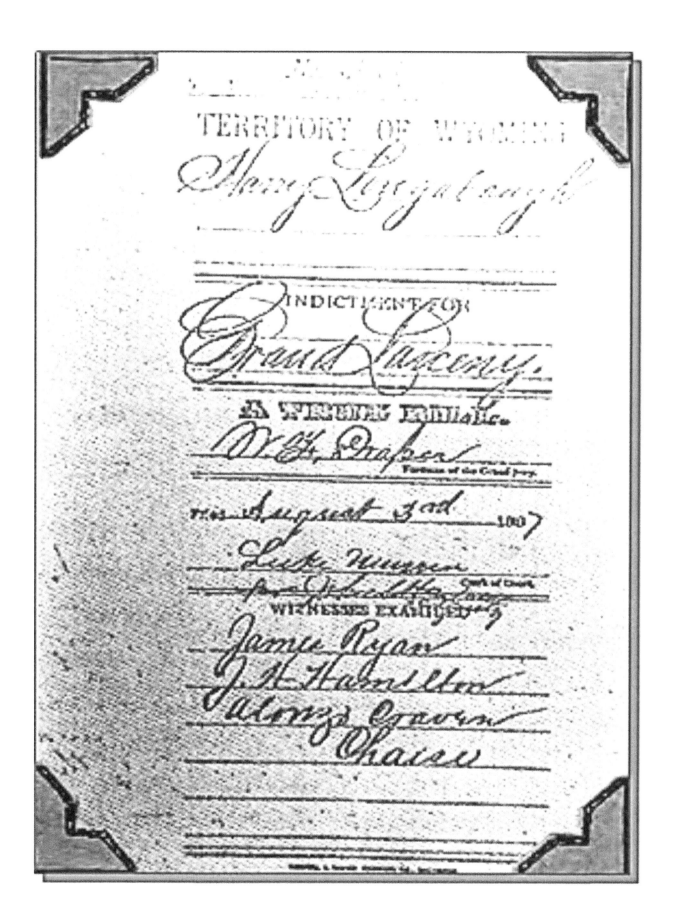

# Pinkerton's National Detective Agency.

FOUNDED BY ALLAN PINKERTON, 1850.

**OFFICES.**

DENVER, OPERA HOUSE BLOCK.
JOHN C. FRASER, Resident Sup't.

NEW YORK, 57 BROADWAY.
BOSTON, 30 COURT STREET.
MONTREAL, MERCHANTS BANK BUILDING.
BUFFALO, FIDELITY BUILDING.
PHILADELPHIA, 441 CHESTNUT STREET.
PITTSBURGH, SECOND NAT'L BANK BLDG
CLEVELAND, GARFIELD BUILDING.
CHICAGO, 201 FIFTH AVENUE.
ST. PAUL, ERNST BUILDING.
ST. LOUIS, WAINWRIGHT BUILDING.
KANSAS CITY, 622 MAIN STREET.
OMAHA, NEW YORK LIFE BUILDING.
PORTLAND, ORE. MARQUAM BLOCK.
SEATTLE, ARCADE BUILDING.
SPOKANE, PEYTON BUILDING.
LOS ANGELES, BRYSON BUILDING.
SAN FRANCISCO, CROCKER BUILDING

ROBT. A PINKERTON, New York,
WM. A. PINKERTON, Chicago. } Principals.

GEO. D. BANGS.
General Manager, New York.
ALLAN PINKERTON.
Assistant General Manager
New York

JOHN CORNISH, Manager, Eastern Division, New York.
EDWARD S. GAYLOR, Manager, Middle Division, Chicago.
JAMES McPARLAND, Manager, Western Division, Denver.

Attorneys:—GUTHRIE, CRAVATH & HENDERSON,
New York

TELEPHONE CONNECTION.

REPRESENTING THE AMERICAN BANKERS' ASSOCIATION.

## $2,000.00 REWARD.

**CIRCULAR No. 3.**

**DENVER, Colo., November 14th, 1904.**

THE FIRST NATIONAL BANK OF WINNEMUCCA, Nevada, a member of THE AMERICAN BANKERS' ASSOCIATION, was robbed of **$32,640** at the noon hour, September 19th, 1900, by three men who entered the bank and "held up" the cashier and four other persons. Two of the robbers carried revolvers and a third a Winchester rifle. They compelled the five persons to go into the inner office of the bank while the robbery was committed.

At least **$31,000 was in $20 gold coin; $1,200 in $5 and $10 gold coin;** the balance in currency, including one $50 bill.

Since the issuance of circular No. 1, dated Denver, Colo., May 15th, 1901, and circular No. 2, dated Denver, Colo., February 3rd, 1902, it has been positively determined that two of the men who committed this robbery were:

**1. GEORGE PARKER,** alias "**BUTCH**" **CASSIDY,** alias **GEORGE CASSIDY,** alias **INGERFIELD.**

**2. HARRY LONGBAUGH,** alias "**KID**" **LONGBAUGH,** alias **HARRY ALONZO,** alias "**THE SUNDANCE KID.**"

PARKER and LONGBAUGH are members of the HARVEY LOGAN alias "KID" CURRY band of bank and train (express) "hold up" robbers.

For the arrest, detention and surrender to an authorized officer of the State of Nevada of each or any one of the men who robbed the FIRST NATIONAL BANK OF WINNEMUCCA, the following reward is offered by THE FIRST NATIONAL BANK OF WINNEMUCCA:

**$1,000** FOR EACH ROBBER. ALSO **25 PER CENT., IN PROPORTIONATE SHARES** ON ALL MONEY RECOVERED.

Persons furnishing information leading to the arrest of either or all of the robbers will be entitled to share in the reward.

# SEDUCTION INTO "The Outlaw Life"

In 1884, George Longenbaugh (cousin to Harry with different spelling but still related) headed West to homestead land in Cortez, Colorado, and Harry came with them.

A special bond formed with George, his wife Mary, and their children. George and Mary worked the family homestead, and Harry stayed for two more years. When Mary and George's son Walter married, he named his second son "Harry." The town of Cortez, Colorado is more of a tent city by 1866, and it grew fast and wild.

The Longenbaugh family moved 48 miles from Durango, to Cortez. The area appealed to other families as well. The Maddens were in nearby Mancos and the McCarty brothers Tom and Bill, (William Henry) McCarty, moved to Cortez from the neighboring, La Salle Mountains, in Utah. The McCarty's ranch is one mile away from the Longenbaugh ranch.

In later years, by 1885, Harry and Bill Madden robbed at least one train together. Robert Leroy Parker (Butch Cassidy) and Willard Erastus Christiansen (Matt Warner) also lived in the Cortez area.

Harry is in the wrong place at the wrong time. Half a dozen outlaws within a 75-mile radius, seduced young Harry to become part of their gang. The ability to raise and handle horses probably appealed to "Butch Cassidy" and Harry is one of his first recruits.

The skills Harry learned as a good horseman served him well, especially when relay horses were used for escaping the law. Butch, Tom, and Matt, saw "Sundance's" talent working with horses and noticed how fast he could draw a gun. Harry had now joined "Butch Cassidy's" gang. "Sundance" and Harvey Logan began working together. Harvey's also part of the gang.

In 1895, the "N BAR" headquarters moved to Oswego, Montana. Harry Longabough once again worked for them as one of the fifty ranch hands listed at that time. Dutch Henry is the head of a small gang of rustlers headquartered just north of Culbertson, Montana, and Dutch would use the "Hole in the Wall" hideout in Wyoming.

"Dutch Henry's" and the "Nelson-Jones" gang would rustle cattle together. Frank Jones became head of the gang and he must have made an impression on Harry because in later years, "Sundance" used the name "Frank Jones," as an alias.

In June of 1900, an informant from Malta, Montana, wrote the Pinkerton's about several outlaws living near Culbertson, Montana. There is a party named Longenbaugh (sic) which was supposed to have been implicated in the holdup which occurred at Malta a number of years ago. Some people here think he is one of the "Jones" or "Roberts" boys... I would like to see Valley County rid of this class of her population. They rustle cattle and horses, do many misdeeds and either hide in Canada or across the border.

In the early 1900's, Dutch Henry went to South America for a while. He may have visited "Sundance and Butch" on their ranch in Cholila, Argentina. Dutch Henry returned to Montana and is eventually killed by the Canadian Mounted Police.

On February 27, 1887, young Harry stole a light gray horse, a revolver, and a saddle outfit from Alonzo Craven, from the VVV Ranch. He headed up to Miles City, Montana. Clay had the employees of the VVV Ranch spread out over the area in search of a smooth-faced, gray-eyed boy, and the stolen goods. It was not until March 15, 1887, which James Wedner, of the VVV Ranch, finally rode into the town of Sundance, the Crook County Seat, to file charges with Sheriff James Ryan.

Ryan then found Harry's trail and followed it to Miles City. By April 8, 1887, Ryan had arrested Harry but did not immediately leave Miles City. Harry was housed in the small jail located on the north side of the new courthouse at Main and Seventh Streets, until April 12th. For reasons unknown, Ryan and young Harry then boarded the Northern Pacific Railroad to St. Paul, Minnesota, nearly 700 miles away. Then they headed to the Fremont, Elkhorn and Missouri Valley train to Rapid City, South Dakota. Somewhere near Duluth, Minnesota, Harry and an accomplice picked the locks of his shackles and handcuffs and jumped off the moving train while Ryan was in the bathroom.

Some researchers believed "Butch Cassidy" was in the Miles City area at this time and came up from Wyoming about 1886. Sheriff Ryan offered a $250 reward; he was very frustrated that Harry had escaped again. Foolishly, Harry returned to the Miles City area. Deputy Sheriff Eph K. Davis and the Stock Inspector, W. Smith, caught up with Harry near the "N Bar Ranch" on the Powder River outside of Miles City. Harry was again shackled and handcuffed; Davis and Smith were left to guard him in the Custer County Jail. Smith fell asleep and Davis pretended to do the same. Harry again picked the locks and made for the windows to escape, but Davis pulled out his gun and stopped him. By morning, Sheriff Tom Irvine had telegraphed Ryan to pick up his prisoner. Irvine also put in a claim for the reward money. In May 1888 at the Crook County, Wyoming, commissioners meeting, they refused to pay the reward to Ryan or Irvine."

# "GUILTY" As Charged

"Sundance" ended up in jail only once in his life. He is 20 years old. He robbed Alonzo Craven of his horse, saddle, and gun. The time, 1887 and he went to jail at the Sundance Wyoming Jail for 18 months of hard labor.

When a lawyer goes into a court of law, he needs to prove that the person that has been arrested is "innocent" or "guilty!"

Here we have the case of Bill Long of Duchesne, Utah. There are many, many leads about William Henry Long as an alias for Harry Alonzo Longabaugh, "The Sundance Kid?" But that "DARN" DNA! Bill Long's DNA does not match the mother, Ann Place Longabaugh. We will have the father's DNA when we locate a living Longabaugh from Conrad's children Jonas or Samuel. Can we convict William Henry Long of being "The Sundance Kid" without DNA? We are doing DNA Genealogy with DNA from William Henry Long's remains.

## Evidence:

*Dr. John McCullough's photo analysis of William Henry Long, "The Sundance Kid" is a 99.9% match. This is scientific evidence that holds up in a court of law.

*Bill Long's sisters' picture matched "The Sundance Kid's" sisters' picture.

> *What is William Henry Long doing with a picture of "The Sundance Kid's" sisters?
> *Matt Warner and Bill Long had a joint bank account in Price, Utah. The money is lost in 1929 during the "Great Depression." Matt Warner is a "known" member of the "Wild Bunch." What is Bill Long doing with a joint account with Matt Warner, a former member of the "Wild Bunch?"

"Sundance" assumed the name, William Henry Long. He appeared at the Hogan Ranch in Loa, Utah, October of 1893. William Henry Longabaugh's brother, Harvey Sylvester Longabaugh, is the father of a son named William Henry Longabaugh, born October 28, 1893.

Bill Long gave his children names that Samanna had given to her daughters who died in infancy: "Bertha Viola"- Florence Viola; "Florence Ann"- Evinda Ann (Vinda). Other family names: "Emma Elva"-Elva O'Neal (great granddaughter); "Etta Place"- Etta Robison (step great grand-daughter). Bill Long used to tease Etta telling her that she was named after "The Sundance Kid's" girlfriend, "Etta Place."

Time Line—Bill Long is absent from Duchesne and left six step-children, and his own girls, Florence Viola (Viola) and Evinda Ann (Vinda), fatherless until he shows up ten years later speaking "fluent" French. No one is to ask where he has been or they would be in trouble. Money is never a problem and yet no one works and their home is a show place in Fremont, Utah. Luzcernia, wife of Bill Long, bought land in Bill Long's name twice—once in 1903 and again in 1907.

William Thadeus Phillips of Spokane, Washington wrote a manuscript in 1929 after he had lost all of his money in the "Great Depression." The manuscript, "The Bandit Invincible," by William Thadeus Phillips states; "At Paris, he entered a private hospital where he submitted to several minor operations. In three weeks (he) left the hospital and he could see very little trace of himself in the mirror, so clever had the transformation been worked out." "Butch and Sundance" went to Paris, France. That is why Bill Long could speak fluent "French." (Chapter 29 "The Last Stand" p. 58, para. 7) "In Search of 'Butch Cassidy'" by Larry Pointer. Larry has documented William Thadeus Phillips' life. Several minor operations: (1) Nose (2) Ears (3) Jaw line.

*Janet Taylor, Texas Ranger Anthropologist, in 2004, in her photo and hand analysis of William T. Phillips, compared to "Butch Cassidy" photos and hand writing. With all the evidence about "Butch Cassidy's" face lift in Paris, France, at a private institution, would her conclusion have been... conclusive?

*Harry Alonzo Longabaugh played in New Jersey with William Henry Longabaugh, (Harvey Sylvester Longabaugh's son) in 1903, when the boy was ten years old. "Sundance and Etta" had come from Bolivia to visit family in New Jersey and Philadelphia. Harry Alonzo Longabaugh, went to the ocean with 10-year-old William Henry Longabaugh to collect sea shells on the Jersey shore, according to Donna Ernst's book, "Sundance, My Uncle." William Henry Long is absent from his family. Then we have William Henry Longabaugh from New Jersey and William Henry Long of Duchesne, Utah. Long/Longabaugh.

122 Jacobs Street, Mont Clare, Pennsylvania, the birth place of "The Sundance Kid." I have contacted Kurt and Joan Callow; they now own the property where "The Sundance Kid" is born in Mont Clare, Pennsylvania. Joan said that the building had been a ten-room boarding house, with one large suite; it caught on fire in 2004 when they were on vacation. They wanted to have the building restored as a historical site, but were unable to do so. The boarding house had to be torn down, but Joan gave us pictures of what the boarding house looked like before the fire. She is also searching to find who owned the property in 1867. We would like the birth year (a record to support the federal census) of "The Sundance Kid." The family of Josiah and Ann (Annie) Longabaugh on the 1870 census lived on a farm in Port Providence, Pennsylvania, about a mile down the Schuylkill Canal. I have the number of the farm that is listed on the census record and we are in the process of locating where the Longabaugh's lived; what years they were there. We may have the Longabaugh family living in Port Providence in 1867, and Harry A. Longaabaugh is born in Mont Clare. "Sundance" is 3 years old when he appeared on the 1870 census record living with the Longabaugh's. Some questions still need answers, but we believe we have the bulk of our research completed.

*Emma Longabaugh is conceived when Josiah Longabaugh fights in the Civil War. Is Josiah her father? The family bible only has the year she was born, 1863. Didn't the Longabaugh's know when Emma is born? Harry Longabaugh only has "abt. Spring" 1867. Why didn't the family know the day and month Harry is born? Were both Emma and Harry adopted into the family and they didn't know their birthdays?

With all the evidence our TEAM has provided; William Henry Long of Duchesne, Utah, is "The Sundance Kid." Bill Long (William Henry Long) is the "missing" piece. "The Sundance Kid" changed his name to William Henry Long to avoid capture and death. William Thadeus Phillips is an "alias" for Robert LeRoy Parker, "Butch Cassidy." Ann Bassett is an "alias" for "Etta Place." They all lived to old age here in the United Stated of America.

Pretend that you are on the jury and they are alive today; what would be your vote as a member of the jury? My vote would be "guilty" of robbing what would be equal to two and a half million dollars today and killing innocent people. There were five lawmen that lost their lives. I say, "GUILTY!" As Charged!

# A Wanderlust

Elwood, Harry's oldest brother is an upstanding citizen; a single sailor who lived in San Francisco, while his brother Harry Alonzo Longabaugh became an outlaw? Samanna his sister is a law-abiding wife and a mother. His other sister Emma, an unmarried seamstress. Emma, along with a partner, owned a tailoring shop in Philadelphia, Pennsylvania. Harvey Sylvester, his brother, became a husband and father and businessman who had never had any trouble with the law.

Early on, Harry A. (Alonzo) Longabaugh is said to have been an unsettled child, "a-wanderlust," a disturber. I gather that he didn't want to go to church with the family or be that involved when it came to participating in family functions? Harry is very close to his sister Samanna and really loved her children, and yet, Harry ended up being one of the world's most notorious outlaws of all time. The entire family went to church. Harry's grandfather, Harry Place is a preacher. Fritz Longabaugh of Rochester, New York, (related to The Sundance Kid) is a minister today and carries on the call to serve. Fritz is the first person I contacted and he has been most helpful with the family history and genealogy charts.

We are doing the DNA for the male side of the family to compare it with Bill Long's DNA. Is Josiah Harry's father? We want to leave no stone unturned as far as possible scenarios concerning Bill Long's DNA. "Sundance's" hands and Josiah's hands both look very similar; unusually long fingers. "Sundance" is the youngest child of Ann and Josiah Longabaugh. Look at all the times they were uprooted and had to move because of poverty. They were just poor farmers looking for a way to survive. So... let's track the birth place of all the children of Josiah (Jas, Jesaias) and Ann (Annie) Longabaugh. Let's show the dates and places they were born.

## Josiah Longabaugh (spelled Jesaias): ("Jas" in Census Record)
Born: 14 June 1822, New Hanover Lutheran Church, PA.
  Died: 9 August 1893, buried Morris Cemetery, Phoenixville, PA., heart disease.
  Married: Ann (Annie) G. Place, August 1855, Phoenixville, PA. Josiah was 33 when they married in 1855, he was 45 when "Sundance" was born.

## Ann (Annie) G. Place:
  Born: 27 September 1828. One report said she was born about 1820. Conflicting reports.
  Died: 18 May 1887 (Sundance was 20 years old when his mother died). Went to jail in Sundance, Wyoming and told the prison that his parents were dead. Ann had passed on but Josiah his father was still alive in 1887.
 Note: *Josiah was in Civil War H Column of 175th Infantry, received pension—sent home, too ill to fight.*
  1850 Census-- Chester, County, and Schuylkill Township #126 says "farmer"
  1860 Census--Montgomery, County, Upper Providence #597
  1870 Census--Montgomery County, Upper Providence #552877, #455/496
Elwood Place:
  Born: 23 June 1858, Montgomery County, PA.
  Died: 11 May 1930, San Francisco, CA.

## Samanna ("Sam"--"Anna") C. Longabaugh:
### (Josiah < Jones (Jonas)< Conrad)
Born: 22 April 1860, Phoenixville, Pennsylvania. Died: 1920, Mont Clare, PA, buried Morris Cemetery, Phoenixville, PA.1880 Census, Chester County, Phoenixville, PA. #58611 pt. 1831 (#2), New Hanover Lutheran Church Records, New Hanover, PA., Falkner Swamp Lutheran Church records, New Hanover, PA., Family Bible in possession of William Hallman.
Married: Oliver F Hallman, 1878, Phoenixville, PA. (born 20 Feb, 1856, died 24 Nov, 1941) Child: A. Adella Hallman (married Henry Weber, died young)
Ferman A "Bud" Hallman (m. Adelaide Sturges, at least one son)
Granville L. Hallman (married Alice Brower, at least one son)
Emma Elva Hallman (died in infancy)
Bertha Viola Hallma (died in infancy)
Emma owned a tailoring shop at 2015 Poplar Street, Phoenixville, Pennsylvania.
Note: *Emma Longabaugh changed spelling of her name because of "The Sundance Kid." She was ashamed to be associated with the*
*"Outlaw." Emma cut "Sundance" out of her will... "If he is alive or dead?"*

## Harvey Sylvester Longabaugh:
Born: 19 May 1865 Upper Providence Township, Montgomery Co, PA.
Died: 6/7 Jan 1937, buried Zion Cemetery, Flowertown, PA.
Married: Katherine Gercke 1886/7 (b. 1 Oct 1865, d. 1949)
Children: Harvey Sylvester
b. 1888, PA, died 8 Feb 1915, age 27, buried Flowertown , PA., unwed.
*William Henry Longabaugh
Florence Ann (died at age 12)

Note: Harvey Sylvester Longabaugh was exhumed in 1992 to compare DNA with skeleton believed to be "Sundance." "WANTED: Butch and Sundance" documentary, Bodies exhumed in Bolivia for NOVA Documentary, with Anthropologist Clyde Snow. Harvey's DNA matched our living descendant, Carl Schuch's DNA on Ann Place Longabaugh's side of the family.

## *William Henry Longabaugh: (Nick name "Bill") Harvey Sylvester Longabaugh <Josiah Longabaugh <Jones (Jonas) Longabaugh<Conrad Longabaugh
Born: 28 October 1893, Philadelphia, PA. (William Henry Long appears at the Hogan Ranch, October 1893)
Died: 9 March 1976, buried: Roslyn, PA.
Married: Rose Sippel, 9 April 1917, Philadelphia (born 3 June 1897, died 1 July 1977) (Bill married Rose - "Bill Rose" an alias for "The Sundance Kid")
Children:     William Henry Longabaugh Jr.
Florence Catherine Longabaugh
William David Longabaugh

Note: *"Sundance and Etta" came to visit Family (according to Donna Ernst) from Bolivia. "Sundance," at that time, was living an honest life and they looked forward to seeing him. During the time Harry Alonzo Longabaugh was visiting family in Pennsylvania, Bill Long was missing from Fremont, Utah. He was an absent husband for ten years while his wife, Luzernia, six step-children, and two daughters lived in Fremont. Bill Long and Luzernia's two children, Florence Viola Long and Evinda (Vinda) Ann Long, were now part of this very large family. Bill Long lived a double life, with a mistress and all. This is where we want to tell about Matt Warner's book, "Last of the Bandit Riders." In the book, Matt does not mention "The Sundance Kid," but there was mention of an outlaw by the name of "Bill Rose." Harvey Sylvester Longabaugh's son, William Henry Longabaugh (Bill), married Rose\* ... "Bill Rose." What a clever way to tell about an outlaw without coming right out and calling him "Sundance."*

All the information came from Donna Ernst genealogy book she donated to the Church of Jesus Christ of Latter Day Saints Genealogical Library in SLC, Utah. Continued from Longabaugh Genealogy Book:

## Harry Alonzo Longabaugh, alias, "The Sundance Kid."
  Born: "abt. Spring" 1867, 122 Jacobs Street, Mont Clare, Pennsylvania.
  Died: 6 November 1908, San Vicente, Bolivia.
  Possibilities:
  Married 1st: Anna Marie Thayne in 1900 and divorced in 1901?
  Child:   Harry Jr.
  Married 2nd: Ethel, ("Etta Place").

## Harry Longabaugh Jr. (?Harry <Josiah) real name probably Harold Thayne Longabaugh
  Born: 2 Feb 1901 or 4 Jan 1901
  Died: 19 Dec 1972 Missoula, Montana
  Source: his own claims and death certificate shows he had a brother, John.
      The strange story of Harry Jr. had papers and documents that he was "The Sundance Kid's" son, down-and-out on welfare, living in a hotel in Missoula, Montana, when someone set a fire underneath him and he died of smoke inhalation in his bed. He was possibly murdered.

## Josiah and Ann Place Longabaugh's children:
  Elwood
  Born: 23 June, 1858, Montgomery Co, PA.
  Samanna
  Born: 22 April, 1860, Phoenixville, PA.
  Emma T.
  Born: 1863, Zeighersville, PA. (no day or month listed)
  Harvey Sylvester
  Born: 19 May, 1865, Upper Providence, Montgomery County, PA.

  Harry A. (Alonzo)
  Born: "abt. Spring" 1867, 122 Jacobs Street, Mont Clare, PA.

## Josiah and Ann (Annie) Longabaugh

1858-Montgomery Co., PA., Elwood's birthplace

1860-Phoenixville, PA., Samanna's birthplace

1863-Zeighersville, PA., Emma's birthplace

1865-Upper Providence, PA., Harvey's birthplace

1867-122 Jacob's Street, Mont Clare, PA., Harry A's birthplace. The 1870 Census---Family living in Port Providence—Mont Clare to Port Providence, is one mile away. History records they were "poor farmers" – unstable financially. Note: I need to go back to Pennsylvania and find actual documentation.

1870 Census---The Longabaugh Family were farmers. The Longabaugh's were living on a farm in Port Providence from 1865 to 1870.

## "Sundance Kid's" Father - Josiah Longabaugh

Civil War Record 175th Regiment Infantry

Organized at Philadelphia, November 6, 1862. Moved to Washington, DC. December 1; thence to Fortress Monroe and Suffolk, VA.

Attached to Gibbs' Brigade, Division at Suffolk, VA, December 1862. Spinola's Brigade, division at Suffolk, 7th Corps, to December 1862.

1st Brigade, 5th Division, 18th Corps, Department of North Carolina, to May 1863.

District of the Pamlico, Dept. of North Carolina, to June 1863. Well's Brigade, Harper's, Ferry, W. VA, 8th Corps, Middle Department, to July 1863.

SERVICE -- Duty at Suffolk, VA, until December 28, 1862. Moved to New Berne, North Carolina December 28 -- January 1, 1863, and duty there until April 1863.

Expedition from New Berne to Trenton, Pollocksville, Young's Cross Roads and Swansborough March 6-10. Operations on the Pamlico April 4-6.

Expedition to relief of Little Washington April 7-10. Expedition to Swift Creek Village April 13-21. Garrison duty at Little Washington until June. Moved to Fortress Monroe, VA.

Thence to Harpers Ferry, W. VA, and to Frederick, MD. Mustered out August 7, 1863. Regiment lost during service 21 by disease.

*Emma was born in 1863 (no day or month of birth in family bible) and Josiah was at war in 1862 when she would have been conceived.

November 6, 1862 and came home because of illness, August 7, 1863. Josiah was at war and may not have been home for Emma's conception?

# Donna Ernst

Sue Balsamo from Philadelphia happens to be related to the Longabaugh's on the Henry Longabaugh line. She is not on the direct line to "Sundance," but she is related, none the less. I met Sue on-line several years ago and she has been most helpful in helping me with research. I get a sense of the area and where things are located because of Sue.

Sue sent me pictures of the graves of the Longabaugh family and she said that some 20-plus years ago, she ran around with Donna Ernst, author of "Sundance My Uncle," with babies and strollers in hand. They went to Josiah, Ann, Samanna, Harvey, and Emma's graves; as well as places that the Longabaugh's lived and worked.

They were friends and shared a love for family history and research. Since our TEAM made the news several years ago, Donna has disconnected her phone and has an unlisted phone number. She has also taken down her website and we have not been able to contact her.

Sue Balsamo lives in Philadelphia and she has not been able to find Donna. Sue explained to me that Donna has all the family photos and research that could help shed more light on what really happened in "Sundance's" life.

Donna has moved since Sue knew her, but she saw with her own eyes the stacks and stacks of research, photos, and family documents, that could possibly help us with our project. Our TEAM has been able to prove with DNA Genealogy that Josiah Longabaugh is a cousin to William Henry Long. We have also found Harry Alonzo's father, Alonzo. You will know all the details when you continue to read the section on "That 'Darn' DNA."

We know that William Hallman, the male descendant of Samanna Longabaugh (Sundance's sister) owns the Family Bible with the days, months and years of Elwood, Samanna and Harvey, but the same bible only has Emma T. (1863). Harry A. Longabaugh has his birthday listed as "abt. spring of 1867." Donna says that the family is not really sure what the "A" in Harry A. Longabaugh stands for. They just assume his name is "Alonzo" because one of his outlaw names was Harry Alonzo.

It is my hope that there could be a spirit of cooperation between our group, the Hallman's, Ernst's, and Longabaugh's. Fritz and Edward Longabaugh have been most helpful and are thrilled to help. Sue Balsamo has become a sweet friend and I look forward to meeting her when our project takes us back east for more research and our UNSOLVED MYSTERY CRUISE to the Eastern Caribbean, with cruise director Randy Hobday. We will meet Sue in Miami on January 17, 2015. So... excited to finally meet Sue!

We are searching for the truth about Harry Alonzo Longabaugh of Mont Clare, Pennsylvania. We want to know more details about his life and times.

All our research lines up, Bill Long is truly "The Sundance Kid!"

According to Donna Ernst, "Sundance" is born at 122 Jacobs Street in Mont Clare, Pennsylvania, about spring of 1867. We will also meet the Callow Family and they will join us on board ship for the cruise. The Callow Family knew "Sundance" came into the world at their boarding house.

The Long Family now knows who Grandpa Long's (Longabaugh's) parents are. The family line continues with Harry Alonzo, Alonzo (Harry's father) and Lewis, their great-great-great grandfather. Yvonne Martinez and Betty Bird, along with the rest of the family are thrilled to have a family tree!

So... it is my hope that in the spirit of cooperation we could come together to find out more details about the fascinating and perplexing story of Harry Alonzo Longabaugh, alias, "The Sundance Kid." The Hallman, Ernst and Longabaugh families would be so helpful in gathering more clues. Besides, I want to meet Donna and Paul.

This is history in the making and I sincerely hope that Donna and Paul Ernst and the William Hallman family would cooperate with us.

We have examined Josiah Longabaugh's photo and our TEAM feels there is a strong family resemblance compared to Harry A. Longabaugh. Harry and Josiah's hands are unusually large and Josiah has long fingers just like William Henry Long. Our scientists are anxious to do a hand analysis of all the photos.

I would ask that anyone who knows how to contact the Longabaugh's, Ernst or Hallman Families I have just mentioned, to please come forward with information.

Thank you for your time and interest and you may contact me on: FACEBOOK, www.sundancekiddna.com, or marilyngrace@gmail.com.

# Ah' The Movies

Movies are my passion; I love the movies more than I can say.  It is my choice not to watch television, I don't even have cable in my home; I just watch movies.  My library of films keeps growing and I enjoy loaning the movies out to family and friends.  When I have way too much going on in my life, there is nothing better than putting on a new or old favorite movie and I am lost in another time and place.  I get to escape into a fantasy world that lifts my spirits.  I make it a rule not to watch films that are negative, violent, or don't have a happy ending.  Life is too short to view a film that makes you sad or unhappy, or traumatizes you because of the violent content or language.  Films that have a positive message and can teach life lessons are the best.

The movie "THE NATURAL," starring Robert Redford, is a wonderful life affirming film that explains consequences for your actions and second chances.  I really like the scene in the hospital where Glen Close is talking to Robert Redford's character, Roy Hobbs, after he has had his stomach pumped.  What a classic scene; the doctor found a silver bullet that had been in Roy's stomach for many years.  My favorite line of all time is: "I believe we have two lives: the one we learn with, and the life we live after that."

I have noticed that some films I only watch once and others I watch over and over again, because of the captivating story.

Who doesn't love the film, "Butch Cassidy and the Sundance Kid?"  What a fun adventure that takes you to "Wild Bunch Country," with daring excitement and breath-taking scenery.  What a great time they are all having and it comes across on film.  Recently I purchased the "Anniversary Edition" with documentaries and interviews included.  The very first time that I saw the "Hollywood" Blockbuster, "Butch Cassidy and the Sundance Kid," I am 16 years old.  It is just a classic that will always be around for our enjoyment.  The film has obviously had an impact on me or I would not have spent around 20 years of my life looking for answers as to what really happened to "Butch and Sundance."

The television shows I watched as a child were: "Hardy Boys," "Nancy Drew," and "Murder She Wrote."  One of the great all-time "Unsolved Mysteries" regarding what really happened to "Butch and Sundance," had been begging for an answer.  Here is my line: "If they didn't die in Bolivia, where did they go?"

After all the evidence, I have presented to you, William Henry Long is the real "Sundance Kid." Harry Alonzo Longabaugh of Mont Clare, Pennsylvania vanished and appeared in the wilderness area of Loa, Fremont, and Duchesne, Utah.  He lived a double life and his wife and family hid him out so no one ever knew he is really, "The Sundance Kid."

We have also solved "The Wild Bunch Mystery."  We can reveal the science that proves who they really are: "Butch Cassidy" - William Thadeus Phillips of Spokane, Washington; "Sundance Kid" - William Henry Long of Duchesne, Utah; "Etta Place" - Ann Bassett of Browns Park on the Utah/Colorado border.

I am having the time of my life and I hope you have been educated, informed, and even entertained by the research that we have included.  If it were not for modern science, the Internet, and the media, we would never have discovered the truth about William Henry Long.

Visualize watching a movie about the true story of what really happened to our notorious outlaws. "Cussin' Charley" and Bill Long are roping and branding cattle at Charley's ranch. Luzernia is at home with her six children and the two darling girls, Viola and Vinda, Luzernia and Bill had together. Picture Viola and Vinda walking towards a weeping willow tree holding hands. The sheriff, Irwin G. Robison, shoots the heads off nails down by the shed with "The Sundance Kid" so he can become the sheriff of Wayne County. Little "Etta" is on her pacer pony and "Grandpa Billy" is teaching her how to ride; he teases her that she is named after "The Sundance Kids" girlfriend, "Etta Place." Bill rescues 6-year-old granddaughter Elva, from nearly being crushed by a plow horse. Grandpa Long is rocking on the porch holding a sweet grand-baby, humming the tune, "In the Good Old Summer Time."

All these characters come to life and we fall in love with them the same way we fell in love with the original movie. Remember the scene where the rail road cars are being blown up; "Use enough dynamite there, Butch?" "The Wild Bunch Gang" at the "Hole-in-the-Wall," with "News Carver," "Flat Nose Curry," and that big guy, "Harvey Logan," gets kicked in the b__ by "Butch Cassidy," during a knife fight. What a romance between the beautiful "Etta Place" and "The Sundance Kid." The lines: "You just keep think 'n there, Butch, (laugh) that's what you're good at." "Who are those guys?" Then there is the sexy bicycle scene with Paul Newman and Katherine Ross. Song by Burt Bacharach, and B.J. Thomas sings, "Rain Drops Keep Falling On My Head," and how could anyone forget "Butch and Sundance" both holding on to a belt and jumping off a cliff! "Oh... sh**!"

They were just living life the best they knew how and we get to go back in time and "peek" in on their lives. We revisit "The Old West" with scenes from days long ago that take you back to the "Turn of the Century."

We experience the ultimate in "Story Telling!" Just imagine the thrill of watching the continuing story of "Butch Cassidy and The Sundance Kid!"

*Marilyn Grace*

Elwood Longabaugh absolutely and Harvey Longabaugh absolutely and in the event of my brother Elwood dying before my death his share is to be equally divided between my said sister Mrs. Samanna Hallman and my said brother Harvey Longabaugh.

(Note: On account of my not knowing whether or not my brother Harry Longabaugh is living, and to avoid any difficulty in settling my estate, I made no bequest to him. This note is merely explanatory, and whether my said brother Harry be living or dead, is not to change or affect this will)

AND LASTLY, I nominate, constitute and appoint CLARENCE L. MITCHELL to be the Executor of this my last will and testament.

IN WITNESS WHEREOF I have hereunto set my hand and seal this *Nineteenth* day of *Sept.* A. D. 191*.*

*Emma F. Longaba* (SEAL)

Signed, sealed, published and
declared by the above named
testatrix as and for her last
will and testament, in the presence
of us, who in her presence, at her
request and in the presence of each
other have hereunto subscribed our
names as witnesses.

*Isabel M. Lowry*
4830 Hazel Ave. Phila.

*Morris M. Paretts*
1703 North Eleventh St. Phila.

# CHAPTER EIGHTEEN
## What's Next?

Seventeen years ago, I set out to discover what really happened to "Butch Cassidy," "The Sundance Kid," and "Etta Place." I have collected reams of information about the "Wild Bunch." There are recorded interviews with several descendants who have told thrilling stories about William Henry Long. They described him as a man devoted to his wife and children. Their stories also shed light on the wild and mysterious past that Bill Long had concealed his whole life.

Each day in my personal journal I detailed all the information from everyone who knew William Henry Long. I have spent my time unraveling the mystery of "The Sundance Kid." We have now captured his story of otherwise unknown information about our beloved outlaw.

This exciting ride has taken me to places I only dreamed about. I have gone on a four-wheel drive adventure to desert caves in search of stolen treasures. Our TEAM filmed the examination of the remains of William Henry Long at Soreneson Forensic Laboratories in Salt Lake City, Utah. We also filmed the exhumation of William Henry Long at the Duchesne City Cemetery in Duchesne, Utah. John Hollenhorst of KSL 5 News did several stories on our discovery. I have met so many wonderful people. I feel grateful to everyone for their willingness to participate in this amazing journey with me. I have the best job in the world!

Our TEAM is wrapping up more scientific research and will travel back east to Pennsylvania. Mont Clare is the birthplace of "The Sundance Kid." We will be able to hunt for more clues when we film back east. Also, we will ask for help from the FBI. "The Sundance Kid" project is such a high-profile case that it is only logical that we ask for the FBI's help.

Our book, "Finding Butch Cassidy and The Sundance Kid' ~ Solving the 'Wild Bunch' Mystery with that 'Darn' DNA" with key evidence, is just the beginning. The past twenty-year journey of capturing family stories has given us critical research that helped bring all the puzzle pieces together.

William Henry Long has been re-interned and Jerry Peck, Diann Peck's husband conducted a graveside ceremony in Duchesne, Utah. Many descendants were at his graveside at the re-internment. So many details had to be left out to keep our book concise and to the point. In the future, we will unfold in vivid detail all our research with more books, documentaries, and of course, more movies of the "Wild Bunch."

# WILLIAM HENRY LONG'S DNA GENEALOGY

## SEARCH RESULTS

Matching User ID on at least 10 markers, allowing a maximum genetic distance of 3

| User Id | Last name | Haplogroup | Tested With | Markers Compared | Genetic Distance |
|---------|-----------|------------|-------------|------------------|------------------|
| 6TW7E | Long | German | Other-Sorenson Genomics | 16 | 0 |
| SKX78 | Long | German | Other-Sorenson | 16 | 2 |
| 5TJF3 | Nield | German R1b1a2 (tested) | Family Tree DNA | 12 | 3 |
| WEPMC | Hill | German | Family Tree DNA | 10 | 3 |
| ZX2GM | Allen | German | Other-Sorensen Molecular Geneal-ogy foundation (SMGF) | 10 | 3 |
| 98TXP | Pennington | French/USA | Family Tree DNA | 10 | 3 |

History Lesson:

"Harry" was a much too common name in Bavaria, Germany back before the 1700's, and it became very confusing. With so many "Harry's" in this small village, the local people began distinguishing them according to where they lived. For example "Harry by the long brook." Long in German is LANGE, and brook is BACH, hence LANGEBACH. These titles eventually evolved into group or family surnames, such as the LANGENBACHERS of Bavaria, Germany.

With the onset of plagues, pestilence, taxes, poverty and war the LANGENBACHERS chose to emigrate to America along with many other Europeans. They sailed on the Morning Star to land on Ellis Island. During registration upon entrance to America, many names were changed or shortened at the whim of the registrars. They wrote whatever seemed close or a best guess to the names they heard from many different dialects and foreign languages. At this time, "LANGENBACHER" became "LONGABAUGH".

As time went by and they became more Americanized through each generation, the name was changed and eventually condensed to the very short and generic "LONG." Now that they were truly Americans, they wanted their children to enjoy all the privileges without the persecution. Especially when we went to war with Germany.

They changed their name to "LONG", but the DNA is still "LANGEBACH"

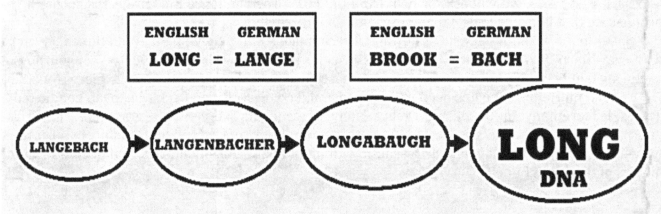

| ENGLISH | GERMAN |
|---------|--------|
| LONG = LANGE | |

| ENGLISH | GERMAN |
|---------|--------|
| BROOK = BACH | |

LANGEBACH → LANGENBACHER → LONGABAUGH → LONG DNA

## There are 59 different spellings in the DNA Genealogy Database

# CHAPTER NINETEEN
## Great Sleuthing!

On November 19, 2010, I attended a meeting with Brent Ashworth at his book store, "B. Ashworth Books," in Provo, Utah. He asked me to come and see his collection of "Wild Bunch" documents. Jim Petty, our genealogist, as well as Yvonne Martinez, (Bill Long is her great grandfather) attended the meeting. Jim Petty and Brent Ashworth are high school and college buddies and had not seen each other for 43 years. They were excited to share all the events in their lives.

We were having a delightful time looking at all of the things Brent has collected over the last 40 years. I have worked with Jim Petty to find the living relative of Ann Place Longabaugh, "The Sundance Kid's" mother. He worked miracles locating Carl Schuch of Rancho Mirage, California.

Jim and I had a chance to talk alone when the meeting was over. I asked him, "Is there anything else we should do to prove our case?" Jim said, "Has anyone thought of doing a DNA test on Josiah Longabaugh, 'The Sundance Kid's' father?" I said, "No! Why haven't we thought of this before?"

When I came home to St. George, I finally had some time to look for the living male descendant of Josiah Longabaugh. We have a new airport with flights to LAX as well as direct flights to Salt Lake City. I went to the observation booth and there were no other people in the room so I could focus. I looked at Conrad Longabaugh, Josiah Longabaugh's grandfather, and I looked for male children to find a living relative. It only took me fifteen minutes and I had found a Longabach, different spelling but still related. I saw that he was born about the same year I was born, so I was hopeful that I could find him. I called directory assistance in California and I found Jay. I can't explain the "magic" leading me to Jay. I talked to Jay's wife, and when I told her how I found her husband, she said, "Great Sleuthing!"

Then I arranged for the DNA kit to be sent to Jay's home. We also mailed a DNA kit to George Longabaugh Senior, for his DNA. We now have Jay and George's DNA, and they are cousins. In Donna Ernst's book, she said that the George Washington Longabaugh's line has not been verified. We did not have that information when we did the DNA testing. Jim Petty has followed two more male descendants of Jonas and Conrad, but they have died out. We have received information from the Historical Society in Pennsylvania, about Josiah Longabaugh's brother Nathaniel. Nathaniel was a doctor and a pharmacist. Nathaniel had a son by the name of William Wood Longabaugh, but his line has died out.

Robert Longenbaugh in Fort Collins, Colorado is a descendent of George and Mary Longenbaugh. I have made a trip to visit with Don Greenlee in Cortez, Colorado. Don called his cousin Robert, and Robert was willing to donate his DNA. We now have Robert and Ronald Longenbaugh's DNA and it is an exact match.

Our TEAM has worked for two years on the DNA and I showed our book to some folks and they were all excited that we have discovered what really happened to the "Wild Bunch!" Yvonne Martinez gave us William Henry Long's DNA profile from his bones on October 30th, 2011. William Henry Long's closest relative on his male line (father) was a LONGABAUGH! William Henry Long's DNA profile from his bones:

- Long>Longabaugh>Langbach>Langenbach>Langenbachers from Bavaria, Germany.
- Nield, (Germany)
- Hill, (German)
- Allen, (German)
- Pennington, (French/USA)

We were just overwhelmed with such great news.  The mother, Ann Place Longabaugh's, DNA did not match William Henry Long, but Bill Long's bones are Longabaugh bones.  There is a story that we will find!  Maybe we have discovered a "Family Secret?"  (That "Darn" DNA explains everything!  Keep reading!)

We now know that Bill Long is "The Sundance Kid," with DNA evidence from his bones.  I have been "sleuthing" since May of 1997 and I am so excited that we have the final piece to the puzzle, the living Longabaugh.  On May 27, 2017 on a Saturday, "Memorial Day" we will be at "Butch Cassidy's" grave in Circleville, Utah.  It will be 20 years since I first started searching for "Butch, Sundance, and Etta Place."

Tim Kupherschmid is our DNA expert at Sorenson Forensics in Salt Lake City.  Tim is so brilliant to work with and has gone above and beyond the call of duty to solve the DNA mystery.  Tim said, "What a great story the DNA will help uncover."

Our TEAM will go to all the places "Butch, Sundance, and Etta," lived and escaped from the law.  We have completed Bill Longs DNA and 7 Long and Longabaugh DNA tests.  Josiah Longabaugh is a "cousin" to Harry Alonso Longabaugh.  Now it is time to tell our story.

At a family reunion, George Longabaugh Jr. talked to Tammy and David Longabaugh.  Tammy told him that a friend went to Paris on vacation and saw a picture of "Sundance and Etta" in a café.  The owners of the café said that everyone knew they were in Paris and "Sundance" could speak fluent French.  On July 14, 2011, Dr. McCullough went to Paris, France.  John went searching for the private hospital where "Butch Cassidy" had a face-lift.  Unfortunately, Paris is so large he could not find the hospital or the café.  We now know that "Butch Cassidy" had drastic plastic surgery at the Parisian Hospital, and the café may be close by.  We will search for the photo and hospital later.  Fun!

# CHAPTER TWENTY
## Reunion of the Children of
## "Butch Cassidy" & "The Sundance Kid"

**"The New Wild Bunch Gang"**
**Willow Creek Ranch at the Hole-in-the-Wall, Kaycee, Wyoming**
**July 2nd and 3rd, 2012**

"Hole-in-the-Wall" is a remote hideout located in the Big Horn Mountains of Johnson County in northern Wyoming. The site was used in the 19th Century by the "Hole-in-the-Wall Gang," a group of cattle rustlers and other outlaws. "Butch Cassidy," "The Sundance Kid," and other desperados met at a log cabin in the "Hole-in-the-Wall" country which has been preserved at the Old Trail Town Museum in Cody, Wyoming. Alexander Ghent built the cabin in 1883.

The area is so remote and secluded, easily defended because of its narrow passes, and impossible for lawmen to approach without alerting the outlaws. From the late 1860's to around 1910 the pass is used frequently by numerous outlaw gangs. Eventually it faded into history, with gangs using it less frequently. At its height, it featured several cabins that gangs used to lay up during the harsh Wyoming winters, and it had a livery stable, a corral, livestock, and supplies, with each gang contributing to the upkeep of the site.

Story Teller Productions launched our book, "The Sundance Kid and that 'Darn' DNA," at "Willow Creek Ranch at the Hole-in-the-Wall." I invited 35 members of the Long, Longabaugh, Longenbaugh family, as wells as relatives of the Morrell family and friends. We called our get together, "The Reunion of the Children of Butch Cassidy and The Sundance Kid."

What an AMAZING time we had together. We sold books and had a "Meet and Greet" where everyone stood up and told us who they were and where they were from. We wanted to know how they were related to "Butch Cassidy and The Sundance Kid." I explained my DNA findings for "The Sundance Kid."

Our gracious hosts served up a "Chuck Wagon" dinner and we had an old fashioned "sing along" as the sun went down. The very last song, "Amazing Grace" just for me! Tears of joy at the surprise of singing "Amazing Grace." I am touched by singer's kindness. That was on July 2nd. The next day our hosts had arranged for a caravan of four-wheel drive vehicles and trucks and we made it to "The Hole-in-the-Wall." Young and old hiked to the top where "Butch Cassidy" and his "Gang" hid out and escaped the law. No one would dare come after them. The law knew that they would be killed instantly if they tried to go into The Hole-in-the-Wall.

What an exciting time we had and we bonded with all the folks that are related and have contributed to our project.

We had candy for the little ones and everyone had such a marvelous time, me included!

Rod Morrell owns the rifle that William Henry Long, (Sundance Kid) used for hunting and he shot off a round. The "echo" was so loud; it sounded like a bomb went off! What a surprise to have Rod bring his rifle and shoot off a round in the air. It was really exciting! We were in the "Old West" with "Butch and Sundance!"

You sure can't say that we don't have fun at Story Teller Productions. We were able to visit the cabin at Hole-in-the-Wall where Butch Cassidy's Gang hid out. We had a "Storyteller" come and you felt like you were there when they were on the run.

Now we have combined both books so you can have more history on Butch, Sundance, and Etta, as well as our research as to how we found our three lost outlaws here in the United States.

We have more adventures and projects to complete, but going to "The Hole-in-the Wall" at Willow Creek Ranch with my friends, family and business associates, must be the most exciting adventure I have ever had in my life!

Life could not possible get any better than when I launched our book, "The Sundance Kid and that 'Darn' DNA," at Willow Creek Ranch at "The Hole-in-the-Wall!"

"Hole In The Wall Country"

# PART II
# THAT "DARN" DNA

*By Marilyn Grace and Dr. John McCullough Ph.D.*

William Henry Long

# "THE SUNDANCE KID AND THAT "DARN" DNA"

*by Marilyn Grace and Dr. John McCullough*

STORY TELLER PRODUCTIONS

www.sundancekiddna.com

marilyngrace@gmail.com

## OTHER BOOKS BY MARILYN GRACE:

Hitler Escapes To America

Amelia Earhart
*Mystery Solved*

SCREAM BLOODY MURDER
The Truth about the Life and Death of Marilyn Monroe

The ASSASINATION OF JOHN FITZGERALD KENNEDY
*Mystery Solved*

"Living Green"

"The Adventures of Fuzzy Bear"
{Children's Book}

*Cover designed by Cyndee Carr*

# CHAPTERS

## CHAPTER I
The Struggle

## CHAPTER II
William Henry Long's DNA Profile

## CHAPTER III
DNA Genealogy

## CHAPTER IV
Alonzo Long, Oregon Pioneer

## CHAPTER V
Cousins

## CHAPTER VI
All The Pieces Come Together

## CHAPTER VII
Science

## CHAPTER VIII
Digging Deeper

## CHAPTER IX
"Who Are Those Guys?"

## CHAPTER X
"Hollywood"

# CHAPTER I
## The Struggle

Our TEAM has worked so hard to solve the William Henry Long mystery. Could William Henry Long, (Bill) of Loa, Fremont and Duchesne, Utah really be Harry Alonzo Longabaugh, "The Sundance Kid?" The photo transparencies that Dr. John McCullough of the University of Utah completed were spot on. William Henry Long is indeed Harry Alonzo Longabaugh, "The Sundance Kid." The name analysis, timelines, sister's pictures compared to The Sundance Kid's sisters, body analysis and family stories, all proved our case. Everything right down the line of evidence matched, but that "Darn" Annie Place Longabaugh, "The Sundance Kid's" mother's DNA, did not match the DNA from William Henry Long's bones?

When Dr. John McCullough and I went on the news with investigative reporter John Hollenhorst, of KSL 5 News, Dr. McCullough told the truth that the mothers DNA did not match our body. He tried to explain that the bones were degraded and DNA from another individual may have contaminated the bones, but it was too late. Our project and research were dismissed as just another story that did not pan out.

We were going to go back on the news to keep the story fresh and in everyone's minds. We did not want the information out that the DNA did not match the mother, but the truth came out and no matter how John tried to say, "We need more time to figure out the DNA," it was over! Everything fell apart.

Dr. McCullough and I knew William Henry Long is really "The Sundance Kid," but how do we prove it? We had all the tangible evidence that William Henry Long is Harry Alonzo Longabough, but how do we solve the whole "darn" thing?" One day at a time, that's how!

With a computer program that allows you to print out your own books, I started to compile all the photos and information. It took me three years to finish up all the evidence so we can now tell our story. After our former partnership ended, the "magic" of our new project started to happen. I would get stuck and family members of William Henry Long came forward and donated money. We figured out that we could "share" in a new project and we formed a company.

Family members, friends, and relatives of William Henry Long all wanted to see the project finished. They came forward with photos, stories, time, talent and money to help us cross the finish line and win! Lightning would strike if I said that this was my book. This is "our" book! Our discovery, and our passion! Our TEAM made all the difference!

As the Creative Executive Producer of Story Teller Productions, I led the way and moved the project forward with a ton of help. Starting in May of 1997 to July 12, 2014, we finally have the answer, William Henry Long's daughter, Florence Viola Long, asked the question, "Who is my Father?" William Henry Long is an alias for Harry Alonzo Longabaugh, "The Sundance Kid." The struggle is over and now I manage the project and can get the word out. We found Sundance!

Now let's walk you through the journey of discovery and that "Darn" DNA.

If I may, I would like to take a moment to explain that this is truly a story about never giving up! We have left no stone unturned and did whatever it took to make it happen!

While living in Park City, Utah from 1997 to 1999, I heard a story that I will never forget. There was a famous mine that a man had worked for years. The miner became discouraged and sold out. The new miner just one "foot" away, hit one of the biggest silver deposits in all of Park City history. The new owner received millions. Something like $25 Million dollars came from that one mine. We all know the moral of the story, "Never give up!" No matter what it takes, if you have a goal, stick with it until you cross the finish line.

My favorite saying when I was raising my children is, "Rest if you must, but don't you quit!" Our TEAM did not quit! Our Company of 25 people are now FAMILY. We all risked and invested in a high-risk venture. Now that we have solved the mystery, we can enjoy the fruits of our labor.

WILLIAM HENRY LONG'S BONE

First, we exhumed the bones.

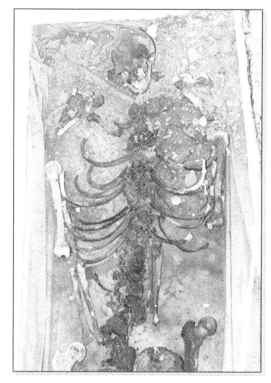

Then we analyzed the bones and tested for DNA.

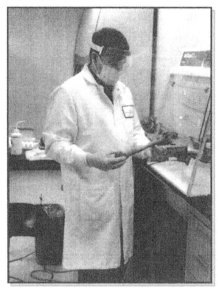

Tim Kupherschmid

Marilyn Grace and Dr. John McCullough

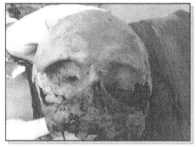
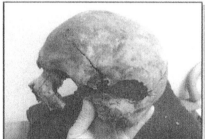
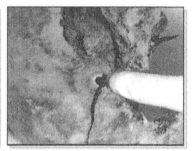

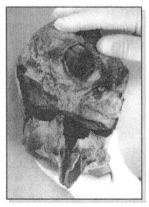

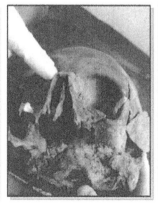

# CHAPTER II
## William Henry Long's DNA Profile

Yvonne Martinez and Betty Bird are sisters.  They have a story in our book, "Finding 'Butch Cassidy and The Sundance Kid' ~ Solving 'The Wild Bunch' Mystery With That 'Darn' DNA," called "Sisters."  Their stories and investigative work have been invaluable.

In October of 2011, Yvonne is determined to find out who Bill Long identity, so she did a search on YSearch.com and found William Henry Long's DNA profile.  Since it is now public information, we had the DNA profile from his bones.  Yvonne is family and deserves to know who her ancestors are!

***See Chart #1***

She instantly forwarded the DNA profile to me, along with a DNA genealogy chart.  The moment I saw "0" Distance LONG, I knew William Henry Long is a Longabaugh!

You will see in the chart that there were too many Harry's in Bavaria, Germany, so the folks in the village started to say, "Harry by the long brook."  Long is Lange and Brook is Bach = Langebach, and changed to Langenbachers of Bavaria, Germany.  When they came to America and passed through Ellis Island, they were illiterate and could only sign with an X.  When asked what their names were, they would say Langebach.  The scribe wrote down Longabaugh.  There are 59 different spellings in the Longabaugh genealogy book.  In Donna Ernst's genealogy book, George and Mary Longenbaugh are cousins to Harry Alonzo Longabaugh.  Same DNA – just spelled their names with an "en" instead of an "a" and the list goes on.

Now, we had the DNA chart from William Henry Long's remains and his family group sheet.  The mother's DNA, (Ann Place Longabaugh) did not match Bill Long's remains.  We now had the science we needed to see if Josiah Longabaugh's DNA matched William Henry Long.

Yvonne is brilliant, she is not only a great sleuth, but she knows so much about computers.  She gave us our final clue.  We owe our project being successful to Yvonne Martinez!  Thank You Yvonne!

# WILLIAM HENRY LONG'S DNA GENEALOGY

## SEARCH RESULTS

Matching User ID on at least 10 markers, allowing a maximum genetic distance of 3

| User Id | Last name | Haplogroup | Tested With | Markers Compared | Genetic Distance |
|---------|-----------|------------|-------------|------------------|------------------|
| 6TW7E | Long | German | Other-Sorenson Genomics | 16 | 0 |
| SKX78 | Long | German | Other-Sorenson | 16 | 2 |
| 5TJF3 | Nield | German R1b1a2 (tested) | Family Tree DNA | 12 | 3 |
| WEPMC | Hill | German | Family Tree DNA | 10 | 3 |
| ZX2GM | Allen | German | Other-Sorensen Molecular Geneal-ogy foundation (SMGF) | 10 | 3 |
| 98TXP | Pennington | French/USA | Family Tree DNA | 10 | 3 |

History Lesson:

"Harry" was a much too common name in Bavaria, Germany back before the 1700's, and it became very confusing. With so many "Harry's" in this small village, the local people began distinguishing them according to where they lived. For example "Harry by the long brook." Long in German is LANGE, and brook is BACH, hence LANGEBACH. These titles eventually evolved into group or family surnames, such as the LANGENBACHERS of Bavaria, Germany.

With the onset of plagues, pestilence, taxes, poverty and war the LANGENBACHERS chose to emigrate to America along with many other Europeans. They sailed on the Morning Star to land on Ellis Island. During registration upon entrance to America, many names were changed or shortened at the whim of the registrars. They wrote whatever seemed close or a best guess to the names they heard from many different dialects and foreign languages. At this time, "LANGENBACHER" became "LONGABAUGH".

As time went by and they became more Americanized through each generation, the name was changed and eventually condensed to the very short and generic "LONG." Now that they were truly Americans, they wanted their children to enjoy all the privileges without the persecution. Especially when we went to war with Germany.

They changed their name to "LONG", but the DNA is still "LANGEBACH"

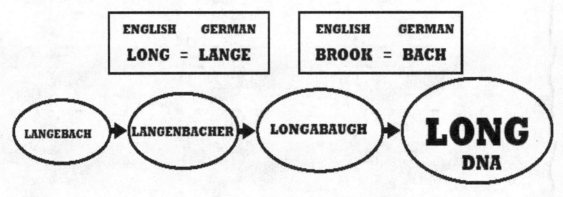

ENGLISH   GERMAN

LONG  =  LANGE

ENGLISH   GERMAN

BROOK  =  BACH

LANGEBACH → LANGENBACHER → LONGABAUGH → LONG DNA

There are 59 different spellings in the DNA Genealogy Database

---

156

# LONG, LONGABAUGH, LONGENBAUGH, LANGENBACHER'S

Just for fun, let's list all the names of William Henry Long's descendants and compare them to George and Mary Longenbaugh, Josiah Longabaugh's, Harvey Sylvester, Alonzo and Samanna's descendants. The family names come up a lot that are the same. You could circle all the similar names. It would only be a guess that Harry Alonso knew that Alonzo Long/Longabaugh is his father.

| William Henry | Samanna | Harvey Sylvester | George | Alonzo* | Josiah |
|---|---|---|---|---|---|
| (Luzernia) | | | (Mary) | (Julia Ann*) | (Ann Place*) |
| Florence Viola* | Bertha Viola* | William Henry* | Jacob | Ida Bell | Elwood Place* |
| Evinda Ann* | Emma Elva* | Harvey Sylvester | Barbara Ann* | Charles | Samanna |
| Etta Forsyth* | | Florence Ann* | William* | (Charlie*) | Emma |
| (Etta Place) | | | Elizabeth | Clara May | Harvey S. |
| (Ann Place) | | | Mary* | John R. | Harry Alonzo* |
| (granddaughter) | | | Sarah | Viola Ann* | |
| Elva O'Neal* | | | Elanor | Thomas Sylvanis | |
| | | | Julia Ann* | William* Oscar | |
| | | | Caroline | Alford M. | |
| | | | George M. | James Lewis* | |
| | | | David | Lee Cleveland | |
| | | | Cynthia | Archie | |
| | | | Noah | Ray | |
| | | | | Lora Ellen | |
| | | | | George Emel | |
| | | | | Rose Odelia | |

# Florence Viola Long Letter, "Who Is My Father?"

The story of my father as near as I know. My father, William Henry Long, left his home as a small boy and went to a cowboy camp. It seems Grandfather went for him several times but the cowboys hid him and kept my Grandfather from finding him. In later years, he met up with a fellow who had a picture of two girls which my father recognized as his two sisters. My father got this picture and at the age of about 21 as near as he could remember, he came to Utah and later married my mother and had two girls. I am the oldest and am very anxious to locate some of my father's people.

My father died last November 26, 27, 1936. Sometimes I wonder if his real name is Long? But I think I can see family resemblances in the pictures. My father never would talk about his past life but very little. I think my grandfather was French and I do remember his saying his father was a cattleman, lived somewhere near Boise. The record of my father as near as I know:
My grandfather James* Long, Mother Ann, * Brothers and Sisters: Charlie, * Frank, William Henry (my father),* Nelson, Sarah Salina, Mary,* Mahalia.

These names are not in order of age but I don't know which is the oldest. But the picture which I have was taken at Lewiston, Idaho - J.W. Riggs Photography.

## COMMENT:

The photo that Florence Viola is referring to is a picture of William Henry Long's sisters that just happen to match "The Sundance Kid's" sister's picture. Bill's photo is when they are young and "The Sundance Kid's" sisters are older. The original photo of the two young sisters does not have the J.W. Riggs Photography studio on the back and Sherma Payton owns the original photo. There are several copies of his sisters that have J.W. Riggs Photography on the back and we can only assume that Bill Long or Florence Viola had copies made in Lewiston, Idaho. Diann Peck (Etta Foryth's daughter) and Ersel Nye (granddaughter of Bill Long), own the Lewiston, Idaho copies and Sherma Payton own's the original. Sherma is the step great granddaughter of William Henry Long. Silas Morrell and Luzernia Allred Morrell Long are her great grandparents.

The photo had been given by Luzernia, Bill Long's wife, to her son Hiett. Hiett gave the original photo to his son Silas, named after his grandfather Silas Morrell and Silas gave the photo to Sherma for safe keeping.

The photo of Bill Long is the photo that we compared to Harry Alonzo Longabaugh in the Fort Worth Five photo and is the reason we could prove that William Henry Long is "The Sundance Kid."

The Long, Longabaugh, and Longenbaugh, as well as Samanna, (Harry Alonzo Longabaugh's sister) and George and Mary Longenbaugh and the Alonzo and Julia Ann Taylor Long families have so many similar names, it is hard to believe that they did not know each other or at least knew that they were all cousins.

# CHAPTER III
## DNA Genealogy

With the DNA chart and the DNA genealogy, I went to work hunting for William Henry Long's father. Remember the "0" Distance is the DNA from William Henry Long's bones. The "0" Distance went straight to Alonzo Long/Longabaugh/Langebach. Harry Alonzo Longabaugh is the real name of "The Sundance Kid."

For an entire month, I worked with a genealogist in St. George, Utah and we found Alonzo Long's photo. The resemblance is shocking. When you compare a 50-year-old Alonzo Long with a 60-year-old William Henry Long, they are definitely father and son!

Alonzo Long/Longabaugh would have been 19 years old when he fathered Harry Alonzo Longabaugh and 20 when Harry is born. Alonzo is born in 1847 and Harry is born in 1867. This is where people's mouths drop open and say, "WOW!" Is your mouth open? I am still in "awe" at the science it took to find the identity of William Henry Long's father. DNA does not lie! William Henry Long is the son of Alonzo Long/Longabaugh.

The Miracle is we have DNA genealogy and we have a "male" from the Alonzo Longs line. Several Long family members donated DNA for the data base at YSearch.com. On Ancestry.com we found beautiful, full color photos of William Oscar Long, Harry Alonzo's half-brother. Also included were photos of Julia Ann Taylor and Alonzo Long so that we could complete a photo comparison of Alonzo and Harry Alonzo, obviously, father and son. If you don't see all the "miracles," then I just give up!

Dr. John McCullough will complete his scientific report at the end of our book and you can put the transparencies together for yourself. The family similarities are unmistakable. The measurements match. The notch on the chin, 1 in 100,000 people have a notch on the chin. The mustache is the same. It is obvious that Harry Alonzo Longabaugh may have never known his father Alonzo, but they both grew their mustaches in the exact same way. Harry had broken his nose at some time in his life, but the similarities are still so unmistakable in the eyes, nose, ears, jawline, etc. There are stories of twins separated at birth who have come together as adults. The twins like the same food and wear their hair alike and have never even known each other. This DNA genealogy is just fascinating! Just think about all the evidence. Our final clue is DNA and DNA genealogy. We could now solve the mystery with science.

Here is where the story gets interesting. Alonzo Long is not married as far as we know when he turned 19 years old. He fathers a child and Harry Alonzo Long/Longabaugh appears on the scene in the spring of 1867. Who is the mother? We know Alonzo is the Father! I had totally dismissed the story that William Henry Long told his daughters, Florence Viola and Evinda Ann Long, about being born in the Big Horn Basin of Wyoming. That just seemed like a lie to cover the fact that he is in reality, "The Sundance Kid."

History proves that there were no whites living in the Big Horn Basin of Wyoming. That was Indian Territory in 1867 when Harry is born. When we did a search of the Mother's DNA from William Henry Long's bones, there were no matches in the database. Then I remembered a Wanted Poster that said, "Looks like quarter breed Indian."

Was Alonzo Long with an Indian woman and they had a child? After the "Reunion of the Children of Butch Cassidy and The Sundance Kid," on July 2nd and 3rd, 2012, I planned on going to the Big Horn Basin of Wyoming to ask for mouth swabs of Native American Indian Women. We will see if we can get a match. Dr. John McCullough is 1/8th Indian and he said that there are two tribes that live in the Basin; Shoshone and Arapaho.

Dr. McCullough is also an avid genealogist with 25,000 names of his ancestors that he keeps on file in his basement. Talk about an exciting project for John!

Every time we think we have finished the project, another clue pops up and we are off again! What fun we are having! Now we have the DNA chart with the "0" Distance of Alonzo Long/Longabaugh, Harry Alonzo Longabaugh, son of Alonzo Long and the photo comparison that is undeniable. They are father and son. Now we just need to discover the mother's DNA.

We need to be sensitive to the Alonzo Long/Longabaugh Family In Baker County, Oregon. Alonzo Long/Longabaugh married two years later to Julia Ann Taylor. Her photo is included in our research.

Alonzo Long/Longabaugh/Langebach was a prominent pioneer and had 15 children. We hope the family will not be too alarmed to learn that their father had a child that became one of the West's most famous outlaws, "The Sundance Kid." DNA does not lie and Alonzo, is definitely the father of Harry Alonzo Longabaugh.

We did break the news to the Long family of Oregon. Only one person is upset. What can you do? This is all our research, with DNA genealogy and family group sheets in a finished book. Our project is about FAMILY and we need to bring the Long, Longabaugh, and Longenbaugh families together.

Our project is still ongoing with the research we have completed so far. It is just not possible to include all our research... at this time.

Florence Viola and Evinda Ann Long

# Alonzo Long & Family

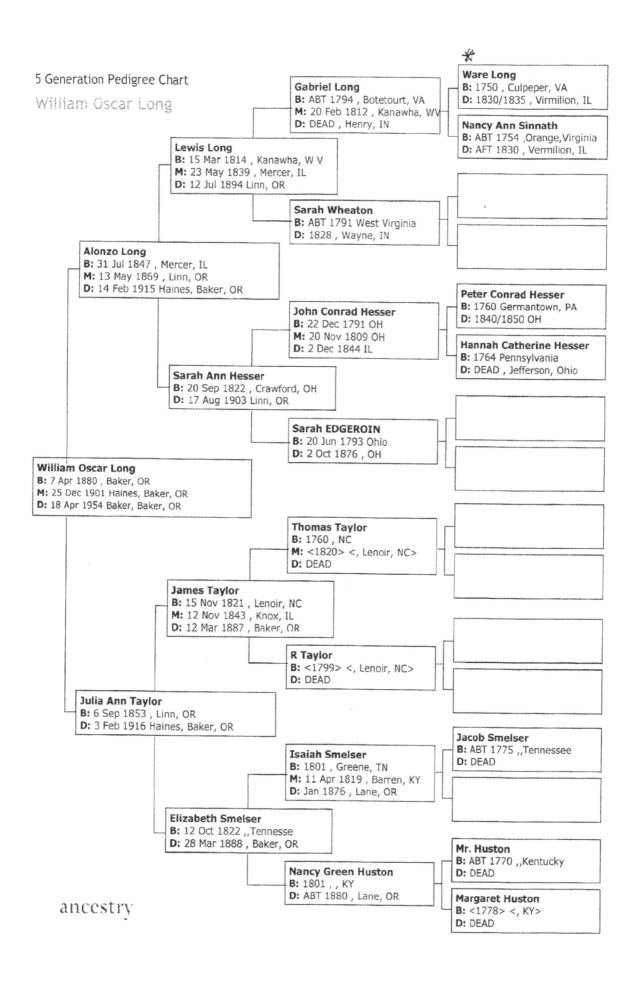

5 Generation Pedigree Chart

William Oscar Long

**Gabriel Long**
B: ABT 1794 , Botetourt, VA
M: 20 Feb 1812 , Kanawha, WV
D: DEAD , Henry, IN

**Ware Long**
B: 1750 , Culpeper, VA
D: 1830/1835 , Virmilion, IL

**Nancy Ann Sinnath**
B: ABT 1754 ,Orange,Virginia
D: AFT 1830 , Vermilion, IL

**Lewis Long**
B: 15 Mar 1814 , Kanawha, W V
M: 23 May 1839 , Mercer, IL
D: 12 Jul 1894 Linn, OR

**Sarah Wheaton**
B: ABT 1791 West Virginia
D: 1828 , Wayne, IN

**Alonzo Long**
B: 31 Jul 1847 , Mercer, IL
M: 13 May 1869 , Linn, OR
D: 14 Feb 1915 Haines, Baker, OR

**John Conrad Hesser**
B: 22 Dec 1791 OH
M: 20 Nov 1809 OH
D: 2 Dec 1844 IL

**Peter Conrad Hesser**
B: 1760 Germantown, PA
D: 1840/1850 OH

**Hannah Catherine Hesser**
B: 1764 Pennsylvania
D: DEAD , Jefferson, Ohio

**Sarah Ann Hesser**
B: 20 Sep 1822 , Crawford, OH
D: 17 Aug 1903 Linn, OR

**Sarah EDGEROIN**
B: 20 Jun 1793 Ohio
D: 2 Oct 1876 , OH

**William Oscar Long**
B: 7 Apr 1880 , Baker, OR
M: 25 Dec 1901 Haines, Baker, OR
D: 18 Apr 1954 Baker, Baker, OR

**Thomas Taylor**
B: 1760 , NC
M: <1820> <, Lenoir, NC>
D: DEAD

**James Taylor**
B: 15 Nov 1821 , Lenoir, NC
M: 12 Nov 1843 , Knox, IL
D: 12 Mar 1887 , Baker, OR

**R Taylor**
B: <1799> <, Lenoir, NC>
D: DEAD

**Julia Ann Taylor**
B: 6 Sep 1853 , Linn, OR
D: 3 Feb 1916 Haines, Baker, OR

**Isaiah Smelser**
B: 1801 , Greene, TN
M: 11 Apr 1819 , Barren, KY
D: Jan 1876 , Lane, OR

**Jacob Smelser**
B: ABT 1775 ,,Tennessee
D: DEAD

**Elizabeth Smelser**
B: 12 Oct 1822 ,,Tennesse
D: 28 Mar 1888 , Baker, OR

**Nancy Green Huston**
B: 1801 , , KY
D: ABT 1880 , Lane, OR

**Mr. Huston**
B: ABT 1770 ,,Kentucky
D: DEAD

**Margaret Huston**
B: <1778> <, KY>
D: DEAD

ancestry

Julia Ann Taylor and Alonzo Long 1896

# Alonzo Long Family 1896

Back row: Charles Long holding Ellen, Ida Hodges Long, Alonzo Long, William Welch, George Wm. Jackson holding Charlie.
3rd row: Daisy Toney Long, Kitty Long, Emma Welch, Clara Long Welch.
2nd row: Lee Long, Laura Long, William Long, Nina Jackson, Ida Long Jackson.
Front row: John Long holding Elsie, Archie Long, Viola Long Anderson, Rose Long, Julia Taylor Long.

Lewis and Sarah Long

William Oscar and Bride

# CHAPTER IV
## The Life and Times of Alonzo Long, Oregon Pioneer

The Life and Times of Alonzo Long, Oregon Pioneer ID: I06157
Name: Alonzo LONG
Sex: M Birth: 31 JUL 1847 in Mercer Co., Illinois
Death: 14 FEB 1915 in Haines, Baker Co., Oregon died of angina pectoris
Burial: Haines Cemetery, Baker Co., Oregon
Event: Census 1880 Oregon, Baker Co., North Powder Twsp., FHL Film 1255080 National Archives Film T9-1080 Page 57D
Event: Boarder 1880 Roland George, b. 1860-1861 in Missouri
Notes for Alonzo* Long:
"The Centennial History of Oregon," 1912, Gaston, Volume III, page 179.

### Alonzo Long

One of the notable pioneers of Oregon, who by successful business management has long since been enabled to retire from active work is Alonzo Long, residing in Haines, Baker County. He was born in Mercer County, Illinois, July 31, 1847; the son of Lewis and Sarah Ann (Hesser) Long, the former of whom was a native of Virginia." (See note on Lewis Long)

"Alonzo Long remained at home with his parents until 1869, when he began farming on his own account in Linn County. He remained in that county following agricultural pursuits until 1872, when he removed to Baker County and bought a ranch near Haines. This ranch which he still owns and which he has finely improved and brought under an excellent state of tillage, consists of five hundred and sixty acres and is one of the most valuable pieces of farming property in Baker County. On this magnificent ranch Mr. Long lived and labored until 1899, when he retired to the fine residence which he now owns in Haines."

"On May 13, 1869, Mr. Long was married to Miss Julia Ann Taylor, a native of Linn County, her birth having occurred September 6, 1853. She was a daughter of James and Elizabeth (Smelser) Taylor, the father being a native of Indiana and the mother of Illinois." (See note on James Taylor)

"Mr. and Mrs. Long have become the parents of fifteen children: Ida B., who was born April 26, 1870; and died in September, 1905 and who was the wife of William Jackson; Charles D., of Baker County, who was born March 16, 1872; Clara M., born February 24, 1874; the wife of W. J. Welch, of Haines; John R., who was born February 20,1876; and resides in Baker County; Viola A., born January 7, 1878; who is the wife of R. P. Anderson, of Baker County. Thomas A., who was born December 31, 1878; and died July 21, 1879; William O., who was born April 7, 1880; and is a resident of Baker County; Alford M. who was born February 12, 1882, and died June 27,1883; James L., who was born July 6, 1883; and died October 15 of the same year; Lee C., of Baker County, who was born March 10, 1885; Archie J., of Baker County, who was born April 23, 1886; Ray, who was born July 20, 1888 and died September 8th of the same year; Lora E., born September 17, 1889; who is the wife of S.W. Loy; George E., who was born September 17,1890; and died August 22,1891; and Rose O., born April 11, 1894; who is now the wife of John Joseph Longueville. Besides raising his own family, Mr. Long has also brought up his grandson, Charles Emery Jackson, who at present is ten years of age. He was two years and four months old when his mother, Ida B. Jackson died, and four years when he joined Mr. Long's family."

"In his political faith, Mr. Long is a democrat but he has never paid a great deal of attention to politics. He takes a lively interest in educational matters and served for some time on the school board. He is an active member of the Farmers Union, the only fraternal organization to which he belongs. Both Mr. and Mrs. Long are earnest and consistent members of the First Baptist Church, being among the most prominent of those affiliated with that religious body in Haines.

By the long residence of Mr. Long in Baker County, the arduous pioneer labors which he performed and the large family which he reared he has rendered valiant service in the upbuilding of the agricultural interests and the public institutions of Baker County. His life being that of a pioneer, he and his family in the earlier days were compelled to submit too many hardships which the younger generation is fortunate in escaping. He was always industrious, economical and frugal and his estimable wife is deserving of much of the credit for the success of her husband. Members of the Long family are well known throughout this entire section and Alonzo Long is numbered among the most esteemed and respected citizens of Haines, where he is now living in retirement, enjoying the fruits of his earlier life of toil as a pioneer."

"History of Baker, Grant, Malheur and Harney Counties" 1902...Book at Baker City Library

"ALONZO LONG... for many years one of the progressive farmers of the county and at present an enterprising grain dealer in Haines, the subject of this review is deserving of rank among the forceful factors in the county's development and it is but fitting that due presentation as such should be accorded him in this portion of our volume.

Mr. Long is a native of Mercer County, Illinois, born July 31, 1847, his parents being Lewis and Sarah Ann Long. In 1854, he crossed the plains with his parents, making the journey by the aid of the slow moving oxen as was the custom at the time. Eventually they settled in Linn County, Oregon, where our subject devoted himself to the basic art of agriculture until 1872, during which year he came to Baker County. In due time he settled on Muddy Creek and engaged in the business of farming and raising cattle. As above stated, he was for many years a leader in this dual industry in the county, and he still owns his original home and superintends the operation thereof, but at present he is himself engaged in managing his grain handling establishment in Haines and has been since 1899. As a business man he is energetic and progressive, possessed of the good judgement and foresight essential to success in commercial pursuits, and as a citizen and member of society he enjoys a very enviable standing.

In Linn County, Oregon, on May 13, 1869, our subject married Miss Julia Ann Taylor, a daughter of James and Elizabeth and a native of Oregon. They have fifteen children: Ida Bell, wife of William Jackson, living west of Haines; Charles Denino, married to Ida Hodges, a native of Arkansas, and living on the home place; Clara May, wife of William J. Welch, of Haines; John R., living on the home place and married to Daisy E., daughter of A.J. Toney; Viola Ann, wife of R. P. Anderson, a residence of Haines; William Oscar; Lee Cleveland; Archie Jackson; Lora Ellen; Rosa Odelia."
Died after a brief illness of Heart trouble.

### Alonzo Long's Will
"IN THE COUNTY COURT OF THE STATE OF OREGON FOR THE COUNTY OF BAKER"
(Keith Long's papers)
PETITION FOR LETTERS OF ADMINISTRATION
In the Matter of the Estate of Alonzo Long. deceased
TO THE HON. J.B. MESSICK, JUDGE OF THE ABOVE ENTITLED COURT:
"The petition of Charles D. Long of Baker County, Oregon respectfully shows:

That Alonzo Long died intestate in Baker County, Oregon on or about the 14th day of February 1915.

That said deceased, at the time of his death, was 67 years old and a resident and inhabitant of Baker County, Oregon.

That said deceased left assets in Baker County, Oregon consisting of real and personal property of the probable value of $37,700.00, and said real property being of the probable value of $35,700.00, and said personal property being of the probable value of $2,000.00.

That the names, ages and residence of the heirs of said deceased are as follows: Charles D. Long, your petitioner, son of deceased, aged 42, and residing in Baker, Baker County, Oregon; Clara M. Welch, daughter of deceased, aged 41 years, and residing in Haines, Baker County, Oregon; John R. Long, son of deceased, aged 39 years, and residing in Baker County, Oregon; Wm. O. Long, son of deceased, aged 35 years, and residing in Baker County, Oregon; Viola Anderson, daughter of deceased, aged 27 years, and residing in Baker, Baker County, Oregon; Lee C. Long, son of deceased, aged 30 years, and residing in Haines, Baker County, Oregon; Arch J. Long, son of deceased, aged 29 years, and residing in Baker County, Oregon; Rose Longuville, daughter of deceased, aged 20, and residing in Haines, Baker County, Oregon; Lora Loy, daughter of deceased, aged 25, and residing in Farina, Illinois; Nina Dahl, daughter of deceased, aged 24, and residing in Haines, Baker County, Oregon; the following heirs of the late Ida B. Jackson, deceased, a daughter of deceased: John Jackson, son of said Ida B. Jackson, deceased, aged 20 years and residing in Haines, Baker County, Oregon; Ora Jackson, daughter of said Ida B. Jackson, deceased, aged 15 years, and residing in Haines, Baker County, Oregon; Charles Jackson, son of said Ida B. Jackson, deceased, aged 12 years, and residing in Haines, Baker County, Oregon; and Roy Jackson, son of said Ida B. Jackson, aged 10 years, and residing in Haines, Baker County, Oregon; and Julia Long, widow of deceased, aged 61 years, and residing in Haines, Baker County, Oregon.

That your petitioner is the eldest son of said deceased, a resident and inhabitant of Baker, Baker County, Oregon, and files this petition at the request of the other heirs of said deceased, and is therefore entitled to Letters of Administration and said estate, upon his filing with the Clerk of this Court his bond, to be approved by this Court, in double the probable value of the personal property, which is of the probable value of $2,000.00, plus double the probable value of the rents and profits of said real property, which is of the probable value of $2,000.00.

Wherefore, your petitioner prays that Letters of Administration on said estate be issued to him as administrator of said estate."
Signed: Charles D. Long
(Note: The error that Nina Dahl is listed as a daughter of Alonzo instead of the daughter of Ida Jackson.... she was daughter of Ida.)

Alonzo donated one fourth acre of land to the Muddy Creek district to build the last Muddy Creek School. Two other small schools had been built prior to this time. A large brick two story school was built on this site but has since been torn down and just the school bell remains as a memorial to the site.

## Children

1.  Ida Bell LONG b: 26 APR 1870 in Linn Co., Oregon
2.  Charles Devino LONG b: 16MAR 1872 in Lin Co., Oregon
3.  Clara May LONG b: 24 FEB 1874 in Rock Creek, Baker Co., Oregon
4.  John R. LONG b: 20 FEB 1876 in Baker, Baker County, Oregon
5.  Viola Ann LONG b: 7 JAN 1878 in Baker, Baker County, Oregon
6.  Thomas Sylvanis LONG b: 31 DEC 1878 in Baker County, Oregon
7.  William Oscar LONG b: 7 APR 1880 in Muddy Creek, Baker Co., Oregon
8.  Alford M. LONG b: 12 FEB 1882
9.  James Lewis LONG b: 6 July 1883
10. Lee Cleveland LONG b: 10 MAR 1885 in Baker Co., Oregon
11. Archie Jackson LONG b: 23 APR 1886 in Muddy Creek, Haines, Baker Co., Oregon
12. Ray LONG b: 20 JULY 1888 in Baker Co., Oregon
13. Lora Ellen LONG b: 17 SEP 1889 in Baker, Haines Co., Oregon
14. George Emel LONG b: 17 SEP 1890 in Baker Co., Oregon
15. Rose Odelia LONG b: 11 APR 1894 in Haines, Baker Co., Oregon

## Alonzo Long and Julia Ann Taylor

The next thing we need to do is discover who William Henry Long's mother is. We are looking for living descendants of Julia Ann Taylor and Alonzo Long's daughters. We want to test the living females to see if Julia Ann is the mother of William Henry Long.

Let's say that they are not a match, we will then go to the Big Horn Basin of Wyoming and ask for DNA from the Arapaho and Shoshone Tribes to see if we can prove that Sundance was part Indian as stated in a wanted poster.

## Comments

When I found this information on the life of Alonzo Long, I wanted to add his history to our research. This is the most positive and charming story about… a really good man. The way they spoke at the turn of the century is rather Old English and we don't take the time to speak in such a proper manner. The way they speak is so elegant and so respectful compared to modern times.

Alonzo Long was admired, respected and loved by everyone, especially his family. I have no doubt that whatever we may find in the future, Alonzo did his best to give his first son Harry Alonzo Longabaugh a chance at life. With DNA from William Henry Long's bones, we now know that Alonzo and Harry Alonzo Long/Longabaugh are father and son. That means that Alonzo Long had 16 children, not just the 15 that are listed with Alonzo and Julia Ann Taylor Long.

We can only imagine what may have happened to Alonzo when he is 20 years old at Harry Alonzo's birth. Until we find Julia Ann Taylor's female descendants and we do DNA testing, we will not know if Julia Ann Taylor Long is Harry Alonzo's mother or not. Julia Ann is 14 when Harry came into the world. We are looking for living females on Julia's line for DNA. We can only speculate until the DNA comes back. Julia could have become pregnant out of wedlock at 14 and being religious, they gave the baby away so no one would find out. Then two years later they married.

I wanted to take the time to tell Alonzo's story so that you get the same information that I have. He was honest, faithful and a hard worker and his history helped me to envision what his life was like. All I can do is paint a picture with my words and I hope you can see the life and times of Alonzo Long the way I see him.

To me, Julia Ann is a really good woman and I can't imagine her giving up her baby boy. All we can do is search for her daughters and granddaughters and ask for DNA.

The wanted poster for "The Sundance Kid" that said Harry, "Looks like quarter breed Indian," is a clue that I think we should take seriously. Finding Arapaho and Shoshone female Indians will be challenging, if Ann's DNA does not match William Henry Long, alias, Harry Alonzo Longabaugh. Who knows what will turn up?

When you look at the photo comparison of William Oscar Long and Harry Alonzo Long, I can see that Harry looks darker than his brother, half-brother, William. Of course, Harry broke his nose and William did not. Look and see if you see how much darker Harry looks compared to William. He may just be dark because of his exposure to the sun, but I think Harry does look like he is part Indian.

You have to admit, this is really exciting research and I hope you enjoyed getting to know Alonzo. I wish we could all have such a wonderful legacy written about our lives when we are gone.

## Alonzo and Harry Alonzo Long

What could have happened in the life of Alonzo Long to have given up his first-born son, Harry Alonzo, to his cousin Josiah Longabaugh to raise as his own child? This is a BIG QUESTION MARK for our TEAM!

Until we do the female descendants of Julia Ann Taylor, Alonzo's wife's daughters, granddaughters we do not know if Julia is Alonzo's mother? It is just a guess, but I don't think Julia is Harry Alonzo's mother.

Julia and Alonzo were very solid citizens and Julia had 15 children with Alonzo. It would be hard to imagine Julia giving up her child and she was born September 6, 1853 and Alonzo was born July 31, 1847. Julia was six year younger than Alonzo and they married May 16, 1869. Julia is 16 when she married Alonzo is 22 years of age. Julia would have had to have been 14 when Harry Alonzo was born. Many women married at 14 at the turn of the century, so why would Julia have given up her child?

Alonzo is 19 years old when he father's Harry Alonzo and 20 when Harry is born. With prejudice of Native American Indian and whites, he asks Josiah Longabaugh, a cousin, to take his son. The really amazing thing is he names him Harry Alonzo, so we have the name connection of Alonzo and Harry Alonzo, father and son. Note that none of Alonzo and Julia's children are named Alonzo.

## Pieces of the Puzzle

1. Alonzo Long has a son and names him Harry Alonzo and something happened in his life to give him to his cousin Josiah Longabaugh and his wife Ann in Mont Clare, Pennsylvania. Alonzo and Harry Alonzo name connection.

2. Harry leaves with cousins George and Mary Longenbaugh (different spelling with "en" but still Longabaugh's, really Langenbacher's of Bavaria, Germany). Samanna is the sister of Harry Alonzo Longabaugh and she writes in her husband's business ledger that Harry leaves for the West with cousin's George and Mary Longenbaugh. George and Mary are married cousins and their grandfather is Jacob Longenbaugh. Samanna knew they were cousins and Josiah, George and Mary and Alonzo and Harry Alonzo are ALL cousins.

3. The DNA from William Henry Long goes straight to Alonzo Long of Baker County, Oregon and the photo comparison of Alonzo Long and William Henry Long photo comparison have all the markings and measurement that they are father and son. They even grow their mustaches out in the exact same way.

With science, our TEAM solved the mystery as to why Ann (Annie) Place Longabaugh's DNA did not match William Henry Long's DNA and we now know that Josiah Longabaugh is a cousin to Harry Alonzo Long/Longabaugh, "The Sundance Kid." Fascinating!

William Henry Long

Alonzo Long

Overlay of Transparencies
Alonzo & William

"There seems to be a strong family resemblance between the two. They look alike. A complete photo analysis will be completed for the final."

Dr. John McCullough

# CHAPTER V
## Cousins

Harry left home in October 1882, to go West with cousins George Longenbaugh and his wife Mary. Samanna, Sundance's sister, wrote in her husband's business journal that Harry Longabaugh left for the West to help cousins George, Mary and family. Harry would have been 14 or 15 years old when he traveled to Colorado. Mary is pregnant and had a small child, a son, Walter. George handled the horses and Harry worked alongside of him. Their destination is Durango, Colorado where George homesteaded with his family.

At age 17, Harry joined the "Wild Bunch" and is the first member of Butch Cassidy's Gang. He served 18 months' hard labor for horse theft and had a full pardon when he is released from the Sundance Wyoming Jail. He is pardoned and released because he is under the age of 21.

We needed George and Mary's living descendent to compare to the DNA taken from the remains of William Henry Long. We had two lines of ancestors from the Donna Ernst genealogy book that I made a copy of in Salt Lake City in 2007. Donna donated the book February 11, 1998 to the Church of Jesus Christ of Latter Day Saints Family History Library. One family line is Conrad Langebach and the other is Balser or Baltzer Lonabach. Remember they all have the same DNA and are all Langenbachers of Bavaria, Germany.

We found both George Longabaugh Junior and Senior from Brownstown, Pennsylvania. They donated their DNA and George Sr. gave us a mouth swab. Then I found Jay Oldhem Longabach who lives in San Luis Obispo, California. George and Jay are on the Conrad Langebach line. They matched each other but they did not match our William Henry Long. That "Darn" DNA! Do we give up or do we keep going? We keep going!

It is my opinion that a lot of people would have thrown in the towel right about now. We had come so far and worked so hard, but the DNA did not match. Then I remembered the story that you just read about cousins George and Mary Longenbaugh and how Harry Alonzo Longabaugh left home at 14 and traveled out West to homestead in Durango, Colorado. The family moved to Cortez later.

While looking through the genealogy book, I found Don Greenlee who lives in Cortez, Colorado. I traveled to Cortez and had a delightful time visiting with Don. He is the one that gave us the photo of George and Mary Longenbaugh and the photo of Walter and his wife Edna, Harry, Gailen and Dillon. Gailen is Don's mother. Don told me the story of how George and Mary Longenbaugh traveled West with Harry. George worked with Harry and he became a skilled horseman.

When we completed the genealogy search, we discovered that George and Mary both had the same grandfather, Jacob. They married cousins. Back then, they did not think anything of marrying cousins. Today, knowing about the possibility of mental illnesses and birth defects, we simply would not marry cousins. The fun part of the story is, they were both cousins and Mary hid out The Sundance Kid and brought him food when he is on the run. Walter is only two when they crossed the plains in a covered wagon and Harry stayed with the family until he turned 17.

Walter loved his cousin Harry so much, that when he married, he named his first son Harry. This Harry had a son by the name of Robert Longenbaugh and he is the great-grandson of George and Mary Longenbaugh. Fortunately for us, Robert Longenbaugh is of a different line. He is a descendant of Balser or Baltzer Lonabach, so it has been worth the effort.

Don Greenlee and I became friends and the family has always wanted to know if Conrad and Baltzer were father and son or brothers. Don asked Robert Longenbaugh for a DNA sample. Robert agreed and we were all waiting with anticipation for the results. We found out that Jay and George's DNA matched each other, but Robert's DNA did not match Jay and George. The family finally had their answer. Conrad and Baltzer were not father and son or brothers. They are "cousins!"

We were disappointed, but when we compared William Henry Long's DNA to Robert's, the genealogy research shows that they are cousins. We traced William Henry Long's DNA back to a Ware Long/Langebach. He was a stone mason that would chisel stone into the shape of a brick.

Ware Long is born in 1691 in Germany. He emigrated from Germany as Lang, changed to Long when he went to England and then onto Wales. This shows Ware's son Gabriel; Gabriel's son Lewis and Lewis is the father of Alonzo Long/Longabaugh/Langebach. Alonzo is born on July 31, 1847 in Mercer County, Illinois. He died on February 14, 1915 in Providence, Hardin, Iowa, of angina pectoris.

Alonzo married Julia Ann Taylor in Darlington, Montgomery, Indiana on May 13, 1869. They had a large family: Ida Gelle, Charles Devino, Clara May, John R., Viola Ann, Thomas Sylvenes, William Oscar, Alfred M., James Lewis, Lee Cleveland, Archie Jackson, Ray, Lora Ellen, George Emel, Rosa Odelia, and Nina Long – 15 Children!

Alonzo's father Lewis is born on March 15, 1814 in Greenbriar County, Virginia. He served in the military in about 1832 in Fulton County, Illinois. He completed a land purchase on June 18, 1853 in Fulton County, Illinois. He emigrated on October 12, 1854 from Iowa to Oregon, where he completed a land claim on March 3, 1855. He appeared in the Census in 1870 in Brownsville, Linn, Oregon. Lewis Long was buried in Alford Cemetery, Halsey, Linn, Oregon on February 16, 1897.

Lewis lived on 40 acres that he paid $0.0 for, in Fulton County, Illinois. He purchased land from the Federal government. He arrived in Oregon on October 12, 1854. Alonzo was 7 when the family left Illinois and moved to Oregon.


## Newspaper: Albany, Oregon, July 1894

Died: At his residence near Rowland, July 12, 1894, Lewis Long, aged 80 years, 4 months and 28 days.

Lewis Long was born in Greenbriar County, Virginia, March 15, 1814. He moved with his parents to Indiana about 1820, thence to Mercer County, Illinois in 1830. He volunteered in the Blackhawk War of 1832. He was married to Sarah Ann Hesser in 1837, moved to Wappolon County, Iowa in 1840: thence across the plains to Oregon in 1854 and settled on the farm where he died respected by all who knew him. He leaves a wife and four sons and one daughter in Linn County, and one son and daughter in Eastern Oregon. Another of Linn County Old Pioneer's gone.

## Newspaper: Browsville Times: Browsville, Oregon, 21, August 1903.

Sarah Ann Hesser Long aged 82 years died at her home near Rowland, Oregon, on Monday August 17, 1903. Sarah born Sept 20, 1821 in Crawford County Ohio moved with her parents to Mercer County, Iowa, where she married Lewis Long in 1839 moved from Iowa to Illinois in 1844, crossed the plains with ox team to Oregon in 1854. Settled on the old homestead in Linn County in 1855, where she lived ever since. She has never been away from the old home except once, when she visited her sons, Alonzo and Gabriel, in Baker County with her husband in 1888.

She experienced a change of heart in the year 1840, but never made an open confession until her sickness when she confessed her faith in Christ and her assurance of a home in Heaven. She was a good neighbor, a kind and loving mother and is sincerely mourned by all who knew her.

## George and Mary Longenbaugh

George Mayers Longenbaugh, born 22 February 1853, Ohio. Died 2 June 1923 or May 28, 1923 and buried in June? Buried Arriola Cemetery, Cortez, Colorado.

Mary Alice Yantis Longenbaugh Married 29 March 1879. Born 20 March 1861, Illinois, Pickaway County, died 28 August 1933, Cortez, Colorado. While working with a genealogist, we discovered that Mary is born in Pickaway County, Illinois, and Alonzo Long is born in Mercer County, Illinois. They were born in the same state and could possibly have known each other.

## All Cousins

George and Mary, and great grandson Robert Longenbaugh: Langenbacher's of Bavaria, Germany.
William Henry Long: Langenbacher's of Bavaria, Germany.
Alonzo Long's Line: Langenbacher's of Bavaria, Germany.
Josiah Longabaugh: Langenbacher's of Bavaria, Germany.

Josiah and Ann place Longabaugh took in a relative's child, a "cousin," and raised him as their own. On the census records it states that Harry's birthday is "abt the spring of 1867." Parents know the birth of their child. They would have known his exact birthday. Elwood, Samanna, Harvey Sylvester, all have the day, month and year in the Longabaugh Family Bible. Emma and Harry Alonzo only have the year they were born. William Henry Long states on his marriage license to Luzernia Allred Morrell that he is born in 1867, the same year that The Sundance Kid is born.

## Close Cousins

William Henry Long is a "close cousin" to George, Mary, and since Robert Longenbaugh is George and Mary's great grandson, William Henry Long is also a "close cousin" to the living Longenbaugh.

Josiah Longabaugh is just a "cousin" to William Henry Long with DNA from his bones and DNA Genealogy.

## Long > Longabaugh> Langebach> Langenbacher's.

DNA has helped us prove that Josiah and Ann Place Longabaugh were not as closely related to William Henry Long/Harry Alonzo Longabaugh, as George and Mary were.

DNA and DNA genealogy is the only way we could have solved the mystery. DNA from William Henry Long's bones captured, "The Sundance Kid."

## Evidence

"0" Distance means DNA from William Henry Long's bones goes straight to Alonzo Long/Longabaugh/Langebach, born in Illinois. William Henry Long's father is Alonzo Long. This is Alonzo and Harry Alonzo name connection.

We do not have permission to publish Robert Longenbaugh's DNA (still living). Robert Longenbaugh is the only person that can publish his profile and he has not given us permission to do so.

Josiah Longabaugh is still a cousin (family) but a distant cousin to George, Mary, Alonzo and Harry Alonzo. They are part of the Langenbacher's of Bavaria, Germany. Remember there are two different family lines, Conrad's and Baltzer's.

Ann Place and Josiah Longabaugh took in a "cousin" and raised him as their own child. They did not know the day or month he was born because he is not their biological child.

This author, Marilyn Grace, suspects that Emma, a sister to Harry Alonzo Longabaugh is also adopted. The family bible only has 1863. Why doesn't Emma have a day and month instead of just a year that she is born?

Harry Alonzo Longabaugh only has "abt spring" of 1867, born at 122 Jacobs Street, Mont Clare, Pennsylvania. The place Sundance was born was a 10 room boarding house with one large suite. The Josiah and Ann Place Longabaugh family lived one mile down the canal on a farm. The Skukyll Canal was a water way and travelers would stay at the boarding house because they were weary from traveling.

The Longabaugh's may have met Alonzo Long/Longabaugh at 122 Jacobs Street in Mont Clare, Pennsylvania in order to adopt Harry Alonzo into their family. Or could he have been born there and something happened to his mother?

The story of Harry leaving for Colorado with cousins George and Mary makes sense to me. Samanna, Harry's sister, wrote in her husband's journal (ledger at his place of business) that Harry left with cousins George and Mary to homestead in Colorado at 14. To me, this means the family had to have known that Harry was a "close" cousin to George and Mary Longenbaugh.

This is all new information. We have presented the living Longabaugh's DNA and the "close cousins" information. We also have the DNA for William Henry Longs mother. She was Eastern European not Indian. You the reader are absorbing the information for the first time. Robert Longenbaugh, a descendant (great grandson), of George and Mary Longenbaugh is our latest clue.

I have been doing research on Sundance, Butch and Etta for 17 years. We have been gathering one piece of evidence at a time and carefully placing the pieces of the puzzle together. When you step back and look at the whole picture, it all makes sense.

The Alonzo Long/Longabaugh and Harry Alonzo Longabaugh connection is something no one could have ever guessed. DNA from William Henry Long's bones went straight to his father Alonzo Long/Longabaugh. What an amazing "twist" to our story.

This is a research project. Take all the information in and let it all organize in your mind and you will come to the same conclusion our Team has. William Henry Long is an alias for Harry Alonzo Longabaugh, the West's most notorious outlaw. Alonzo Long/Longabaugh is his biological father. All we have left to solve is to find Harry's mother.

William Henry Long telling his family that he was born in the Big Horn Basin of Wyoming is a clue. That is all we have ever had throughout the entire project is clues. That is our job, to follow the clues and see where they lead us. You have to admit, this is fascinating stuff... the kind of stories movies are made of.

# William Henry Long's DNA Profile
## Mothers DNA Father's DNA

### MITO

16126 T-C
16294 C-T
16296 C-T
16304 C-T
16519 T-C
73 A-G
263 A-G
309 1C
315 1C

### Y-STR

DYS456 17
DYS389 I 13
DYS390 23
DYS389 II 28
DYS458 17
DYS19 15
DYS385 11, 14
DYS393 13
DYS391 12
DYS439 12
DYS635 23
DYS392 13
GATAH4 12
DYS437 14
DYS438 13
DYS448 19

# George Longenbaugh & Family

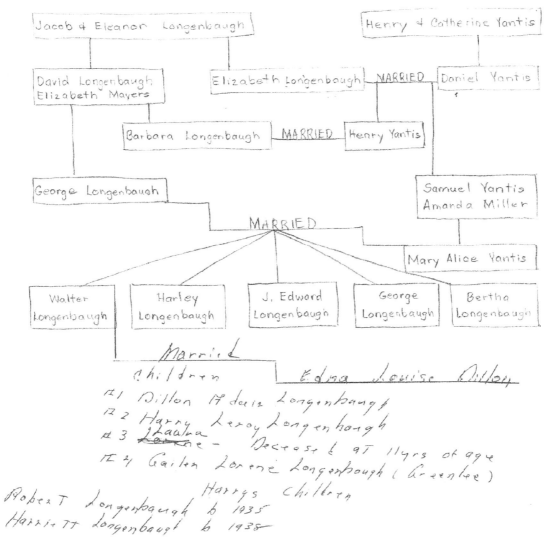

Sent to Harry Longenbaugh
by Mrs. Gerard
Aug. 1983

Three Marriages Between the
Longenbaugh and Yantis Families

Jacob & Eleanor Longenbaugh

Henry & Catherine Yantis

David Longenbaugh
Elizabeth Mayers

Elizabeth Longenbaugh — MARRIED — Daniel Yantis

Barbara Longenbaugh — MARRIED — Henry Yantis

George Longenbaugh

Samuel Yantis
Amanda Miller

MARRIED

Mary Alice Yantis

Walter Longenbaugh

Harley Longenbaugh

J. Edward Longenbaugh

George Longenbaugh

Bertha Longenbaugh

Married

Children          Edna Louise Dillon

#1 Dillon Adair Longenbaugh
#2 Harry Leroy Longenbaugh
#3 ~~Laura~~ — Deceased at 11 yrs of age
#4 Gailen Lorene Longenbaugh (Greenlee)

Harrys Children
Robert Longenbaugh b 1935
Harriett Longenbaugh b 1938

---

187

George and Mary Longenbaugh

The Walter C. Longenbaugh Family

George and Mary Longenbaugh & Family

David Longenbach 12-29-1812 DOD. 10-16-1888
Elizabeth Mayers Longenbach 3-30-1816
Died 7-29-1872

Their Children
Jacob Longenbach 4-14-1837
Barbara Ann Longenbach 2-11-1840 --- 11-7-1913
William Longenbach 1-25-1842
Elizabeth Longenbach 2-21-1843
Mary Longenbach 4-18-1844
Sarah Longenbach 11-10-1845 --- 11-11-1918
Eleanor Longenbach 5-23-1847
Julia Ann Longenbach 12-3-1848
Caroline Longenbach 2-24-1851
George M. Longenbach 2-22-1853 --- 5-28-1923
David Longenbach 11-25-1854 --- 4-4-1924
Cynthia Longenbach 3-11-1858
Noah Longenbach 12-16-1860
Picture Left to Right
Bottom row          David, Elizabeth, David, Cynthia,
Middle row                          Noah,
Top row George, Barbara, William, Jacob

This information was Compiled by
George M. Longenbach 2-22-1853 Carlazi Co.
Sometime between 9-9-1912 and 5-28-1923.
Copied by Harry L. Longenbaugh 1-27-1904 on 10-29-27

# Robert Longenbaugh

Chart no. _____
No. 1 on this chart is the same as no. _____ on chart no. _____

**16 Balzer or LONGENBACH**
b:
d:

**32 Mr LANGENBACH**

**33 Mrs LANGENBACH**

34

35

**8 Jacob LONGENBACH**
b:
p: , , Pennsylvania, USA
m:
p:
d:
p:

**17 Elizabeth**
b:
d:

36

37

**4 David L. LONGENBACH**
b: 29 Dec 1812
p: , , Ohio, USA
m: 2 Oct 1836
p: , Pickaway, Ohio
d: 15 Nov 1888
p: , , Ohio, United States

18
b:
d:

38

39

**9 Eleanor SHOFE OR SHOPE**
b: Ohio
p:
d:
p:

19
b:
d:

**2 George LONGENBACH**
b: Feb 1853
p: , , Ohio, United States
m: 30 Mar 1879
p: , Shelby, Illinois
d: aft 1920
p: Colorado, United States

20
b:
d:

40

41

10
b:
p:
m:
p:
d:
p:

21
b:
d:

42

43

**5 E MAYERS OR MOYERS**
b: abt 1817
p: , , Illinois, United States
d:
p:

22
b:
d:

44

45

11
b:
p:
d:
p:

23
b:
d:

46

47

**1 Walter LONGENBACH**
b: 2 May 1880
p: Shelby, Illinois, United States
m:
p:
d:
p:

24
b:
d:

48

49

**sp: Lois Edna DILLON**

**12 Daniel YANTIS**
b: 15 Sep 1811
p: Maryland
m: 21 Apr 1833
p: , Pickaway, Ohio
d: 30 Sep 1893
p: , Shelby, Illinois

25
b:
d:

50

51

**6 Samuel YANTIS**
b: Apr 1834
p: , Pickaway, Ohio
m: 5 Nov 1857
p: Shelby, Illinois
d:
p:

**26 Jacob LONGENBACH**
b:
d:

**52 Balzer or LONGENBACH**

**53 Elizabeth**

54

55

**13 Elizabeth LONGENBACH**
b: 2 Dec 1809
p: Ohio
d: 16 Feb 1890
p: Illinois, United States

**27 E SHOFE OR SHOPE**
b: Ohio
d:

**3 Mary Alice YANTIS**
b: 20 Mar 1861
p: , , Illinois, USA
d: 25 Aug 1933
p: Colorado, United States

28
b:
d:

56

57

14
b:
p:
m:
p:
d:
p:

29
b:
d:

58

59

**7 Amanda F. MILLER**
b: Mar 1836
p: Ohio
d:
p:

30
b:
d:

60

61

15
b:
p:
d:
p:

31
b:
d:

62

63

1

## Family Pedigree with Details

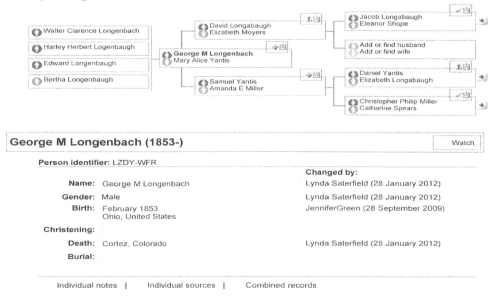

### George M Longenbach (1853-)                                    Watch

Person identifier: LZDY-WFR

|  |  |
|---|---|
| | **Changed by:** |
| **Name:** George M Longenbach | Lynda Saterfield (28 January 2012) |
| **Gender:** Male | Lynda Saterfield (28 January 2012) |
| **Birth:** February 1853<br>Ohio, United States | JenniferGreen (28 September 2009) |
| **Christening:** | |
| **Death:** Cortez, Colorado | Lynda Saterfield (28 January 2012) |
| **Burial:** | |

Individual notes  |  Individual sources  |  Combined records

# Pedigree Chart - Robert Longenbach

9 February 2012

Chart no. _____
No. 1 on this chart is the same as no. _____ on chart no. ___

16 **David L. LONGENBACH**
b: 29 Dec 1812
d: 15 Nov 1888

32 **Jacob LONGENBACH**

33 **E SHOFE OR SHOPE**

34

35

8 **George LONGENBACH**
b: Feb 1853
p: , Ohio, United States
m: 30 Mar 1879
p: , Shelby, Illinois
d: aft 1920
p: Colorado, United States

17 **E MAYERS OR MOYERS**
b: abt 1817
d:

4 **Walter LONGENBACH**
b: 2 May 1880
p: Shelby , Illinois, United States
m:
p:
d:
p:

18 **Samuel YANTIS**
b: Apr 1834
d:

36 **Daniel YANTIS**

37 **Elizabeth LONGENBACH**

38

39

9 **Mary Alice YANTIS**
b: 20 Mar 1861
p: , , Illinois, USA
d: 25 Aug 1933
p: Colorado, United States

19 **Amanda E MILLER**
b: Mar 1836
d:

2 **Harry LONGENBACH**
b:
p:
m:
p:
d:
p:

40

20
b:
d:

41

42

10
b:
p:
m:
p:
d:
p:

21
b:
d:

43

5 **Lois Edna DILLON**
b: 1882
p:
d: 1964
p: Colorado, United States

44

22
b:
d:

45

46

11
b:
p:
d:
p:

23
b:
d:

47

1 **Robert LONGENBACH**
b:
p:
m:
p:
d:
p:

sp: _____

48

24
b:
d:

49

50

12
b:
p:
m:
p:
d:
p:

25
b:
d:

51

6
b:
p:
m:
p:
d:
p:

52

26
b:
d:

53

54

13
b:
p:
d:
p:

27
b:
d:

55

3 **Mrs Harry LONGABAUGH**
b:
p:
d:
p:

56

28
b:
d:

57

58

14
b:
p:
m:
p:
d:
p:

29
b:
d:

59

7
b:
p:
d:
p:

60

30
b:
d:

61

62

15
b:
p:
d:
p:

31
b:
d:

63

# Josiah Longabaugh & Family

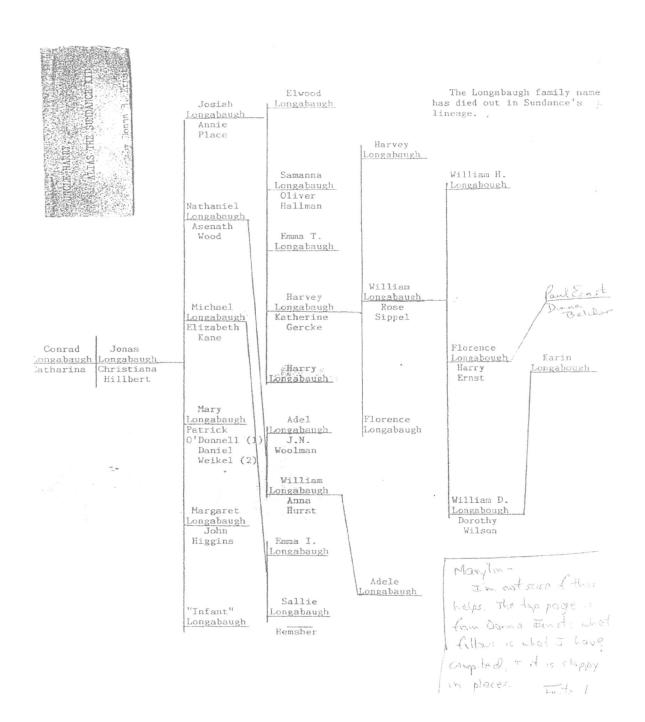

The Longabaugh family name
has died out in Sundance's
lineage.

Harry A. Longabaugh, age 4, with his father Josiah

Annie Place Longabaugh,
Mother of Harry A. Longabaugh

Elwood Place
Longabaugh

Harvey Sylvester Longabaugh, the older brother of Harry Longabaugh, "The Sundance Kid"

Harvey Sylvester Longabaugh

## The Sisters Pictures

Regression Summary
A1 vs. A2

| Count | 8 |
|---|---|
| Num. Missing | 0 |
| R | .978 |
| R Squared | .957 |
| Adjusted R Squared | .950 |
| RMS Residual | 14.152 |

ANOVA Table
A1 vs. A2

| | DF | Sum of Squares | Mean Square | F-Value | P-Value |
|---|---|---|---|---|---|
| Regression | 1 | 26695.911 | 26695.911 | 133.294 | < .0001 |
| Residual | 6 | 1201.670 | 200.278 | | |
| Total | 7 | 27897.581 | | | |

Regression Coefficients
A1 vs. A2

| | Coefficient | Std. Error | Std. Coeff. | t-Value | P-Value |
|---|---|---|---|---|---|
| Intercept | -16.982 | 9.943 | -16.982 | -1.708 | .1385 |
| A2 | 1.365 | .118 | .978 | 11.545 | < .0001 |

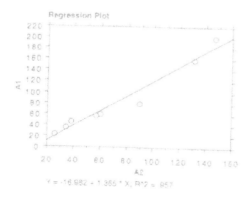

Regression Plot

$Y = -16.982 + 1.365 * X, R^2 = .957$

Sister A1 vs. Sister A2

Standing: Samanna Longabaugh
Sitting: Emma Longabaugh
Sisters of Harry A. Longabaugh

This is the photo mentioned in Viola's 1936
letter on Bill Long's "Sisters Picture."
Bill Long had this photo on his fireplace in
Duchesne, Utah.

# Conrad & Balzer

# Longabaugh Family Tree

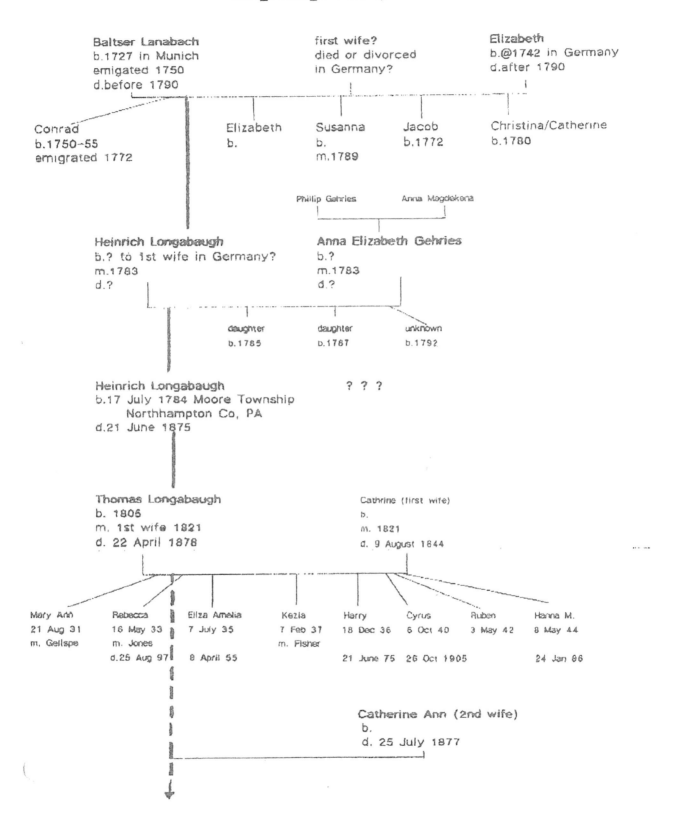

Baltser Lanabach
b.1727 in Munich
emigated 1750
d.before 1790

first wife?
died or divorced
in Germany?

Elizabeth
b.@1742 in Germany
d.after 1790

Conrad
b.1750-55
emigrated 1772

Elizabeth
b.

Susanna
b.
m.1789

Jacob
b.1772

Christina/Catherine
b.1780

Phillip Gehries          Anna Magdekena

Heinrich Longabaugh
b.? to 1st wife in Germany?
m.1783
d.?

Anna Elizabeth Gehries
b.?
m.1783
d.?

daughter
b.1785

daughter
b.1787

unknown
b.1792

Heinrich Longabaugh
b.17 July 1784 Moore Township
      Northhampton Co, PA
d.21 June 1875

? ? ?

Thomas Longabaugh
b. 1805
m. 1st wife 1821
d. 22 April 1878

Cathrine (first wife)
b.
m. 1821
d. 9 August 1844

Mary Ann
21 Aug 31
m. Gellspe

Rebecca
16 May 33
m. Jones
d.25 Aug 97

Eliza Amelia
7 July 35

8 April 55

Kezia
7 Feb 37
m. Fisher

Harry
18 Dec 36

21 June 75

Cyrus
6 Oct 40

26 Oct 1905

Ruben
3 May 42

Hanna M.
8 May 44

24 Jan 86

Catherine Ann (2nd wife)
b.
d. 25 July 1877

# Narrative

Baltser Lanabach (also spelled Baltzar) was the first Longabaugh in this country. He was born in 1727 near Munich, Germany. We know little about him; he emigrated here in 1750 for reasons unknown, and perhaps he brought children with him. He was married to a woman named Elizabeth, also born in Germany near 1742 to parents we do not know. Baltser was quite a bit older than Elizabeth -- by about fifteen years. Together they had at least five children born and baptized in this country: Elizabeth, Susanna, Jacob (born 1772), Mary, and Christina (born 1780).

Baltser also had at least two other children. Conrad, born between 1750 - 1755 in Germany, emigrated on a brig called The Morning Star in 1772 -- the same year Elizabeth gave birth to Jacob. Elizabeth would probably have been too young to be Conrad's mother, so we theorize that Baltser had a first wife in Germany who either died or was divorced. Perhaps this first wife gave birth in Germany to Heinrich, our anscestor. Or maybe Conrad was Baltser's brother. According to one record Heinrich had a brother named Christian. Could this be "Conrad"? The name is a clue to the religious streak that is one theme we see running through the generations.

Baltser settled first in Somerset County, Pennsylvania. Pennsylvania has remained the "homeland" of this branch of the Longabaughs even to this day. Espey and Grandmama, Hans and Paula, and Heidi and Jim live in counties that Longabaughs called home seven generations ago.

Baltser fought in the Revolutionary War, and according to lore he served under General George Washington. In a 1776 census he was found living with Elizabeth in Frederick County, Maryland. By 1790, though, Baltser had died and Elizabeth had moved to Washington County, Maryland with some of her children still with her. We know that Conrad's family stayed in touch with the American-born children; Conrad's great-grandson Harry traveled West in a covered wagon with one of Baltser's great-grandchildren. Harry became know as the Sundance Kid, one of the most notorious bandits of the Wild West.

We know less about Heinrich than we do about his father Baltser. I estimate he was born between 1755-1765. He was married in 1783 to Anna Elizabeth Gehries (also spelled Gerass), who was daughter of Phillip Gehries and Anna Magdekena. The Gehries were enrolled at Upper Mt. Bethel Evangelical Lutheran Church. Heinrich at some point moved to Anna's home in Eastern PA -- so I guess we knew who wore the pants in that family! Together Heinrich and Anna had four children that we know about: a boy baptized in 1784, two girls baptized in 1785 and 1787, and another child born in 1790. The oldest was our ancestor Heinrich Longabaugh, born 17 July 1784 in Moore Township of Northhampton County, PA. (Jr.)

This Heinrich is a mystery. We don't yet know whom he married, but he did have ten chidren, one of which was stillborn. Heinrich Jr. died on 21 June 1875, leaving Thomas Longabaugh, the next generation in our lineage.

Thomas was born in 1805. Aunt Grace's record says he was born in 1811, but an earlier date jives better because he was married In 1821. Even so, he was only sixteen when he wed Cathrine, his first wife. Our facts must be off, though, because they didn't start having children until 1831 -- so maybe Grace's date for Thomas' birth is correct and the wedding date is wrong. Once Thomas and Cathrine started having children, they didn't stop. They had eight total. Poor Cathrine had a child every two years until her last, Hannah. Cathrine died when Hannah was only four months old. It makes me wonder how many other women in this time period died because they could not stop having children.

One of their children, Cyrus, is remembered fondly by Uncle John, Espey's half-brother. Uncle John recalls visitting Cyrus' farm in Huntington PA and eating all the ice cream he wanted to. This seems to imply some closeness in the family because Uncle John is only distantly related to Cyrus. He was the grandson of Cyrus' half-brother, John Mayes Longabaugh.

John Mayes Longabaugh was born from Thomas Longabaugh's second wife Catherine Ann. Thomas apparently wasted no time in re-marrying after his first wife died. I suppose that with eight children he needed help! But Thomas didn't stop with eight children -- he had seven more with his new wife. Either Thomas was wealthy enough to provide for his fifteen children, or he was too irresponsible to care. Either way, Thomas died 22 April 1878. He is buried at Logan Cemetery in Bellwood, PA near Hollidaysburg.

With John Mayes Longabaugh our story takes an ugly turn. Born 29 December 1849 in Potter Township of Centre County, PA, he competed with fifteenl other children for attention. His daughter Margaret reports that he began drinking at age 16. He never spoke of his mother or father even to his wife. After dating for four years, he married Mary Ann Bonner in 1876. She married late at age 34; John was age 27. Mary Ann was born in London to a man who made horse collars. He too was a drinker and didn't care for the welfare of his children. At age five Mary Ann's mother died and she went to live with her uncle. She attended school by day and worked until 10:00 at night sewing seams for her Uncle's tayloring business.. Her uncle died when she was thirteen and she was sent to live with her aunt in America.

The relationship between John Mayes and Mary Ann was a bitter one. He nearly beat her to death several times. Mary Ann was a devout Christian and though she had offers from John Mayes' family to leave him and stay with them, she refused.. apparently out of duty. Together they had four children: John Rutherford, Alice Bonner, May Spencer, and Margaret Dawson, nicknamed "Ginty". John Mayes was a carpenter and shipping manager at Riter and Conley steel mill, among other things. Mr. Conley tolerated his drinking out of Christian charity, but when Conley died Mr. Riter fired him. Then in 1894 John Mayes had a conversion. According to a letter from his daughter in 1965, John Mayes "was rescued by Rev. E.D Whiteside, a (Presbyterian) missionary in Pittsburgh, and brought to the Lord by His matchless grace. He served the Lord for several (five) years (as a lay preacher in an abandoned church on skid row at the corner of Liberty Avenue and Third). However, he went back into the old life for some time. But God followed him and brought him into His fold before he passed out of this life". John Mayes died in Woodville (or Mayview?), a home for mentally ill or addicted people. Mary Ann Bonner died seven years later.

John Rutherford Longabaugh was born in Pittsburgh on 1 February 1873. Because of his father's alcoholism he spent much of his youth in poverty. He remained a sickly person, due perhaps to the malnourishment he suffered as a child. He was educated to sixth grade, but left school to support his family. He was a self-learner and a math whiz, teaching himself trigonometry. His sister wrote of him: "I thank God every day for the fatherly care of our beloved brother John, who bore the heat and burden of the family when Pop dropped all responsibility, unknown to us all." At fifteen John Rutherford got a job in his father's steel mill. When it was taken over by Andrew Carnegie, it prospered; John Rutherford, a very hard worker, also prospered. He eventually became a director in six banks.

John Rutherford inherited his mother's religous zeal. He dreamed of being a minister or missionary as a youth, but his circumstances did not allow this. As an adult he taught a men's bible study and was reputed to have spent more time on preparation than the minister on the sermon. His children recall (with some chagrin) his lengthy prayers before supper. John Rutherford took in his homeless father for a while, but when his father threatened John Ruterford's first wife Grace, he kicked him out. Grace died early in their marriage. His second wife bore him John Rutherford Jr. before she too died.

His third wife, Anna Federlein (Grammy!), was born of a man who was born in the same German city as Baltser Lanabach. Anna was twenty-one years younger than her husband. Together they had Edward Espey, Grace Mary, and Thomas Bonner. For a time they were quite well off; then came the bank crash and subsequent depression. John Rutherford Jr. writes: "Dad could have gotten out of some banks before the crash but stayed in because friends trusted him and he thought he could weather the storm. So he stayed in and it nearly killed him." His family suffered also as they plunged into poverty. Around 1933 he suffered a "nervous breakdown" and went with Anna to rest in Pultneyville for several months. In 1952, before any of us grandchildren knew him, he died of a stroke. John Rutherford Jr. remembers him in glowing terms; Espey remembers that he was at times oppressively rigid, and worse, harsh with Grammy.

I will not detail the stories of Edward Espey and Mary Jane Kurth. How could one describe one's own parents in two paragraphs? You will have to ask them about their perceptions and experiences. I have some information on the Kurth line, and I hope the inaccuracies with spur Mom to provide more detail.

Mary Jane Kurth is the offspring of Harold Richard Kurth ("Poppy") and Bessie Dodge Neily. Harold was born to German immigrants Gustav Kurth and ? on 22 August 1895 in New Britain, Conneticut; Bessie ("Mimi") to Primrose Neily, a farmer, and Clara Belle on 22 September 1896 in Middletown, Nova Scotia. Harold graduated from Harvard College in 1915 and Harvard Medical School in 1919. He was a surgeon. Mimi was a nurse. They wed in 1921. Their first child was Harold Richard Jr., born on 22 August 1922. He too went to Harvard. He was in the United States Marine Corps and fought in World War II. Later, he was part of Ike's security . Mom was born next, then Wilfred Kurth on 10 May 1933. Two other children were lost by miscarriage.

I remember Mimi barely, but seem to recall that she was rather formidible. I also recall that wonderful farm in New Hampshire. I'm hoping that Mom will relay more. Sadness struck the family when Poppy died on 7 February 1956. Two years later, Harold Richard Jr. died in a plane crash.

Barbara Newell seems to be the person to contact for more Kurth family history at Box 158 / 118 Wentworth Rd. / New Castle, NH 03854.

I hope this is as intriguing to you as it is to me. I feel badly that information on our foremothers is somewhat scarce. Simply because we retain the family _name_ through the male descendants does not mean that our family _identity_ is based in them. It's also worth noting that the information I present here is not irrefutable; conflicts exist. But I hope this gives you a sense of roots. It's interesting to see where we come from, isn't it?

Fritz
9 June 1997

*Descendants of Edward Espey Longabaugh and Mary Jane Kurth*

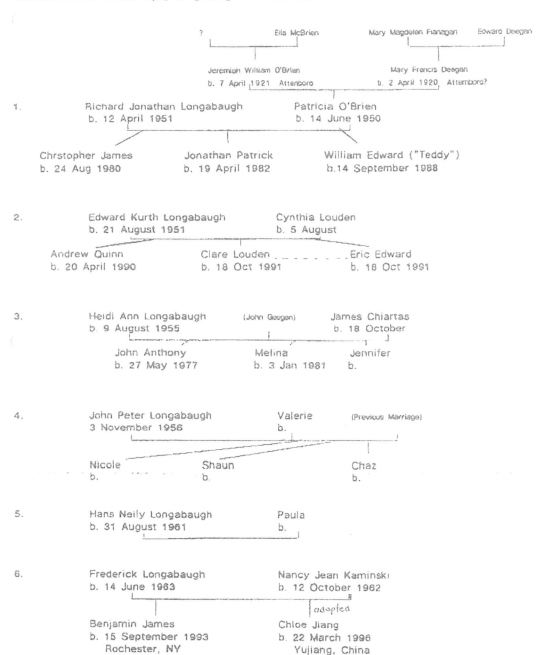

# CHAPTER VI
## All The Pieces Come Together

With all the research from our first book, everyone gets the tangible evidence that William Henry Long is "The Sundance Kid." No doubt about it.

William Henry Long hid out in the Utah wilderness area of Loa, Fremont and Duchesne, Utah and lived a double life. Bill Long's wife, Luzernia, knew about another woman, Etta Place. Bill left for four days in 1925 to attend Josie Bassett's 50th Birthday party in Indian Canyon. Butch, Josie, Ann Bassett (Etta Place) and Matt Warner attended Josie's party.

Luzernia knew about Etta, but she put up with the affair because she loved him. Etta Forsyth (granddaughter) told us that Luzernia knew she would be poor, just like when Grandpa Silas died and left her with six children. Luzernia was dependent on Bill Long to provide for her. She loved her husband and family and had to have known his identity. She married due to desperate times, but stayed with him through it all. She loved "The Sundance Kid."

### All The Evidence
- Photo Comparison: William Henry Long compared to Harry Alonzo Longabaugh – a match.
- Name Analysis matching family members in Pennsylvania.
- Timeline – Bill Long was missing the same time that The Sundance Kid was in Bolivia. William Henry Long's sisters compared to The Sundance Kid's Sisters – they are the same people – Bill's photo is when they are young.
- Body Analysis: Match Harry Alonzo Longabaugh's body all the way down the list.
- Hair color – Same.
- Eye Color – Same.
- Broken Nose – Same.
- Sinus Problem– Same.
- Bullet Wound To Leg – Both the Same.
- Height – Same.
- Weight – Same.
- Build – Same.
- Pictures of Hands - Both the Same.

### Family Stories
Etta Forsyth, step granddaughter filled in all the blanks. Etta said she was teased by Bill Long that she is named after "The Sundance Kid's" girlfriend, Etta Place. While interviewing Etta at age 93, she explained that his eyes were "kindly grey." Etta saw the photo of Sundance and said, "That is Uncle Billy Long, I see it now."

William Henry Long's bones, "0" Distance goes directly to "0" Distance to the father. Alonzo Long/Longabaugh /Langebach/Langenbacher. Hello! Alonzo and Harry Alonzo!

### DNA does not lie!

William Henry Long
Age 25-27
Loa, Utah

Harry Alonzo Longabaugh,
"The Sundance Kid"

Sundance Kid

Sundance Kid

William Henry Long

Sundance Kid and William Henry Long have the same build.
Note how the right hand is curled under.

Harry Alonzo Longabaugh,
"The Sundance Kid"

William Oscar Long
Sundance Kid's half brother

# CHAPTER VII
## Science

How can you trust our research? Science needs to be able to be duplicated, processed again and again, with the exact same results.

William Henry Long's DNA from his bones will lead to his father. The "0" Distance of William Henry Long's father is Alonzo Long/Longabaugh. Every single time without fail, the research goes directly to Alonzo. William Henry Long is an alias for Harry Alonzo Longabaugh, "The Sundance Kid." Alonzo Long is Harry Alonzo's Father.

George and Mary Longenbaugh are "close cousins." Repeat that exercise repeatedly and you will get the exact same results every time.

Josiah Longabaugh is a "cousin" to our William Henry Long, alias, Harry Alonzo Long/Longabaugh, but he is a "cousin." That result will always be the same every time.

The only conclusion will always be that Harry Alonzo Longabaugh's father was Alonzo Long/Longabaugh. Something happened for Alonzo to give his first-born son to his cousins, Josiah Longabaugh and his wife Ann Place.

The mother is still a mystery, but we do have a clue. Tim Kupherschmid analyzed William Henry Longs mother's DNA profile. She is Eastern European, Russian or German.

George and Mary Longenbaugh are stated as "cousins" in Harry's sister Samanna's business ledger. Harry leaves for the West at 14 with his cousin George to homestead. The family knew George and Mary were both cousins, so they had to know Harry is a family member adopted in.

The abt. (about) spring of 1867 is a definite clue that the family did not know the day and month he was born.

Be my guest to all of our research and try to prove us wrong. It is just not possible. The science will come out the same every time!

What a fascinating TWIST to such a Famous Story!

The only piece left to the puzzle is Harry Alonzo's mother. Alonzo knew a woman and had a child with her. Life's circumstances made it necessary to give up his child to cousin Josiah and his wife Ann Place Longabaugh. We solved the "Darn" DNA mystery with a lot of "great sleuthing" from our Story Teller Productions TEAM!

### Conclusion

By now we know that William Henry Long is an alias for Harry Alonzo Longabaugh, "The Sundance Kid". How can you argue with our research and science! Everything can all be checked and double checked and you will ALWAYS get the same result.

### Finale

What fascinating lives they lived. Butch Cassidy, The Sundance Kid and Etta's story did not end in Bolivia! They all shared the same secret. They were in FEAR their whole lives that they could be betrayed, killed or imprisoned. Not a pleasant way to live.

**ALL of what you have read is true!**
**I can't wait to follow through on our final clue, finding The Sundance Kid's mother!**

Overlay of Transparencies
Alonzo & William

Alonzo Long with DNA and DNA genealogy

Alonzo Long with DNA and DNA genealogy
is the father of Harry Alonzo Longabaugh, "The Sundance Kid"

# CHAPTER VIII
## Digging Deeper

"YOU HAVE TO DIG DEEPER!"

When Ann Place Longabaugh's DNA (The Sundance Kid's mother) did not match William Henry Long's DNA, you must ask the question, "Why not?" How could all the photo comparisons and all the other research we completed prove our case that William Henry Long is an alias for Harry Alonzo Longabaugh, "The Sundance Kid," and yet the DNA did not match the mother of Harry Alonzo Longabaugh.

We did not have DNA for Josiah Longabaugh, The Sundance Kid's father. The way my mind works is, what will the DNA from William Henry Long's bones tell us? With the help of Yvonne Martinez, great granddaughter of William Henry Long, we did a search with Bill Long's DNA profile and went to YSearch.com. That led us to Alonzo Long/Longabaugh (the family changed their name to be more American) and then we were fortunate to have photos of Alonzo and his wife Julia Ann Taylor. Anyone can see the resemblance of Alonzo and Harry Alonzo right away. Dr. John McCullough saw the photos and said, "They have a strong family resemblance. They look alike!"

We also needed to find male descendants of Conrad and Baltzer. The two lines of genealogy appear in Donna Ernst book of Longabaugh Genealogy that she donated to The Church of Jesus Christ of Latter Day Saints Family History Center in Salt Lake City, Utah. We had Jay, George and Robert Longenbaugh's DNA reports. Jay and George's DNA matched each other, but Robert did not match Jay and George. That gave the family answers about their ancestors. Conrad and Baltzer were not father and son, but cousins.

When we compared William Henry Long's DNA profile to Robert Longenbaugh's DNA, they had 6 exact markers. We do not have permission from Robert Longenbaugh to publish his DNA. but we can say that they are close cousins.

Digging even deeper, we discovered they are all Langenbacher's from Bavaria, Germany.

Our project is a journey of discovery and we have almost completed all our research. I just came back from Willow Creek Ranch at THE HOLE IN THE WALL, just outside of Kaycee, Wyoming. THE NEW WILD BUNCH GANG just had our very first REUNION OF THE CHILDREN OF BUTCH CASSIDY AND THE SUNDANCE KID at the ranch on July 2nd and 3rd, 2012. We launched this book, "THE SUNDANCE KID AND THAT 'DARN' DNA," on July 2nd. I am adding this update to let you in on more discoveries.

On July 3rd, "The New Wild Bunch Gang" went to THE HOLE IN THE WALL. What a FABULOUS place to launch our book! We went to the cabin where Butch Cassidy and the GANG hid out, and we climbed to THE HOLE IN THE WALL. We sold books and released the news that Harry Alonzo was adopted into the Josiah Longabaugh family and is a "cousin" to Josiah Longabaugh. We wanted to keep this amazing TWIST a secret, until we had a completed book. Everyone is just amazed at what great detective work it took to solve the mystery.

When I came home, I received a call from a member of our "gang," Rod Morrell. Rod is on the Luzernia Allred Morrell side of the family. Luzernia is William Henry Long's wife. Rod suggested that we not only do DNA testing for the Arapaho and Shoshone women of the Big Horn Basin of Wyoming to look for William Henry Long's mother, but he also suggested that we find living descendants of Julia Ann Taylor, Alonzo Long/Longabaugh's wife. He pointed out the combination of both Julia and Alonzo, looks a lot like William Henry Long. I said we would follow through on his information. We do need to leave no stone unturned and "dig deeper!"

I contacted Jim Petty our genealogist and he will help us find the living descendants of Julia Ann Taylor. A good place to start would be where Julia Ann and Alonzo lived in Baker, Oregon. They had 15 children, so that should be easy to find direct descendants of Julia and Alonzo's daughter's. We will let you know what we find. What Fun!

This is such a complicated story. Modern science is THE ONLY WAY we could have figured out the whole "darn" thing. There is always the possibility that we may never find a match for Sundance's mother. What will help is to get our books out and it is AMAZING how people have come forward with information that has helped solve the mystery? You can join our group and become a "sleuth" like the rest of our Team.

When you are working on a project or your life's work, don't forget about DIGGING DEEPER! Our Story Teller Productions Team did and OH MY, look at what we've got! We have changed history and we found Butch, Sundance, and Etta and have been on an adventure of a lifetime. We get to go to all the places that the Wild Bunch hid out and escaped from the law. We have many more adventures in our future. You get to come along and learn about what really happened to THE WILD BUNCH GANG.

Happy Trails Until We Meet Again!

*Marilyn* **AMAZING** *Grace*

# CHAPTER IX
## "Who Are Those Guys?"

Butch Cassidy, The Sundance Kid and Etta Place left Bolivia in 1905. There is a letter that was found in 1997 that is written by Harry Alonzo Longabaugh at his Cholula Ranch in 1905 stating that, "Etta and I have had it with this place; we are leaving for San Francisco, never to return to this country again."

We can find that letter with the help of collector Brent Ashworth in Provo, Utah. That letter is another piece of the puzzle that proves that Butch, Sundance and Etta escaped Bolivia, went to Paris, France where Butch Cassidy had a face lift. Then they all three came back to the United States. They did not die at San Vicente, November 7, 1908. Two other American Bandits died that day.

Percy Sievert, the head of the Bolivian Tin Mines liked Butch and Sundance. Percy and his wife were the only American's at the Concordia Tin Mines and they had them over to dinner and were friends. Percy knew how badly they wanted out of the outlaw life so when two bandits were killed, he did not bother to go down and identify the bodies of the two outlaws, but told the authorities that it was Butch and Sundance so they could escape the outlaw life. Brent Ashworth owns Percy Siebert's journal. We need to do a thorough search of Percy's journal to find more clues.

Sundance could come back to Duchesne, Utah to his six step-children and two girls of his own, but Butch is too recognizable to come back to the United States without being captured. Butch was lucky in the fact that Dr. Louis Ombrédanne, a reconstructive plastic surgeon could perform surgery on his nose, ears and jaw. Surgeons could cut into the front of the chin and push the jaw back to change the shape of the jaw-line. Many people have asked if this type of surgery could be possible as early as 1907. I have included Dr. Ombrédanne's medical background. Paris is on the cutting edge of plastic surgery because of all the wars.

Now for the fun part. Since Dr. John McCullough and I have been on the news three times, I received a copy of a tin type (photograph) taken in Utah in about 1907. Just look at what we have discovered! It is a photo of Robert LeRoy Parker, alias, Butch Cassidy and Harry Alonzo Longabaugh, alias, The Sundance Kid taken with an American Indian. This is possibly the last photo taken together before going their separate ways.

Having been born in 1867, Sundance would be 40 years old in this picture and Butch has the same chubby fingers of William Thadeus Phillips and Butch Cassidy in the Fort Worth Five photo. You can believe we will have a scientist look at this photo. We have no idea who the Indian is but I bet we could find out.

The original tin type is very small, but we enlarged the photo. It is Butch Cassidy and The Sundance Kid. It had to have been taken in 1907. That is when William Thadeus Phillips appeared in Spokane, Washington. I believe the collector that sold the photo was in Utah, so it may have been taken in Utah. More research is needed, but you must admit, this is a great find.

Robert LeRoy Parker appeared in Spokane, Washington in 1907 and went to the library and assumed the identity of William Thadeus Phillips, who had died as a child.

William Henry Long just had to return to his family in Duschene, Utah where they all knew he is really Harry Alonzo Longabaugh, The Sundance Kid.

Just like the vibrato they showed when the "gang" had their picture taken in the famous "Fort Worth Five" photo, and sent it to the bank manager, thanking him for the money, Butch and Sundance were bold to pose for one last picture. Just one last "hurrah" before they went their separate ways, never to see each other again.

We know that there were two tin types that a collector in Utah sold to another collector and we will work with Brent Ashworth to find this other Utah collector of rare photographs.

This is a "Wild Bunch Enthusiasts" dream, to find a photo of Butch and Sundance that no one has seen before.

## Note:

*Dr. John McCullough will work on the photo comparison and we will ask the FBI Labs at Quantico, Virginia for their help. I am also sure that Tim Kupherschmid at Sorensen Forensics lab in Salt Lake City, Utah will be looking over John's shoulder to see what the results are. Tim has been such a great support for our project and we would never have been able to get DNA for William Henry Long without him.*

*This is our "DA TA DA DAH" moment! From the beginning, we have taken one puzzle piece at a time and laid out all of the evidence. Now we leave the best for last. What a magnificent tin type of Butch Cassidy, The Sundance Kid and an unknown Indian! This is probably the last photo taken of them together before they parted ways forever.*

# The Tin Type

Left-Butch Cassidy    Back-Indian    Right-Sundance Kid

## Robert LeRoy Parker alias "Butch Cassidy"

Many people have asked me how "Butch Cassidy" had his ears, nose and jaw changed in 1907 with plastic surgery. Paris is on the cutting edge of plastic surgery because of the war. The most valuable information that needs to be clear is that surgeons can cut into the front of the chin and push the jaw back, changing the outline of the jaw. This is being done today and was also possible in 1907.

I saw a detective show about how criminals in the 1930's and 40's, especially mobsters like Pretty Boy Floyd, underwent plastic surgery to disguise their appearance. Butch Cassidy is just so recognizable that he could not come back to the United States without being captured. Cutting into the front of the chin and pushing the jaw back is exactly what took place to change his appearance.

(Notice the difference in the photo comparison of William Thadeus Phillips.
I can see a welt line on the front of William Phillips chin that is vertical. Any dentist could tell you that his teeth would not have matched up. He is desperate to change his appearance. Then he would have trouble eating for the rest of his life without his teeth matching.)

Also read the "Bandit Invincible" document that William Thadeus Phillips published in 1929 during the great depression when he is desperate for money. Phillips states, "From Permabuco (he went) to Liverpool and then England and Paris. At Paris, he entered a private hospital where he submitted to several minor operations. In three weeks, (he) left the hospital (and) he could see very little trace of his old self in the mirror, so clever had the transformation been worked out."

It is important to me that you understand the jaw line reduction that took place in 1907 is the same plastic surgery that is done today.

Butch Cassidy, (Robert LeRoy Parker) underwent plastic surgery for his ears, nose and jaw in Paris, France in 1907. Then he next appears in Spokane, Washington and assumes the identity of William Thadeus Phillips.

Phillips took the identity of a young boy that died. He is cleaver enough to steal his identity so he could drive and become a contributing member of society.

Sundance on the other hand did not ever own a car, let alone drive and is still riding a horse until his death in 1937. Butch Cassidy is the leader of "The Wild Bunch." The mastermind!

# Louis Ombrédanne
From Wikipedia

Louis Ombrédanne (March 5, 1871 – 1956) was a French pediatric and plastic surgeon born in Paris. He was the son of general practitioner Emile Ombrédanne.

In 1902 he became surgeon to Parisian hospitals, becoming a professor of surgery in 1907. [1] From 1921 to 1940 he was head of pediatric surgery at the Hôpital Necker.

Ombrédanne's primary field of research was development of new methods of surgery. In 1906 he was the first to describe the use of the pectoralis minor muscle for breast reconstruction following mastectomy. He also introduced transscrotal orchiopexy for surgical repair of an undescended testis.

In 1907, after two fatal anesthetic accidents, Ombrédanne created a prototype of an inhaler as a safe anesthetic device. It consisted of a tin container as reservoir that was fitted with felt to absorb ether, a graduated air inlet, and a respiratory reserve chamber. This device was tested successfully on over 300 patients, and design modifications were later made.

In 1929 Ombrédanne provided an early description of malignant hyperthermia, a condition he described as pallor with hyperthermia in newborns during anesthesia. The disorder was historically referred to as "Ombrédanne Syndrome".

Dr. Louis Ombrédanne

# Note:

## Marilyn Grace Journal Entry April 22, 2009 Wednesday

*Dr. John McCullough invited a colleague from the University Anthropology Department (Jane) to examine the remains of William Henry Long at Sorenson Forensics DNA lab in Salt Lake City, Utah.*

*I do not have permission to use the anthropologist's name, so we will call her Jane. Jane has known Dr. McCullough for many years and has previously helped with research and a book on Amelia Erhart. I was impressed with her expertise and professionalism.*

*Tim Kupherschmid, Dr. McCullough, Jane and I were in a clean and secure room while they examined the remains of William Henry Long. Jane had her gloves on and I was sitting on a chair in the corner when all of a sudden, Jane came over and held up the skull of William Henry Long and exclaimed, "This skull belongs to this photo!" Jane had her finger on my notebook with the side by side photos of William Henry Long and Harry Alonzo Longabaugh, "The Sundance Kid." She had another finger on the famous photo of "Sundance" taken at the turn of the century in the famous "Fort Worth Five" photo. She saw the skull matched "The Sundance Kid."*

*I am the lead on the project and I have been to every event since we started filming in September of 2007. Anthropologists can take clay and reconstruct the skull. We have all the photos and we will work on a new documentary and do exactly that. We will make a plaster cast of the skull and the scientist will add clay, and you will see Harry Alonzo Longabaugh "The Sundance Kid" appear before your very eyes.*

*I wanted YOU to understand that we really have FOUND THE SUNDANCE KID!*

**Marilyn Grace Journal Entry March 15, 2013 - Friday**

*Dear Journal,*

*Yesterday, Thursday, March 14, 2013, was such an amazing day! The DNA for William Henry Long's mother (DNA sample from his bones) did not match Julia Ann Taylor – Alonzo Long's wife in Haynes, Oregon.*

*The mother of William Henry Long is Eastern European. That means she could be German, Italian or Russian etc. Yvonne Martinez is doing a search on a DNA data base for females to see if we can find Bill Long's mother. Yvonne now knows that William Henry Long's father is Alonzo Long/Longabaugh. (Yvonne is the great granddaughter of William Henry Long, "The Sundance Kid"). With DNA from William Henry Long's bones, the Long family has a family tree. The "0" distance is "Father and Son." DNA does not lie.*

# $6,500 REWARD

REWARD FOR THE CAPTURE, DEAD OR ALIVE OF

## HARRY LONGBAUGH

ALIAS

# THE SUNDANCE KID

Age, 35 to 40 years

Complexion, dark.
(Looks like quarter breed Indian)

Eyes, Black.

Features, Grecian type.

Height, 5 ft. 9 in.

Color of hair, Black.

Mustache, black.

Nationality, American.

Weight, 165 to 170 lbs.

Build, rather slim.

Nose, rather long.

Occupation,
Cowboy, Rustler.

Harry Longbaugh, alias THE SUNDANCE KID served 18 months in jail at Sundance, Cook Co., Wyoming when a boy, for horse stealing. In December, 1892, the Sundance Kid, Bill Madden and Harry Bass "held up" a Great Northern train at Malta, Montana. Bass and Madden were tried for the crime, convicted and sentenced to 10 and 14 years respectively!

The Sundance Kid escaped and since has been a fugitive.

# Robert Redford & Paul Newman

*Movie Poster*

## "BUTCH CASSIDY & THE SUNDANCE KID"

We do not have permission to add the movie poster in our book. We would LOVE to obtain permission from Fox Studios to add the AMAZING photo to our book!

# CHAPTER X
## "Hollywood"

When I think about Hollywood, my own experience of living there comes to mind immediately. My former husband and our three children and I, lived in an apartment in Hollywood and I commuted to Beverly Hills five days a week for work. The Aida Grey Salon on Rodeo Drive and Wilshire is where I had the best job of my career. Aida Grey is in her 90's when she hired me as her assistant and I did hair and make-up for many movie star clients.

Just a few months ago, I went back to Hollywood after a 25-year absence to visit my daughter and her husband. Man am I grateful that they were driving. It felt like they were in "attack" mode. They would say, "Are you driving or navigating?" Then we were off to the races in the worst traffic I have ever seen in my life.

Our destination is "The Farmers Market" in Los Angeles. We went to dinner and a movie and the prices were "double" what I pay in St. George, Utah where I live.

The air quality, the traffic, the cost of living helped me realize why I "choose" to live in Utah. So many times, I have had folks say that I should move to L.A. or New York so I can really get my motion picture company moving faster. I let them know that with the Internet, Skype, and our brand-new airport, I can do business from St. George and fly or drive anywhere I need to go. I believe we need to choose "happiness" over location. We can create a new movie about "Butch Cassidy & The Sundance Kid" without moving to Hollywood.

The beach is wonderful and I lived in Manhattan Beach for a year and a half after my marriage ended in 1989. The air and beauty are amazing and I would run on the beach, Monday, Wednesday, and Friday. I can see myself living on some beach in California like Carmel, why not?

It has been great to dream about who would star in the new movie on Butch and Sundance. My ideal star to play "Sundance" would be Brad Pitt. He starred with Robert Redford in "Spy Games." What an exciting film, and the two look like they could be father and son. Brad, (listen to me, Brad) could play a wonderful middle aged William Henry Long, and Robert Redford could magically become William Henry Long that is shot and murdered by the woodpile at his home in Duchesne. I have been to the exact location where William Henry Long died so it is easy for me to imagine.

Why not Brad Pitt and Robert Redford in the new movie? We are just making it up as we go along. Who knows what will happen in "real life."

Many folks have said that Kurt Russell would make an "excellent" Butch Cassidy. When Kurt Russell played "Elvis," he is almost spooky how he "channeled" Elvis and it felt like he was Elvis. Kurt Russell would be "amazing" to play Paul Newman's character, Butch Cassidy. I think Paul would like that. I sure would!

Angelina Jolie would be just "awesome" to play Etta Place. She is so gorgeous and elegant, but she could be one "tough cookie" that robs banks with the boys. Her father Jon Voight could play her father on the Bassett Ranch in Browns Park. Heck, Angelina, Brad, Jon, and all the kids could all be on set. Remember Robert Redford's line when they were robbing a train and the conductor came out to stare? Sundance says, "What are you doing?" The conductor says, "Just thought I'd watch". Then Sundance said, "Bring the kids why don't ya?" Now I am just having so much fun! I am laughing out loud. Oh my, I love show business! Not going to happen, in light of recent events… Oh my!

Katharine Ross starred as "Etta Place" in the original movie and we could just make Katharine look younger or older. That is always an option. I love how they aged Brad Pitt in the "Benjamin Button" movie. Sam Elliott, acted in the original movie, and as many actors that were in the first movie could do an encore performance for the continuing story of "Butch Cassidy & The Sundance Kid."

We just must invite Tom Selleck to be in the new movie because he is so darn handsome. We will figure out what part he will play later. Maybe he could play Matt Warner who murdered Sundance?

WHAT A FUN SET!

## Your Words Create Your World!

My coach back in New York, Tracy, really worked with me to watch what I say and to not complain about "anything!" She would say, "Your words create your world, watch what you say." I have taken that to heart and I keep myself so busy, I do not have time to complain. I asked the question, "If they didn't die in Bolivia, where did they go?" I found all three outlaws and their true identities. My words and work created the new movie on "Butch Cassidy & The Sundance Kid." Wouldn't it be great if all the stars I just mentioned were hired for the new movie!

I remember talking to our Cruise Director, Randy Hobday about joining him on CRUISING ALASKA WITH COLLIN RAYE. Randy said to come on the cruise and he would create a cruise for our company. His words became reality and we now have our own UNSOLVED MYSTERY CRUISE and WILD BUNCH CRUISE!

## Family

Yvonne Martinez and Betty Bird, sisters, now have a genealogy chart with family names and pictures of their ancestors, where they had nothing before. Bill Long did not have any family and their genealogy line stopped. Now they have Harry Alonzo, Alonzo, Lewis and the entire line back to the Langenbacher's of Bavaria, Germany.

The really great news is that a family member came forward with the story that explains the mystery.

## The Ending Is Just The Beginning"

I had a call from the last of the living females of Julia Ann Taylor and Alonzo Long/Longabaugh. Julia and Alonzo are buried in the Haines Cemetery in Oregon. I talked to the great granddaughter for 3 hours on Thursday. She was so generous with her time to explain the family stories. (She wishes to remain anonymous.)

Tim Kupherschmid at Sorenson Forensics, head of the DNA Lab in Salt Lake City, Utah sent us the DNA profile for the living female of Julia Ann Taylor. Julia is not the mother of William Henry Long, but Alonzo is the father.

The family stories of William Henry Long and Alonzo Long's family helps explain what happened to "The Sundance Kid."

The living female and I went through every relative in her genealogy to see if anyone else could have been the father of William Henry Long/Longabaugh. Only Alonzo could have been William Henry Long's father. The dates all line up perfectly for Alonzo and Harry Alonzo.

The family story of the Long family is rather complicated, but I will do my best to explain the details.

There are only 2 living females left and we have their DNA profiles at Sorenson Forensics.

We cannot possibly know the details in Alonzo's life, but we can fill in the blanks when Alonzo Long fathered Harry Alonzo Longabaugh, "The Sundance Kid." The story does give us an idea of what happened to Alonzo from 1866 to 1867 – when the Sundance Kid is conceived and born.

## Rite of Passage to Manhood

Imagine that Alonzo is 19 when he went on a hunting trip with his father Lewis in 1866 to possibly the Big Horn Basin of Wyoming? The Big Horn Basin of Wyoming is Indian Territory, but there were mines and pioneers coming to Wyoming in 1866-67. The Long female descendant believes that Lewis Long took his son Alonzo on a "rite of passage to manhood" and explained the family story and all the details.

## Mormon Pioneer Story

The Hans Peter Olsen Company of Mormon Pioneers passed through the area in 1851. An Indian stole a cow and Hans demanded that the Indians return the cow.

The Indians offered a horse for the cow. Hans refused the horse that was now more valuable, but Hans would have none of it. A battle took place and Hans and his men were killed. Hans is "dead right."

## Big Horn Basin of Wyoming

The Hans Peter Olsen Company of Mormon Pioneers is an example story that shows there were white settlers in the area at the time and Alonzo may have traveled with his father Lewis to the Big Horn Basin of Wyoming?

The history of the Big Horn Basin of Wyoming is bloody, and the Indians were treated badly, to say the least.

Alonzo and his father Lewis Long went on a hunting trip in 1866. The family lived in Linn, Oregon.

A Long family member, (do not have permission to use his name and lives in Haines, Oregon) said that he owns the rifle that Lewis and Alonzo took on the hunting trip. He told me this story.

Lewis wanted to take his son on a trip as a possible "rite of passage to manhood." Father and son are alone in the wilderness on a hunting trip. Alonzo Long is 19 years old at the time.

Lewis is an abusive father and a prominent rancher in Linn, Oregon. He owned a large ranch and ruled his wife and 6 children with fear.

On the hunting trip, Alonzo saw an Indian in the distance and Lewis pressured him to kill the Indian for sport. Lewis bullied Alonzo into killing the Indian as if he were like any other animal. The Long male family member said that when he inherited the rifle of Alonzo Long, the family told him the story about Alonzo's rifle that he used to kill the innocent Indian.

The living female said that all we can do is guess and fill in the blanks to Alonzo's life.

The Long family members are not proud of the family story about Alonzo killing an Indian for sport, but they wanted me to know the truth. We all have skeletons in our closets that we do not want the world to know about, but what a story I have captured. I am so grateful for the family member that wanted the truth to be told.

The female Long family member suggested that since the trip was a "rite of passage to manhood," in 1866, and Lewis pressured Alonzo to kill an Indian, it is possible that his father Lewis may have pressured Alonzo to have his first sexual experience.

Alonzo fathered Harry Alonzo Long/Longabaugh, "The Sundance Kid," in 1866 and the female descendant told me the story about Lewis, Alonzo's abusive father. She felt that at least Alonzo took responsibility for the child and named him Harry Alonzo, his name sake. Alonzo gave his son to his cousin Josiah Longabaugh in Mont Clare, Pennsylvania. Josiah is a cousin to Alonzo Long/Longabaugh and Josiah and Annie Longabaugh raised Harry Alonzo Long/Longabaugh as their adopted son. They took in a relative, a "cousin."

Story Teller Productions submitted seven DNA Kits to Sorenson Forensics and Tim Kupherschmid, the head of the DNA Lab. Tim processed all our DNA samples. We have every line of Long/Longabaugh/Longenbaugh family members giving us their DNA, as well as Julia Ann Taylor's living female descendant. We started with the Conrad and Baltzer line and helped the family prove that Conrad and Baltzer were not father and son, but two separate lines. We have DNA samples from George Junior and Senior Longabaugh, Jay Langebach, Robert Longenbaugh, the two female descendants of Julia Ann Taylor, (want to remain anonymous, and another male that wants to remain anonymous). We also have proven our case with DNA and DNA Genealogy. The most important DNA is Harry Alonzo, and Alonzo Long's "0" distance. FATHER AND SON! Alonzo's DNA profile is an EXACT MATCH to Harry Alonzo's DNA profile. The age is the right age and there are no other males but Alonzo that matches Harry Alonzo. The only reason we solved the DNA Mystery was with the help of Yvonne Martinez and her detective work on YSearch.com. (Yvonne Martinez is the great granddaughter of William Henry Long. She wanted to have a family tree and Yvonne helped solve the case.) I took over and handed Yvonne her family tree with the Long Family Genealogy Chart. Harry Alonzo, Alonzo, Lewis and so on. . .

The reason Annie Place Longabaugh had all her children's birthdays listed in her family bible with the day month and year, and she only wrote "about spring of 1867" by Harry Alonzo, is because he is adopted. Josiah and Harry Alonzo were "cousins."

The female descendant found census records for Alonzo Long in Illinois, Oregon and Pennsylvania. She became ill before she could mail the records off to me. She is so ill; we need to leave her alone. We will do our own search later.

I saw the Alonzo Long census record that has Alonzo in Illinois before 7 years old and we will search for the Alonzo Long census record in Pennsylvania. There are also census records for Alonzo Long in Oregon that I have copies of.

The living female felt that Lewis may have arranged for Alonzo's first sexual experience and a woman became pregnant. The mother of Harry Alonzo Longabaugh is Eastern European and the Harry is born in the spring of 1867, Harry Alonzo Long/Longabaugh.

Tim Kupherschmid read the DNA profile for William Henry Long's mother's DNA for me and said that she is Eastern European, not Indian. She is German, Italian, or Russian. She is the same nationality as Harry Alonzo. That solves that "mystery." We have not been able to find the mother and suspect that the mother had no female descendants or we would have found them on the Internet and on the data base for females. It is most likely that she did die in childbirth. We would have to throw a lot of money towards finding Sundance's mother with DNA Genealogy, but it is possible.

The descendant said that at least Alonzo took responsibility for the child and gave him a home with a cousin and named him Harry Alonzo Long/Longabaugh. Note that none of Alonzo's children are named Alonzo.

"The Sundance Kid" appears in Mont Clare, Pennsylvania in the "spring of 1867." Josiah and Ann Place Longabaugh adopt Alonzo's son, Harry Alonzo.

Lewis Long is a prominent rancher in Linn, Oregon and Alonzo is not married and had a son at age 20, Harry Alonzo Long/Longabaugh. William Henry Long's photo matches Harry Alonzo Longabaugh, and William Henry Long's DNA matches Alonzo Long.

## Julia Ann

Two years after the birth of Harry Alonzo, Alonzo courts and marries 16-year-old Julia Ann Taylor. They were the parents of 15 children and 10 lived to be adults.

Alonzo hated his father Lewis and he and Julia Ann moved as far away as possible from Lewis, his father. They claimed 600 acres in Haines, Baker County, Oregon under the Homestead Act. Julia could own 300 acres and Alonzo also claimed 300 acres.

Alonzo did not visit his father for 26 years, until he was dying. I can only imagine the scene between the two men. Alonzo is very successful and had a very large family. To hate his father so much that Lewis never ever visited him and he never sees any of Alonzo's children is just unthinkable. Something awful must have happened.

Wow! What a remarkable story that will help us fill in the blanks as to what happened to Harry Alonzo Longabaugh, "The Sundance Kid."

## Long Family

Thanks to all the Long Family members that helped me with an ending to our 20 years of research.

We will keep looking for the mother of "The Sundance Kid" but unless a living descendant has donated their DNA, we may never find her.

An Oregon Long family member went on a search for the living relatives of Alonzo Long. DNA kits were passed out to the male descendants. Without the living, DNA and a family member sending out DNA kits, and posting the DNA profile on YSearch.com, we never could have solved the whole mystery. I hope to find the person that sent out the DNA kits in the future so I can thank them. What a story!

## NO ONE HAS BEEN ABLE TO PROVE ME WRONG! NO ONE!

DNA Genealogy at YSearch.com helped us find William Henry Long, an alias for Harry Alonzo Longabaugh, "The Sundance Kid."

Our research has been out for two years and many folks have tried to discredit our findings. I have even been threatened by one Long family member in Oregon that said, "You only have a 50/50 chance of being right. I will not allow you to use my great grandfather, Alonzo's, picture in your book."

It is understandable that you would not want the reputation of your great grandfather, Alonzo Long, to be under attack, but DNA does not lie. There is nothing I can do about Alonzo being the father to Harry Alonzo Longabaugh, "The Sundance Kid." How could I possible make all of this up, the clues and evidence lead us to Alonzo, the father of Harry Alonzo, they are father and son with a DNA match that is exact.

You cannot threaten someone for telling the "truth" and expect to win. This is all public information and we have the family photos and comparisons that show Alonzo as Harry Alonzo's father. We have a right to publish his picture because it is posted on the Internet.

This individual has not been able to disprove that Harry Alonzo is the son of Alonzo Long, because the DNA is an exact match. The "0" distant will always be father and son. All the piece's match! We have done our homework.

Because of the opposition from several individuals, I worked even harder to do seven DNA samples to prove our case. Sometimes your enemies are good for you. Sometimes!

## Alonzo Long

Alonzo Long left a legacy as a wonderful father and husband to his family. All the Oregon Long family members love it that they are related to "The Sundance Kid" and only one is upset. What can you do? I am a historical researcher just doing my job.

Thanks to all the Long family members in Haines, Baker County, Oregon and Albany, Oregon that helped with family stories, genealogy and female DNA for Julia Ann Taylor.

When the female descendant that helped with the stories and I worked with for a total of 4 hours, understood and it became clear that the Long family has the exact DNA as William Henry Long, how else could we have found them. The trail of evidence leads to the Long Family and Harry Alonzo Longabugh, "The Sundance Kid." They Are Family!

There are Long family members of Haynes and Linn, Oregon that are excited to add "The Sundance Kid" to their family tree. I have informed Yvonne Martinez and Betty Bird about their new-found relatives and they have called and visited together. FUN!

Thank you, Morrell, Long, Longabaugh, Longenbaugh family members for all your help! So grateful!

## "NEW MOVIE ON BUTCH & SUNDANCE"

What an exciting story I have captured for the new movie. Richard Zanuck knew the truth about "Butch Cassidy, The Sundance Kid, and Etta Place" before he passed away. Richard Zanuck produced "Butch Cassidy & The Sundance Kid" in 1969. I traveled to his Hollywood Mansion in October of 2011 and handed two copies of our books to Mr. Zanuck's personal assistant. His assistant explained that Mr. Zanuck is planning on doing a new movie with our Story Teller Productions TEAM. I screamed with joy all the way home to St. George, Utah. Then he passed away in July of 2012. Mr. Zanuck said that I am an incredible researcher. That makes me very happy. It is so wonderful that I could tell Mr. Zanuck the truth about Butch, Sundance, and Etta.

How I cried when Mr. Zanuck passed away, but I learned a valuable lesson in life, "Be Happy No Matter What!" I made myself sick to think that we had a movie deal with the same producer that produced "Butch Cassidy & The Sundance Kid" 40 plus years ago, then he dies. Because of my experience with his passing, I can truly see that "God Has a Plan!" Look how far we have come and we now have 7 "MAJOR" book and movie deals in the works. Not bad for a girl from Clearfield, Utah.

When I saw the movie, "Get Low" produced by Dean Zanuck, Richard Zanuck's son, I drove to Dean's Beverly Hills mansion after I attended a "COLLIN RAYE CONCERT" at Canyon Lake, California on April 2, 2016. (Remember, Collin Raye and B.J. Thomas will sing songs for our new movie on Butch and Sundance. I planned on going to Beverly Hills and Dean Zanuck's offices, when I saw Collin Raye would be performing close by. FUN CONCERT AND A HAPPY MEMORY.) When I came home to St. George, Utah I called Mr. Zanuck's office to make sure he received our four books, and the exact same assistant, Bert, answered the phone and he remembered me from October of 2011 and I remembered him. Bert let me know that they had received my books and he would help me with getting the information to Dean Zanuck. SWEET! I WOULD LOVE TO WORK WITH DEAN ZANUCK, and Dean would carry on the family legacy. Papa Zanuck would be proud of his son Dean. I have such an AMAZING LIFE!

Paul Newman passed away before he knew the truth and I cried when he died. Such a good man and I feel like I cannot work fast enough to get this information out to the public.

Katharine Ross, her husband Sam Elliott, each have a copy of "FINDING BUTCH CASSIDY & THE SUNDANCE KID." Katharine Ross sent me a lovey letter congratulating me on finding Butch and Sundance. She said that my book is very well organized and researched. She wished me well. Katharine and Sam now know about Butch, Sundance and Etta Place. I love it... Robert Redford is next to let him know that we have found Butch, Sundance, and Etta. It is wonderful that B.J. Thomas has our book and research. Everyone is getting old! It is important to me to give everyone our research!

Now that I am wrapping up this book, "Finding 'Butch Cassidy & The Sundance Kid' ~ Solving The 'Wild Bunch' Mystery With That 'Darn' DNA," it is my hope that Robert Redford, "The Sundance Kid," will be able to read all of our research soon. My attorney Lowry Snow just knows that Robert Redford will be thrilled to know the truth about the historical character that launched his career. Robert Redford named his resort... "SUNDANCE" because of his role in the movie. Robert Redford is "The Sundance Kid!"

## UNSOLVED MYSTERY CRUISE & WILD BUNCH CRUISE

I asked to meet "Country Western Star Collin Raye" December 15, 2012 at Ruby's Inn, just outside of Bryce Canyon, Utah. Jean Seiler, the owner kindly arranged the meeting for me. Jean carried our books at his resort and I let Jean know that I wanted Collin to sing the songs for our new movie. After the concert, I went back stage with my business partners and we met Collin. Collin is just perfect to sing the music for the new movie, "Finding Butch Cassidy & The Sundance Kid."

Collin loved our books and agreed to do the music for our new movie. Collin picked me up around the waist three times and kissed me on the head three time. He said, "God Bless You! You Found Butch Cassidy and the Sundance Kid." I will never forget that meeting and I am amazed at the chain of events that have happened since. We talked about "Hitler" and I told him about my research. Collin said, "Get me a copy!" If Collin had not asked for a copy, the "Hitler" story may still be in my files.

Then a month after I met Collin Raye, I send him the first copy of, "Hitler Escapes To America." Now he also has "Amelia Earhart, Mystery Solved" and "SCREAM BLOODY MURDER, The Truth about the Life and Death of Marilyn Monroe," as well as, "JFK ASSASINATION, Mystery Solved." Not a bad collection!

On March 4, 2015, I saw that Collin Raye and B.J. Thomas, (Famous for singing, RAINDROPS KEEP FALLING ON MY HEAD, from the original, "Butch Cassidy & The Sundance Kid" movie) would sing together in Pocatello, Idaho. I bought tickets at the last minute and could not get into the MEET AND GREET. Collin and B.J. came out on stage and I am so embarrassed when B.J. Thomas said, "There is a person that sent me an e-mail saying that they did not think that I am still living." The whole audience laughed! That would be me. . . I truly did not think to look up information on B.J. Thomas and I did send his agent an e-mail apologizing. I truly didn't know that he is still singing so beautifully. Collin Raye and B.J. Thomas did a FANTASTIC JOB of entertaining all of us.

B.J. told a story about Burt Bacharach and how he went to see Burt at his Malibu home to record RAINDROPS KEEP FALLING ON MY HEAD. B.J. said that those were his drinking days, and he is given instructions on how to get to Burt's home in Malibu, California. He arrives at Bert's home and pushes a code. He is three hours late because he had been drinking. He pushed the button and the garage door opens. Angie Dickenson, Burt's wife at the time, is in the garage. B.J. explained that he is there to rehearse with Burt. Angie yelled to Burt, "Burt honey, your little friend is here!" The whole audience laughed.

Collin Raye said, "Never in my wildest dreams did he ever think he would be singing with B.J. Thomas."

Collin Raye sang his famous song, THAT'S MY STORY and B.J. wowed us with RAINDROPS KEEP FALLING ON MY HEAD. Man, am I a blessed!

Right before the concert started, I hand security my first hand written draft of my newest book, "THE ASSASINATION OF JOHN FITZGERALD KENNEDY, *Mystery Solved.*" The security guard kindly delivered my newest book to Collin. Then at the end of the show I gave security, "FINDING BUTCH CASSIDY & THE SUNDANCE KID," for B.J. Thomas. B.J. Thomas now has our photo transparencies and our book.

Collin Raye and B.J. Thomas at the end of the concert had their arms around each other and they were BUDDIES! I am touched by their affection for each other. When I came back home to St. George, I immediately contacted Collin Raye and B.J. Thomas's agent and offered to have Collin and B.J. sing a song for our new movie. How could I not include this amazing talent to join us and to sing with Collin Raye?

They sang again in Florida a few days later, and Collin said that they were doing a third event together. I knew that Collin is talking about our WILD BUNCH CRUISE to the Western Caribbean with our Cruise Director Randy Hobday. We are working on booking Collin and B.J. for a future event, but everyone's schedules will have to come together, so we will just have to wait and see. We will be on Norwegian Cruise Lines, THE GETAWAY! I LOVE THAT SHIP! THE BEST IN THE WORLD AND I KNOW THE CAPTAIN! I had my own UNSOLVED MYSTERY on January 17, 2015 to the Eastern Caribbean.

B.J. asked Collin, during the standing ovation, if the lady with the long blonde hair that is holding a book is the person that found Butch and Sundance. Collin said, "Yes!" At least B.J. Thomas knows what I look like and he has our research.

I look forward to meeting B.J. Thomas in person when we make the new movie.

Was it God's Grace that brought all of us together? I would like to think so! I had the best time of my life and I came home and wrote EVERYTHING down in my journal. My life is like a MOVIE! COLLIN RAYE AND B.J. THOMAS IN CONCERT! WOW!

I will keep my promise and when I produce the new movie with my publicist Brian Mayes, Collin Raye will write and sing the song for our new movie. *Sweet!* Collin Raye and B.J. Thomas will sing a song together. We will make music history!

Collin Raye is a talented song writer as well as a performer. "She's With Me" is the song Collin wrote for his granddaughter Hayley Bell, who passed away. I saw Collin in concert in Seattle, and the song made me cry. I would like Collin Raye to sing and write a song for Luzernia and Bill Long's two girls, Florence Viola and Evinda Ann. They did not see their father for 8 to 10 years, because he is on the run.

I know this story coming and going and I felt inspired to invite Collin to sing the music for the new movie and look at all the wonderful things that have happened.

I went on Collin Raye's website and saw that he had a CRUISING ALASKA WITH COLLIN RAYE. The cruise sailed from Seattle on August 31, to September 7th, 2013. When I inquired about the cruise with Cruise Director Randy Hobday, Randy said to come on board and he would create a cruise for me and our company.

If I had not met Collin Raye at Ruby's Inn, and if I had not attended his AMAZING CRUISE, we would not have our own cruise. Story Teller Productions had our own cruise, THE UNSOLVED MYSTERY CRUISE! We sailed on January 17, 2015. We went to the Eastern Caribbean and I gave a lecture to our group and even met the Captain of the Floating Hotel. Captain Sir Sean and I talked about telling stories about our books on board ship. We will always be grateful for Collin's involvement that created our own cruise. Thank You Collin Raye!

Next year on our cruise, our whole company will be there along with many fans and family members. Randy Hobday is asking for more time to set up the website and get all our ducks in a row.

Brent Ashworth will be our special guest and he will bring his collection of Butch Cassidy and Sundance Kid documents as well as Hitler, Amelia Earhart, Marilyn Monroe, Joe DiMaggio, JFK and if I ask real nice, Elvis photos and the shirt he wore in "Jailhouse Rock."

Dr. John McCullough will talk about the science and photo transparencies that he completed for Sundance, Butch, Etta, Alonzo and Harry Alonzo. John and I have been partners since 2007. It will be amazing to be with him on board the Norwegian Getaway! We will post the exact dates on our website at www.sundancekiddna.com .

What fun to have a "Wild Bunch" Costume Party and then we will watch the original movie "Butch Cassidy & The Sundance Kid," and celebrate our AMAZING discovery! I will talk about all our books.

On the last night on a Friday, we will have a "TRIBUTE TO HOLLYWOOD" and have our next book on Marilyn Monroe ready for a release. Then Collin Raye & B.J. Thomas will entertain us once we schedule them. We would like Collin and B.J. to sing all the old songs from the movies. We will dance the night away and I will come as Marilyn Monroe and Randy Hobday is thinking about coming as Charlie Chaplin. I would really like Collin Raye to do his "Elvis" impersonation. He can sing just like Elvis! WHAT FUN!

When Randy Hobday our Cruise Director and I were talking about what songs Collin Raye, and B.J. Thomas would sing at our, TRIBUTE TO HOLLYWOOD COSUTME PARTY, we laughed that we may not want them to sing the theme song from the movie, TITANIC. Randy said it would be like watching an airplane disaster movie on board a flight across the ocean. We are a FUN GROUP!

Life could not possibly get any better. We will go on a different cruise every year and "travel the world!" Please come join us! Go to...

www.sundancekiddna.com, or on Facebook and type in Marilyn Grace for more information. There is a video of our FANTASTIC SHIP, "The Getaway." THE SHIP IS THE STAR! I have never had so much fun in my life! The fastest water slide in the world and the ship is designed to not move. I am almost sea sick on CRUISING ALSAKA WITH COLLIN RAYE, but THE GETAWAY is designed to have very little movement. There are 16 stories of absolute luxury! There are FIREWORKS GUYS! Many folks I met on CRUISING ALASKA WITH COLLIN RAYE will be on board the WILD BUNCH CRUISE. Please Come Join Us! You will have the TIME OF YOUR LIFE!

## They did not die in Bolivia!

Butch, Sundance, and Etta did escape from South America and they went to Paris, France. Butch Cassidy could not return to the United States with his square jawline or he would be captured. He had a face lift.

Sundance went back to his wife and two girls in Loa, Utah. Then in 1917 he went to Fish Lake, Utah on a trip and came back with enough "gold coins" to pay cash for the ranch in Duchesne.

The Sundance Kid is murdered by Matt Warner in 1937, a member of his own "Wild Bunch" Gang. There is no honor among thieves. Brent Ashworth owns Matt Warner's hand written manuscript, "Last of the Bandit Riders." Matt and Bill Long had heated arguments about not writing a book about Matt's outlaw life in 1936. The family heard the fights and Betty Bird's mother Eva, always suspected that Matt Warner killed Bill Long.

Dr. McCullough discovers the truth about his death when we examined the skull. Bill is shot with a 22 rifle from 2 to 3 feet away and he is murdered. The family quickly buried him and put "suicide" on the death certificate. An awful way to die when you have changed your life and you are living the life of a family man, then it is over. The past caught up with William Henry Long, an alias for Harry Alonzo Longabaugh, "The Sundance Kid."

There were 3 Etta's that Butch and Sundance would switch to protect Ann Bassett. She was just as wanted as Butch and Sundance and they tricked the law by trading different women and calling her "Etta Place." Etta Place is an exact match to Ann Bassett in the New York City, "Wedding Photo" with "The Sundance Kid." The transparencies are perfect for Ann Bassett and Etta Place.

## It's a Wrap

It was 1997 when I first saw the documentary, "Wanted Butch and Sundance." Clyde Snow, an anthropologist for the University of Oklahoma, exhumed two bodies that were thought to be "Butch Cassidy & The Sundance Kid." Mr. Snow and his Team exhumed two bodies in Bolivia. The DNA did not match and I had the thought, "Where did they go?"

It has taken me 20 years to bring all the puzzle pieces together. What a wild ride I have been on and it is just the beginning. I will finish up our other books on "Hitler," "Amelia Earhart," "Marilyn Monroe" and "JFK," before we sail off to the Western Caribbean on our WILD BUNCH CRUISE!

More stories and more research to be completed, but "I Just Love The Movies!" I would not have it any other way. I cannot wait to be on the set of the new movie for "Butch Cassidy & The Sundance Kid." The ending in the 1969 movie is just all wrong! We will tell the continuing story.

## CREATIVE EXECUTIVE PRODUCER

My job as Creative Executive Producer at Story Teller Productions is to move the project along to completion. My journal has helped me keep all the facts and stories alive so we can remake the movie for everyone to enjoy. Many folks have called me "The Mastermind," and I am flattered.

It has not been a "bed of roses" by any means. I vividly remember one man literally screaming in my face, "Give it up, Butch and Sundance died in Bolivia!" He was my neighbor in 2008 and we just exhumed the body of William Henry Long in the Duchesne City Cemetery. He saw me on KSL 5 News with John Hollenhorst and with Dr. McCullough; he apologized when he saw the photo transparencies come together of William Henry Long and "The Sundance Kid." At least he apologized.

Finding Butch and Sundance led to solving Hitler, Amelia Earhart, Marilyn Monroe's murder, and the JFK assassination with "science." You solve one "Major" Mystery, why not solve them ALL! What I do is find the SCIENCE that proves my case. What I really don't like is "Conspiracy Theories." I must have documentation and science or I will not invest my time in a project. After our cruise, I will write another book on JFK's assassination.

## WILLIAM GOLDMAN

William Goldman wrote the screenplay for "Butch Cassidy & The Sundance Kid" in 1967 and Richard Zanuck bought the rights to make the movie for 400 thousand dollars for Fox Studios. That was the most money ever paid for a screenplay at the time and Mr. Zanuck could have been fired.

Mr. Goldman is still alive and well living in New York City and he goes to a matinee movie every day. He also wrote one of my favorite movies, "The Princess Bride." He wrote the story for his 2 young daughters. Who doesn't love, "The Princess Bride?" I can only dream that he would be willing to do the screenplay. Wouldn't that be something? I have given him all the material he could possibly need. The movie, "The Man from Snowy River" is a poem that the producers made into two "Blockbuster Hits" in Australia. How could William Goldman go wrong with all the information I have gathered.

My favorite scene for our new movie on Butch and Sundance would be "The Lone Tree Dance." "The Sundance Kid" is handcuffed to the "dead" outlaw and he plays the fiddle for the Thanksgiving Day dance. He escapes and the Pinkerton Detective is accidentally killed and the town covers up his death by placing "Harry Alonzo" on the tomb stone. Now that is a GREAT scene for the new movie. Why not "dream" of Mr. Goldman writing the new screenplay?

## MY MOVIE BACKGROUND

From 1983 to 1985, I lived in Hollywood and worked in Beverly Hills doing hair and make-up for the public and may movie stars. I am hired as assistant to the President of the Aida Grey Salon. Aida Grey was in her early 90's when I went to work for her as her assistant. She owned an 11-million-dollar salon and cosmetic company. Her salon was on Rodeo Drive and Wilshire Boulevard, right across the street from the Beverly Wilshire Hotel.

Some of my clients were Beverly Sills, Diahann Carroll, Marilyn McCoo, Gloria Loring and many soap opera stars. I will never forget Tina Sinatra, Frank Sinatra's daughter, bringing her daughter into the salon for her very first make-up lesson. This young girl did not understand why everyone made such a fuss over her, and I am there to teach her how to put on makeup. What a great memory.

My career was wonderful, but my marriage ended and I came back to Utah and worked for the Utah Film Commission. It was in 1997 that "Air Supply" hired me to do their album cover. What fun to run around on their thousand-acre ranch outside of Park City, Utah and do their hair and make-up! I have all the photos that we took that day and they are in my portfolio.

Back in 1976, I went to the movies by myself because I needed to get away. I am a working mother putting my then husband through school at Brigham Young University. Going to the movies that day is something that I really wanted to do. I am worn out and needed some "me time." The movie I paid to see happened to be, "The Adventures of The Wilderness Family." The film had been made for 405 thousand and made 64 million the first year. I just knew that I wanted to be a part of such a great "Family Film." I convinced my husband to go to Medford, Oregon and apply for a job with Pacific International Enterprises.

With the success of "The Adventures of The Wilderness Family," nick named, "The Rocky of 'G' Family Films," it was easy to be hired on the spot and we moved our family with two small children to Medford, Oregon. My role is to support my husband because I had two small children at home. My husband helped put together Pacific International Enterprise's next project, "Across The Great Divide" starring Robert Logan. That film is made for about one million and made 42 million the first year.

Then my husband and I had read the book, "Windwalker." The author is Blaine Jorgensen and we recommended to the president that he could make the book into a great movie. The film starring Trevor Howard is a HUGE HIT! The film is made for about one million and made 200 million dollars the first year. The excitement in the company is OVER THE TOP! One idea for a movie made Independent Film History! The problem is, the film made so much money that the producer became greedy and cut us all out. We lost our jobs and ended up moving back to Provo, Utah with my mother. It was devastating!

I went back to school to be a hair and make-up artists, but I wanted to be back in show business.

How could I forget flying into Salt Lake City, Utah to premier "Across The Great Divide." We rented a limo for the two young stars and stayed at the Hotel Utah, now "The Joseph Smith Memorial Building." We had a catered dinner and we were able to rent Trolley Theatres and premier "Across The Great Divide." We had a packed audience of 500 folks when we announced the movie. "We hope you enjoy the show!"

All I ever wanted to do is make my own movies. I got it! The "Big Aha" was, only the President gets to collect the money. I remember the "Brinks" trucks bringing in the bags of cash from the movie theatres for "Windwalker." Back then they rented the movie theatres and collected the money. We did not have a distributor the way they do today.

Being single and raising my third child on my own and living with my mother in Provo, Utah was not the life I thought I would have. When I saw the documentary "Wanted: Butch and Sundance," a Nova Documentary with anthropologist Clyde Snow, and the DNA did not match Butch and Sundance, I remember saying out loud, "Where did they go?"

For 20 years I have been on their trail and I am just now combining our two books on "Sundance," into "Finding Butch Cassidy & The Sundance Kid ~ Solving The 'Wild Bunch' Mystery With That 'Darn' DNA." That is a long time to stay on task and get the project completed, but I did it with the help of my Story Teller Productions TEAM!

### "Connected To Heaven"

When my former husband and I were in show business, we stopped going to church as a family and everything fell apart. When my marriage ended in 1989 and I am a single mother, I went running back to church. I call myself a "Born Again Mormon." My membership in the church has helped me in so many ways. My family and being a temple worker in the Los Angeles, San Diego, Provo, Salt Lake City, and St. George Temples, has helped me accomplished so much. Do not ever underestimate staying on the "straight and narrow path" that helps you finish your work on the earth. Having a connection to "Heaven" is the ONLY reason I have been able to succeed.

I love what Denzel Washington said about putting your shoes way underneath the bed at night so you "have too" get on your knees in the morning to pray. I am on my knees every morning asking for "guidance from above!" I need lots of help so I can complete our projects. I truly believe that I have accepted the "call" to solve the mysteries and tell the truth. The Lord doesn't like lies.

When you are striving to be good, you know when you are off track. Never again do I want to be "lost" like I was when I lived and worked in "Hollywood." I became an alcoholic because I am sad about my divorce and the loss of my family. I have paid the price and have gone through rehabilitation. For 45 days, I would sweat in a sauna and receive counseling that helped me to achieve a complete recovery. Since 1990 I have been drug and alcohol free. Many times, I have said that Hollywood chewed me up and spit me out, and I went running back to Utah, my church, and my Savior Jesus Christ.

Now I live in St. George, Utah that is just a half an hour away from the Nevada border. The weather and people are just wonderful! Yes... it gets "hot" in the summer time, but it is better than 9 months of snow.

My son Sterling and his wife Mindy, along with my beautiful granddaughters, live an hour away. Many people have said that I have the "best job in the world" and they are right! Researching "Mysteries" and writing books, making movies, is what I love to do. Being with my family on top of that is "Heaven On Earth!"

Brent Ashworth and my mother June knew each other in Provo, Utah many years ago. Brent lost his precious son when he was riding his bike as a child and my mother June is one of the first to be on the scene. I did not know Brent Ashworth when my mother was alive, but Brent said that my mother is VERY SPECIAL! She was! She loved people and Brent said that June took care of their family and loved them when their son passed. How AMAZING that Brent Ashworth is helping me with ALL our books and is giving me permission to take photographs of all of his extensive collection.

My mother June is in her "Heavenly Home" with Brent's boy and Brent is helping me with my work. What a joyous reunion, when we all meet again at Jesus feet.

## CHANGE

Monty Roberts's book, "HORSE SENSE FOR PEOPLE" has changed me forever! The last chapter CHANGE explains the power of being "gentle." "Slow Is Fast" has made an ENOROMOUS difference in my life. Monty teaches you to be an observer of your life and to keep your "adrenaline down" and "learning up." If you want to change your life for the better, I HIGHLY recommend you buying a copy your library, "HORSE SENSE FOR PEOPLE."

Several years ago, I had the privilege of going to Monty Robert's "Flag Is Up Ranch" in Solvang, California. I wanted to ask Monty to share his diet secrets with me and write another book, "The Real Horse Whisperers Diet." Debbie his CEO and daughter arranged for me to meet Monty. What a thrill to spend 6 hours with Monty and Debbie filming a young girl learning how to ride for the 30th Anniversary of The Queen of England's visit. Monty was summoned by The Queen of England 30 years ago to teach her and her staff how to be "Horse Whisperers."

At the end of the 6 hours of filming, Monty left and Debbie his daughter and I went into the office to talk about my idea for another book. I handed Debbie two copies of "Finding The Sundance Kid." We had the scientific evidence for Butch, Sundance, and Etta. Debbie said that her father would love it that I solved the Wild Bunch Mystery. I left and I am back to work and had no idea so many things would happen since meeting with Monty and Debbie at their ranch. We have come so far and I will finish up all our other projects and I will contact Debbie and Monty Robert's again for another very important book.

When I met Debbie and Monty in 2012, I had no idea that I would find DNA Genealogy for William Henry Long and solve the DNA mystery. Then on top of that I am handed Hitler, and solve Amelia Earhart Mystery, find Marilyn Monroe's murderer and JFK's murderer with science. I will finish the book on how Monty Roberts and his whole family stay so healthy and active with their special diet after our cruise. Monty has developed nutritional products for horses, why not for people. I really want to know how Monty, his wife Pat, Debbie and the rest of his family and friends stay so active and young. I hope Monty accepts the "call" to share his diet secrets! I know that I am passionate about writing another book on his diet secrets.

# LOVE

Let's say that I tell the whole truth and nothing but the truth about what motivated me to find "Butch Cassidy & The Sundance Kid." It's time to share the story behind the story. It does not serve anyone to keep this my secret.

There is more to my story and if you will bear with me, I will explain how sometimes life just throws you more than you can handle. Remember I am living with my mother in Provo, Utah with my then 16-year-old son. My mother is elderly and needed care. My divorce was not good and my daughter joined an organization in Hollywood that would not let me talk to her unless I gave them 100 thousand dollars. How on earth could I come up with that kind of money? My mother gave me a thousand dollars and I sent it to her organization and I insisted on a receipt. They never sent me one. I could tell I would have to think "outside of the box" to be able to be with my only daughter.

The real reason I went back into show business was to be with my daughter. How could I pull out of the situation and get my child home safely?

My mind went to work on how I could earn 100 thousand dollars. The only thing that clicked was, "I need another movie like WINDWALKER." That made 200 million in one year, and I would need to be the producer and start my own company. It's my suggestion that the book "Windwalker" could be made into a movie. My former husband who worked for Pacific International Enterprises, told the President about "Windwalker" and the rest is motion picture history. I needed to be the President and collect the money this time around!

Time has flown by and my daughter and I have reconnected. My daughter and her lovely husband spent Mother's Day together of this year, 2014. The money demands turned out to be a mistake and everything has been cleared up with her company. What a JOY to be back with my precious daughter. Life has put me through some tough life circumstances, but I completely trust that God has a plan for me. My trials have made me a better person and I did rise and became President of my own production company.

The truth is, LOVE is the reason I went back into show business. I love my daughter and I would have done anything to get her back. Love is why I will always be in the book and motion picture business. I love my family, my friends and members of Story Teller Productions. Oh, and I love the MOVIES!

## Hey Mr. Producer, spend a little time with me!

Richard Zanuck is in his "heavenly home" now. He did so many wonderful movies, "The Sound of Music," "Jaws," "Driving Miss Daisy," "Yes Man" with Jim Carrey, "Wonderland" with Johnny Depp, and more. I have thought a lot about who else besides Dean Zanuck, that would be wonderful to direct the continuing story of "Butch Cassidy & The Sundance Kid." One of my favorite movies is "The DaVinci Code" starring Tom Hanks and produced by Ron Howard. I will approach Mr. Howard. He is such a "Nice, Nice Man." He is always kind and everyone loves to work with him. I have worked with some real "screamers" as directors, and I will not do that ever again! I have some contacts for Ron Howard. We will have to wait and see what happens.

Robert Redford, James Cameron, Clint Eastwood, Kevin Costner, Jerry Bruckheimer, Steven Spielberg, Chris Columbus, who directed "The Illusionist," would ALL be wonderful directors. The one thing that I know for sure, it will just "feel right" when we meet with potential directors. Fox Studios did the first movie, so why not the second?

So now it is time to complete the last of the information on Butch and Sundance. I wanted you to feel like you were watching a movie when I talked about the relationship between Alonzo Long and his father Lewis. Folks have commented that they like my writing style because it is like I am talking to them. I am not a screen writer but I thought it would be fun to include my version of the story about Alonzo and his father Lewis like a scene from the movie.

# The Continuing Story of
# "Butch Cassidy & The Sundance Kid"

## DEATH SCENE

Alonzo and his father Lewis Long are on a "rite of passage" hunting trip to the "Big Horn Basin of Wyoming." Their ranch is in Linn, Oregon and Lewis feels that it is his duty as a father to teach his son how to be a "man."

Lewis is an abusive father and controls his wife and 6 children with fear and punishment.

Alonzo is only 19 and he does not want to be on the hunting trip with his father, but he feels that he has no choice.

The scene is beautiful with all the fall colors in the background with majestic mountains and flowing streams. The trip is very long as they travel towards the Big Horn Basin of Wyoming for their outing.

Lewis sees an Indian in the distance and orders Alonzo to kill the Indian for sport. Alonzo knows his father is not incapable of killing him. Alonzo has been beaten on many occasions, and he does not have the will to defy his father's command. Alonzo takes aim at the Indian and whispers under his breath, "God forgive me." The Indian is dead and there is silence between the two.

Lewis is puffed up with pride that his son fears and obeys him. His father has more evil plans for his son.

They travel in silence to the closest town where they visit a saloon and brothel. Lewis walks in and asked for two of their best rooms. His very presence commands the employees to jump and they hurry to escort them to their rooms.

Lewis seeks out the Madame of the brothel and whispers to her that he will pay her handsomely for her best "girl" to have Alonzo experience some romance for the night. The Madame is more than willing to help and can see that Alonzo is a virgin. She chooses a young girl that works for her to be his first sexual experience.

The scene moves to a young 16-year-old female, slaving in the kitchen. She is poor, orphaned, and alone. When the Madame approaches the young girl, she succumbs to the temptation of more money than she can make in a month. She rationalizes selling her soul for money. Maybe she could get out of this hell hole.

Lewis orders his son to spend the night with the girl that the Madame dresses up in the finest clothes you have ever seen. Introductions are made by Lewis, and the Madame enters their room. Lewis abruptly states, "Clara, meet Alonzo my son!" Lewis with his whiskey bottle in hand and his arm around the Madame, head off to their room and Alonzo and Clara are finally alone. The sun has gone down and Alonzo is kind enough to blow out the kerosene lamp so they can undress in the dark.

Both innocent, they do as they are ordered and they slip under the covers and begin to kiss. Romance always starts with a kiss, and Alonzo is not sure what to do, but they both mechanically figure it out and the deed is done. They have had their evening of lust and they both feel relieved that it is over.

Lewis is with the Madame and they are at it all night. In the morning, Alonzo knocks on his father's door. Lewis yells at Alonzo, "go away, I'm sick."

Alonzo is alone to himself and he has a day of walking around town and seeing a world he has never seen before. His life on the farm has been all work and his every move has been controlled by his father.

The guilt wells up inside of him and he asks folks in town if there is a church nearby. They give him directions and he walks into the only church in town. He kneels to pray and sobs with guilt over killing an Indian and spoiling a young girl. "God forgive me for I have sinned," as the tears and extreme emotion come to the surface.

Alonzo and his father stay for a week in the hotel and Alonzo barely sees his father. Lewis is like an animal that can't get enough of the whore houses and booze. Clara finishes her work and slips away for a stolen moment to be with Alonzo. They go for long walks in the countryside and the pressure is off, they are becoming friends.

The week is over and Lewis comes out of his drunken and lustful stupor. He orders Alonzo to pack up, they are going home. Alonzo obeys, but he slips away to quickly give Clara his address so they can write and stay in touch. Alonzo and Clara exchange a sweet innocent kiss, and the two men disappear into the landscape.

Father and son are silent as they make the long journey back to their homestead in Linn, Oregon. Alonzo knows that he must never talk about what has happened on the trip. Months pass and nothing from Clara. Alonzo decides to write to her and he receives a letter saying that she is pregnant and showing. If anyone were to find out that she is with child, she will be out on the streets, homeless.

Alonzo is 20 and he wants to do the right thing. He has a confrontation with his father and explains that he wants to marry Clara and bring her home. Lewis goes into a fit of rage! He will not have his son marrying a whore.

Alonzo finally stands up to his father and threatens to tell his mother everything! "If you don't give me the money to go and get Clara, I will tell mother everything." Alonzo threatens.

Lewis is afraid. He knows his wife would leave him for sure. She has put up with his abuse, but she would never stay with him if she knew he was with a prostitute. He could risk losing everything.

Alonzo screams, "You caused this, and all I want is to be with Clara!"

Lewis has to think fast and he tells Alonzo, "You cannot marry her, but I will arrange for you to go to Pennsylvania to my cousin Josiah and he and his wife Annie, will take the baby. You do not need to ruin your life over this girl, and she can get on with her life. No one will know."

They both go over all the details and finally Alonzo realizes that his father is right. He does not even know the girl. She is so young and ill prepared for marriage and a baby. It is decided, Alonzo will leave in the morning. He sends a letter ahead to Clara that he is coming to rescue her.

His father gives Alonzo plenty of money and a horse and wagon for the long journey to Pennsylvania. Clara is so grateful to see Alonzo and their reunion is touching. They leave the next day. The trip is hard on the mother, but they make it to 122 Jacobs Street in Mont Clare, Pennsylvania. Alonzo has never met Annie and Josiah Longabaugh, but they meet and make plans.

Josiah and Annie's farm is a mile down the water way and Clara and Alonzo are grateful that their baby will have a good home.

Months pass and Alonzo is falling deeper and deeper in love with Clara. They stay in the large suite of the 10 room boarding house and now their love making is genuine. It has been 5 months and it feels like a dream, spending time with each other day after day. They put it out of their minds that they are giving their baby away, and are lost in the moment.

The winter is hard, but finally spring arrives and the baby is close at hand. No one in the Josiah Longabaugh family knows about the baby. Lewis is willing to pay for their silence. He must protect his reputation as a respected and wealthy farmer.

It's time, Clara is in labor. Alonzo sends a boy to have Josiah and Annie come to help deliver the baby. Annie and Josiah live only a mile down the canal, so they are there in plenty of time. Clara and Alonzo are just children themselves.

Annie is wonderful with four children of her own. She is a good Christian woman that is amazed that God would allow her to adopt a child.

Clara has a hard labor and things are going wrong. Annie is afraid for Clara and the baby and demands that Alonzo leaves and brings a doctor. The doctor arrives and helps Clare and her unborn baby. He orders everyone out of the room. Alonzo, Josiah and Annie are finally relieved to hear the baby cry. When the doctor opens the door, his expression lets them know that Clara is gone.

Alonzo weeps over the mother of his child and is overcome with grief. The scene is so sad, and Annie and Josiah take the baby to give Alonzo time alone with Clara. Clara is now sleeping with the Angels and Alonzo wants to see his new son.

How foolish Alonzo feels thinking he could secretly give away his baby and slip back into his old life, as if nothing had ever happened. The whole town knew about Clara and the baby. Arrangements needed to be made and they called for the preacher. (Hey, we could look in the Mont Clare Cemetery for a female that could have died in the spring of 1867. Just saying!) There is a quiet ceremony the next day and only Alonzo said a few words. He didn't want the preacher to talk. He didn't know Clara, she is his girl and no one had a right to say anything. Alonzo is bitter and broken; he just wanted to put the whole scene behind him.

The baby is a day old and Annie arranged for a nurse maid. Alonzo could not go back to the suite where he had lived with Clara for five months. He had his horse and wagon ready to go home after the funeral. Alonzo met with Josiah and Annie and they needed to decide what to call the baby. Annie asked if she could name him Harry, a family name that she liked. Alonzo agreed, but he wanted his son to have his name, so everyone agreed that his name would be Harry Alonzo Longabaugh. Alonzo kissed his infant son goodbye, and thanked Josiah and Annie for raising his son. Alonzo is overcome with emotion as he slowly drove away.

All he ever wanted is to be loved. He had been raised with the most abusive father and everyone thinks Alonzo is a responsible father and successful rancher, but Alonzo has the scars to prove that he is a demon. If his father had not ordered him to have an affair with Clara, none of this would have even happened. The day Clara died, Alonzo became a man and he took back his life and now things would be different. He now had the upper hand with his father.

Alonzo had to pick up the pieces of his life and carry on. When he arrives back at his father's ranch, he simply tells Lewis, "Clara is dead, the baby is with Josiah and Annie," and walks away. Their names are never mentioned again.

Lewis never bothered Alonzo after the loss of Clara and his son; they just stayed out each other's way. When Alonzo turned 22, he met and married 16-year-old Julia Ann Taylor. Alonzo is now ready to do things right and he married Julia Ann in church and they moved as far away as they could go from his father. At that time in history, a woman could claim 300 acres and so could a man without it costing them a penny. Haines, Oregon is where Alonzo and Julia Ann homesteaded their 600-acre ranch. Alonzo and Julia Ann were the parents of 15 children, of which 10 survived. They became wealthy and respected pioneers and left a family legacy of honest work and generosity. They donated land for a school and Julia Ann declared Jesus Christ as her Savior before she died.

Alonzo never saw his father for 26 years. Lewis would never be allowed to be near his children or see his 15 grandchildren. He despised his father and he had to protect his family.

Alonzo received word the first week of July 1894 that his father would not survive the week. He did not want his children to see the father that had abused him, so he simply left Julia Ann and his family and traveled by horseback from Haines, Oregon to his father in Linn.

Alonzo walks into his father's bedroom and kissed his mother Sarah Ann out of respect. He always saw his mother as weak for not leaving Lewis, but that is all in the past. Alonzo can see that Lewis is old and frail. He is dying and he cannot hurt him ever again.

A lifetime has passed between them and Alonzo goes to his father and holds him. The two men are face to face and eye to eye. Never seeing his son or his grandchildren is punishment enough and Alonzo and Lewis hold each other in silence. Lewis slips away on July 12, 1894. Now there is peace at last.

Alonzo goes home to his loving wife Julia Ann and he holds his beloved wife and cries. Julia Ann knows what happened without saying a word. It is finally over.

Alonzo passed away on Valentine's Day, February 14, 1915 and Julia Ann passed away a year later in February. Alonzo was loved by his family and the whole town respected him. Alonzo is a man that did not follow in his father's footsteps, but blazed his own trail and broke the chain of abuse and lived a descent and good life.

My job is done and I have dedicated my research "To My Children!" This is my legacy. I found Butch Cassidy, The Sundance Kid, and Etta Place.

With love and gratitude for all who helped,

*Marilyn Grace*

# PHOTO ALBUM

William Henry Long

Cast of Characters

Josiah and Harry Longabaugh

William Henry Long

Sundance Kid

Butch Cassidy

Ann Place Longa-

Harry Longabaugh

Silas Morrell

Luzernia Morrell

Etta Place

Sammana & Emma

Bill Long's

Florence Viola & Evinda Ann Long

Percy Seibert

Matt Warner

Clara Robison

Irwin Robison

Etta Robison

Ann Parker

William Phillips

George, Mary & Walter C. Longenbaugh

Cussin' Charlie & Aunt Mary

Silas Morrell Family

Poster for the Movie

## "RAINDROPS KEEP FALLING ON MY HEAD"

Sung by B.J. Thomas

Bicycle Scene

We do not have permission to add this poster to our book, but will contact FOX STUDIOS for permission to add the poster for our final book. Paul Newman and Katharine Ross are riding the bicycle. Fun and Sexy Scene!

*Luzernia and Bill Long*

Bill Long and Luzernia With their "Giant" Pumpkin

**Tombstone of Luzernia and William Henry Long in the Duchesne City Cemetery**

Luzernia Allred Long was born on April 27, 1857 in Spring City, Utah. Luzernia passed away four months after her husbands death.

William Henry Long said he was born in the "Big Horn Basin" of Wyoming when there were no white settlers.

Etta Forsyth, Bill Long's step grand-daughter, said that the family celebrated his birthday on March 13.

When Bill Long married Luzernia, his license stated he was born in 1867. "The Sundance Kid" had about Spring of 1867 as his birth year.

The Long Family said he was born February 1st or 2nd, 1860? They were not sure when he was born?

William Henry Long died on November 27, 1936. He was 69 years old.

On the porch: Martha Morrell Jobe - Center: Clara Morrell Robison, Irwin G. Robison at the Hogan Ranch, Paradise Valley.
Grandpa Robison owned the Hogan Ranch in the 1930's. The Hogan Ranch is 15 miles east of Loa, Utah.
Bill Long was a "Horse Breaker" at the Hogan Ranch for two dollars a day before he married Luzernia Morrell
in Fremont, Utah. (From Diann and Jerry Peck's Collection)

The Walter C. Longenbaugh Family

Annie Place Longabaugh, the mother of
Harry A. Longabaugh

George Mayers and Mary Alise

Top: Edna and Walter Longenbaugh
Left to Right: Harry, Gailen, Dillon

Josiah Longabaugh with his youngest child,
four-year old Harry A. Longabaugh

Harvey Sylvester Longabough,
the older brother of Harry Longabaugh, "The Sundance Kid"

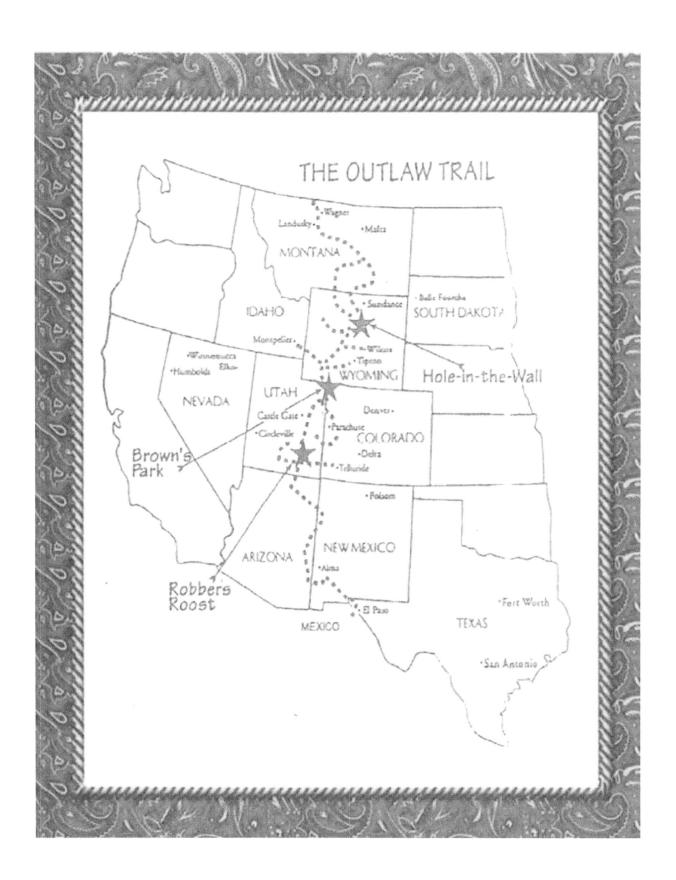

THE OUTLAW TRAIL

Wagner
Landusky · · Malta
MONTANA

· Belle Fourche
· Sundance
IDAHO SOUTH DAKOTA

Montpelier ·
Winnemucca · · Wilcox
· Humboldt Elko · · Tipton
WYOMING Hole-in-the-Wall

NEVADA UTAH
Denver ·
Castle Gate · · Parachute
· Circleville COLORADO
Brown's · Delta
Park · Telluride

· Folsom

NEW MEXICO

ARIZONA · Alma
Robbers
Roost · Fort Worth
· El Paso
MEXICO TEXAS

· San Antonio

Cholila Ranch

Sundance, Wyoming, at the turn of the Century

The Compound in San Vicente, Bolivia,
where Sundance and Butch were reported dead

Cholila Ranch with BUTCH, SUNDANCE, ETTA, and neighbors in Argentina

Percy Siebert was an engineer for the Concordia Mine where
Butch and Sundance worked. He is the source of the 1930
report that Butch and Sundance had been killed in Bolivia.
Siebert never went to view the bodies in San Vicente,
and yet world-wide headlines reported that
Butch and Sundance were dead.

The Concordia Tin Mine, 70 miles north of La Paz, Boliva.
Butch Cassidy and Sundance bunked in the first white
building on the left.

The Silas Morrell Family
Left to Right: Chloe Jane, Luzernia holding Ernest Alma on her lap, (front) Martha,
(rear) Clara Elizabeth, Silas with son Hiette Allen, and Mary Francis
Photo taken shortly before Silas' death, 26 September 1893

### SILAS WILSON MORRELL

Silas was born in Cottonwood, Salt Lake County, Utah, to William Wilson (1830-1907) and Sarah Jane Richards (1833-1909). He married Virginia Morrell while living in Midvale, Utah. Virginia died August 2, 1875. The actual cause of death is unknown, but it is suspected that she died during or shortly after childbirth; it is know that an infant daughter of this couple died during this time period. Silas moved to Rabbit Valley in Wayne County, with his father in 1876. On July 12, 1876, he married Luzernia Allred (daughter of Andrew Jackson and Chloe Stevens Allred) in Fremont, Utah. Luzernia was born on April 27, 1857 in Spring City, Utah. Luzernia and Silas had seven children.

They owned a farm just east of Fremont where they built a two-story, log house. They also had a dairy farm east of Fish Lake, later know as Silas Springs, where in the early summer they herded milk cows to the mountain spring to graze during the warm months.

While working his father's sawmill, Silas was severely injured; he broke his back. He was unable to do manual labor after the accident. Silas never recovered his health completely and died in Fremont, Utah.

CHILDREN:
| | |
|---|---|
| Chloe Jane Morrell Jackson | (1877-1956) |
| Silas Warren Morrell | (1878-1881) |
| Clara Elizabeth Morrell Robinson | (1880-1953) |
| Mary Frances Morrell Anderson | (1883-1953) |
| Martha Morrell Jobe | (1886-1968) |
| Hiett Allen Morrell | (1888-1936) |
| Ernest Alma Morrell | (1891-1968) |

A young Irwin G. Robison (age 17)

Clara Morrell (age 23) Irwin's wife

Irwin G. Robison, Sheriff of Wayne County
Related to Bill Long by marriage

Left: Irwin G. Robison Center: Etta Robison Right: Bill Long
Photo Courtesy of Diann and Jerry Peck

Mr. Long was the father of Mrs. Evinda (nicknamed Vinda or Vinde)
Merkley, Duchesne, Utah. She contributed this picture for publication
in the local paper. Picture taken sometime after 1917.

## TURNED AWAY FROM THE OUTLAW LIFE AND HELPING IN THE COMMUNITY

Putting up ice on the Duchesne River about 50 years ago to have a supply to make that pitcher of cold lemonade for the July 4th
community celebration was quite a process. On the wagon is Bill Long, standing at left, Joe Danner and at right, Fred Oldstrum.
Point of harvest is near the junction of the Duchesne and Strawberry Rivers, directly east of Duchesne. They were not treading on
thin ice; it was 20 inches thick in the block.

Photo: Silas and Luzernia Morrell with their small family at Fish Lake, Utah 1917.
Bill Long made a trip to Fish Lake and came back with cash {gold coins} to pay for the ranch in Duchesne,
Utah. He moved to be near his daughter, Evinda Ann {Vinde} and family.

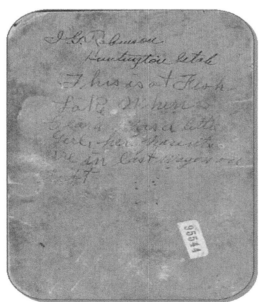

Back of Fish Lake Photo

Turkey picking at the ranch: Bill Long in the cap, behind his wife, Luzernia, holding a large turkey in the center. Turkey's were hung and bled out on the pole behind them. Then the feathers were plucked. In the photo they appear to be having fun while working together. They sold turkey's for their living. They could only afford to eat their own turkey's at Christmas and Thanksgiving.

Photos courtesy of Diann and Jerry Peck Collection

Seated on the right is Bill Long.
Notice his right hand compared to
"The Sundance Kid's" right hand.

**"The Fort Worth Five"**
Seated L to R: Harry Longabaugh, alias "The Sundance Kid," Benjamin Kilpatrick, alias "The Tall Texan," Robert
LeRoy Parker, alias "Butch Cassidy."
Standing L to R: William Carver, alias "News Carver," Harvey Logan, alias "Kid Curry."
"The Wild Bunch"
1900

Left: Young "Sundance Kid" - Brent Ashworth purchased the photo 30 years ago from Matt Warner's family. Matt was a member of "The Wild Bunch."
Center: William Henry Long - compare the thumb and hands of a 14 year old Harry Longabaugh with the thumb and hands of William Henry Long.
See how the hands are curled under. Sundance was known to have unusually long fingers so he curled them under in photo's.
Left to Right: 1. Young Sundance Kid's right hand. 2. William Henry Long's right hand. 3. William Henry Long's left hand. 4. New York photo of
Sundance Kid's right hand. 5. Fort Worth Five photo of Sundance Kid's right hand. 6. William Henry Long's right hand at age 69.

### "Cussin' Charley"

Aunt Mary, Luzernia's first child, and Cussin' Charley,
who was exactly as his name says; there was not a word that
came out of his mouth that was not a "cuss" word.
Cussin' Charley was heavily involved with Bill Long and the outlaws.
Photo courtesy of Diann and Jerry Peck

An older man know as "The Speckled Nigger."
Luzernia Long chased him out of town because
she blamed him for her husband Silas Morrell's back injury.
We do not have any other name for this individual.

Wild photo of
"The Speckled Nigger"
The folks in Fremont, Utah
only knew him by this name.

## Note: Journal Entry of Marilyn Grace – December 24, 2010 "Christmas Eve"

*I went to Cedar City, Utah on Christmas Eve.   I spent time with my son Sterling, his wife Mindy and my four grandchildren.   I showed Sterling our book and he looked at the pictures of "The Speckled Nigger." He said, "Mom, you can't call him 'The Speckled Nigger' you are going to be on 'Oprah'!" He was just horrified!   I had to laugh and explain that I do not have any other name for this man, but I was thrilled that he just knew that we were going to be on" Oprah!"*

### Update:

One of my shard holders Edward (Eddie) Fast, read our book and found Albert Welhouse and his nick name is SPECK!  We both agree that the information includes Brown's Park History, so we are confident that this is our man.  There is also a RARE PHOTO of Butch, Ann Bassett and Albert Welhouse.  Go on Amazon and look for a book on the WILD BUNCH that has rare photos.  This is a major find for our research.  We will see about permission to add the photo to our updated book.

That was some GREAT DETECTIVE WORK!  I am so grateful!

From "Where The Old West" pages 49 and 50.

Thank you so much Eddie!

*Marilyn Grace*

Samanna and Emma Longabaugh

William Henry Long

Samanna and Emma Longabaugh

**Side Story: Marilyn Grace – Journal Entry: At Christmas Time 2009**

*I visited with my neighbor, Ferron Moon, who lived in Vernal, Utah. He was 7 years old when he met Josie Bassett. He said his mother had invited 10 women over for a quilting party. Josie was among the ladies. My mother asked, "Josie how come you have so many husbands?" Josie married five men that are buried on her land in Vernal. One may have "mysteriously" vanished? Josie wasn't saying a thing if you get my drift. Josie said that all these reports came to say that she had poisoned her husbands. She said she didn't poison them, but she didn't say she didn't kill them! Josie told all the ladies at the quilting party, and my neighbor heard Josie's response as to why she had so many husbands, "Well, when you get in the habit of marrying 'Son's a Bitches,' it's hard to break the habit."*

William Henry Longabaugh and Family (Bill)

1946

Left: William Henry Longabaugh

Right: Harvey Sylvester Longabaugh, Jr.

In 1903, "Sundance" came back from Bolivia to visit his brother in New Jersey.

One day he went with young William Henry Longabaugh (age 10 at the time)

To the ocean to collect sea shells.

Luzernia Long on her Duchesne Ranch with one of her grandchildren

Luzernia Long

Viola and Vinda

Vinda and Viola

# $6,500 REWARD

---

REWARD FOR THE CAPTURE, DEAD OR ALIVE OF

## HARRY LONGBAUGH

ALIAS

# THE SUNDANCE KID

Age, 35 to 40 years

Complexion, dark.
(Looks like quarter breed
Indian)

Eyes, Black.

Features, Grecian type.

Height, 5 ft. 9 in.

Color of hair, Black.

Mustache, black.

Nationality, American.

Weight, 165 to 170 lbs.

Build, rather slim.

Nose, rather long.

Occupation,
Cowboy, Rustler.

Harry Longbaugh, alias THE SUNDANCE KID served 18 months in jail at Sundance, Cook Co., Wyoming when a boy, for horse stealing. In December, 1892, the Sundance Kid, Bill Madden and Harry Bass "held up" a Great Northern train at Malta, Montana. Bass and Madden were tried for the crime, convicted and sentenced to 10 and 14 years respectively!

The Sundance Kid escaped and since has been a fugitive.

## William Henry Long

## The Sundance Kid

Dr. John McCullough's photo comparison of William Henry Long on the left and "The Sundance Kid" on the right. The results: 99.9% that William Henry Long IS "The Sundance Kid."

## Sisters Pictures

Standing: Samanna Longabaugh
Sitting: Emma Longabaugh
Sisters of Harry A. Longabaugh

This is the photo mentioned in Viola's 1936 letter of Bill Long's "Sisters Picture." Bill Long had this photo on his fireplace in Duchesne, Utah.

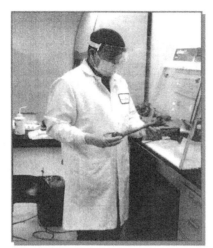

Tim Kupherschmid at Sorenson Forensic Lab

Marilyn Grace and Dr. John McCullough examining Bill Long's remains at Sorenson Forensics Lab in Salt Lake City, Utah.

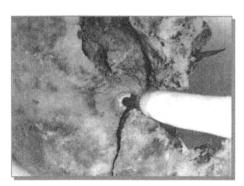

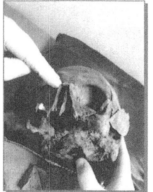

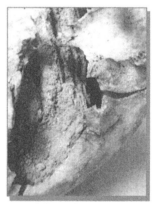

William Henry Long (Bill) had a broken nose and sinus problems and "The Sundance Kid" had a broken nose and sinus problems as well!

Exhumation of Bill Long
Duchesne City Cemetery

Filming Bill Long's Remains
Duchesne City Cemetery

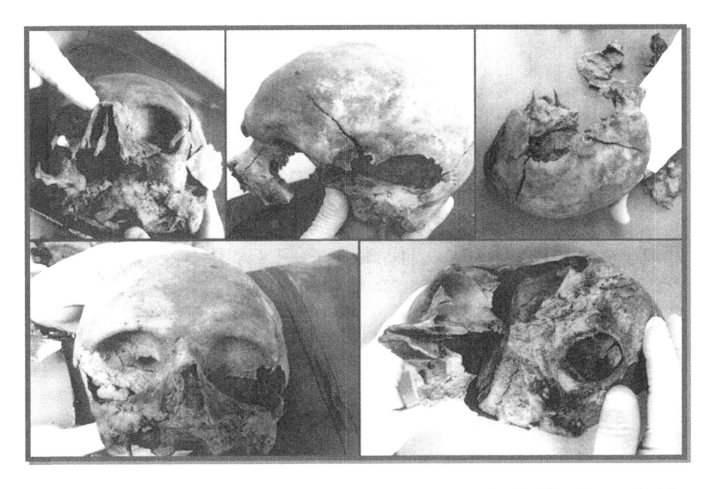

While examining the bones of William Henry Long, Dr. John McCullough proved with forensic science that Bill Long did not commit suicide, but was murdered. It would be close to impossible with the angle of the bullet wound, fired by a 22 rifle from an upward position and two to three feet away, to inflict this type of wound. Bill Long was murdered in cold blood and Matt Warner was suspected of being the murderer. Matt Warner was supposed to be Bill Long's best friend. They even had a joint bank account. The money, however, was lost in 1929, during the depression. Bill Long strongly opposed Matt in his writing a book on his outlaw life. Surprisingly enough, Bill Long was found dead after Matt Warner went on a four-day hunting trip. Bill's body was found on the ranch with a rifle by his side and he was slumped over a pile of wood. We believe that the family made up the "suicide" story in order to close the case and not have the authorities probe into his past as an "outlaw."

Dr. John McCullough and film crew -
Exhumation of Bill Long

DNA was extracted from this bone fragment
of Bill Long's remains

Tim Kupferschmid -
Exhumation of Bill Long

# DESERET NEWS

## SUNDANCE KID STORY

GOOGLE

Is Sundance really buried in Duchesne?

December 16, 2008

By Geoff Liesik

## THE DESERET NEWS
## DOUBLE THEIR READERSHIP THE DAY
## THEY PUBLISHED OUR STORY ON

## "THE SUNDANCE KID"

WE DO NOT HAVE PERMISSION TO PUBLISH THE
NEWSPAPER STORY IN OUR BOOK

# ETTA FORSYTH

## GRAND DAUGHTER OF WILLIAM HENRY LONG

## "THE SUNDANCE KID"

Newspaper story

2009

GOOGLE

THE NEWSPAPER STORY

WE DO NOT HAVE PERMISSION TO ADD THE
STORY TO OUR BOOK

**Sundance and Etta's "Wedding" Photo**
Etta Forsyth, Bill Long's step-granddaughter (age 93)
said, "I see the resemblance, that's Grandpa Billy Long!"

# LULA PARKER BETENSON

Consultant on the set of…

## "BUTCH CASSIDY & THE SUNDANCE KID"

## (PHOTO OF LULA, PAUL NEWMAN
## &
## ROBERT REDFORD)

We need to get permission from FOX STUDIO'S to put the photo in our book.

# Gaylen Robison's Family

Back Row, left to right: Viola Long Ehlers, Elva (daughter of Bill Long), Beverly, Gaylen, Mahonri Ehlers, Robert Alvin Robinson
Front Row, left to right: Barry, Lance, Marilyn Robinson (not misspelled but a different father)
Elva married a Robison and then a Robinson.

The Pinkerton's

Joe Lafores and Posse

The Uintah County Jail

Marilyn Grace Journal Entry

March 15, 2010 - Monday

# Photo Comparison of William Thadeus Phillips and Robert LeRoy Parker

William Thadeus Phillips

Robert LeRoy Parker
"Butch Cassidy"

Combined Overlay

Photo Comparison of Ann Bassett and Etta Place

Ann Bassett

Etta Place

Combined Overlay

Photo Comparison of William Henry Long and Harry Alonzo Longabaugh

William Henry Long

Harry Alonzo Longabaugh
"The Sundance Kid"

Combined Overlay

On the left is Ann Gillies Parker, Butch Cassidy's mother. In the middle is William Thadeus Phillips of Spokane, Washington. On the right is Robert LeRoy Parker also known as Butch Cassidy. I saw the family resemblance between Ann Parker and William Phillips 14 years ago when I read "In Search of Butch Cassidy" by Larry Pointer. It's exciting to have the photos side by side for YOU to see the resemblance.

The Last of the BANDIT RIDERS

MATT WARNER
MURRAY E. KING

Matt Warner in 1937, the year before his death (far left)

Turn of the Century "Cowboys"
Right: Lasse Allred,  Left: Unknown
Lasse Allred is Clara Morrell's Uncle
Making a Trip to the Canyons of Escalante,
The Grand Staircase,
and the Kaiparowits Plateau.

Clara and Irwin G. Robison Homestead
Loa, Utah 1910
Etta Robison Forsyth (daughter)
Etta is Diann Peck's mother

Photo's from Diann and Jerry Peck collection

**The Green River Saloon**
Harry Longabaugh leaning against the tree.
"Butch Cassidy" sitting in the chair next to the tree.
Sheriff Tom Fares sitting in front of the door.

**Miles City, Montana
At the Turn of the Century**

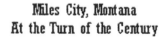

The Candy Box

The Union Pacific Railroad Train Posse
The Possee was formed after the
Wilcox robbery
Left to Right: George Hiatt, T.T.
Kelliher, H. Davis, Sifunk, Jeff Carr,
Joe Lefores
In the Movie "Butch Cassidy and
The Sundance Kid" Paul Newman's and
Robert Redford's characters are
chased by the "Super Posse."
The famous line, "Who are those
guys?"

Union Pacific Train ~ Tipton, Wyoming 1900
Robbed by the "Wild Bunch"
Mr. Woodcock was robbed by Butch Cassidy, Kid Curry and others possibly
involved were Ben Kilpatrick, O. C. "Deaf Charlie Hanks," William Cruzan
and Bill Carver

Union Pacific "Posse Train"

Great Northern Express Car
Wagner, Montana 1901

"The Curry Brothers"
Left to right: John, Harvey and Lonie
Kid Curry (Harvey) a bronc-twister
Harry Longabaugh knew them and worked
the Coburn Spring Cattle round-up, 1893

"Sundance" and "Etta"
at Cholila Ranch, Bolivia

This is the birth place of "The Sundance Kid" - 122 Jacobs Street, Mont Clare, Pennsylvania.
(A 10-room boarding house with one large suite - burned down in 2004)
Kurt and Joan Callow own the property and Joan was so kind to send me a stone that was shaped into a brick
from the boarding house that had to be torn down because of a fire.
THANK YOU JOAN!
I love my stone brick and I carry it everywhere and show everyone!

Top left shows how the cabin looked originally, the others show the destruction of time and nature.

Center photo shows a view from above the cabin and how easily it could be defended.

"The New Wild Bunch Gang"

Willow Creek Ranch at the Hole-in-the-Wall, Kaycee, Wyoming

July 2012

# THE BRENT ASHWORTH COLLECTION

Brent Ashworth is the "World's Largest Private Collector" of historical documents, memorabilia and photographs.

Brent was born in Albany, California and grew up in Provo, Utah. He graduated from Brigham Young University "cum laude" with a BA in History and Political Science. He served in the US Army Reserves and was called to active duty at Ft. Ord, California. Then he met his wife Charlene at Brigham Young University and they have raised 9 children together and have thirteen grandchildren.

In 2006, Brent founded "B. Ashworth Books, Inc.," a Provo, Utah business dealing in rare documents, books, art, collectibles and other curiosities. His firm deals primarily in rare LDS and Western material, but handles other significant items from around the world.

The television and radio celebrity Glenn Beck asked Brent to help him with his "Mercury One" organization and has been a significant contributor to Mr. Beck's "Man in the Moon" museum. The display was staged at the Grand American Hotel in Salt Lake City, Utah over the Fourth of July, 2013, and was the Fiftieth Anniversary of the Kennedy Assassination.

Brent Ashworth helped Glen Beck to display for "Mercury One" at the Omni Hotel in Dallas, Texas in November, 2013.

Mr. Beck also asked Brent Ashworth, historian David Barton and Rick Harrison of the TV reality show "Pawn Stars" to be on Glenn Beck's first "Collector's Showcase" television show. The show aired on "The Blaze" network, on November 2, 2013. Brent read one of Marilyn Monroe's letters on the show. Marilyn wrote to her first husband saying she is thinking of becoming a model. Brent said, "Becoming a model is an understatement." We all know Marilyn became one of Hollywood's biggest stars.

Some know Brent for sharing his many experiences from his varied and wide collecting career, enthusiastically pursued for over half a century. Brent feels that his most important accomplishment he is most proud of is his relationship with his wonderful wife Charlene and their great family.

What a "thrill" to be able to do a photo shoot with Brent at his bookstore and wear "Amelia Earhart's" leather jacket and goggles. The photos will go in our book, "Amelia Earhart Mystery, Solved."

Then I am invited back and we take over 30 shots of "Marilyn Monroe's" wardrobe, her photos and Joe DiMaggio collection. I have a photo of me wearing the gown Marilyn wore to the premier of "Gentlemen Prefer Blonds" and I put on her jewels and then hold her shoes and gloves. That photo shoot will go in our book, "SCREAM BLOODY MURDER, The Truth about the Life and Death of Marilyn Monroe."

We have also completed a photo shoot of "Butch Cassidy & Sundance Kid" items with the 200 page "Bandit Invincible" document. Without the "Bandit Invincible" document we would not have known that Butch went to Paris, France and had a facelift. Brent owns that document also! The "Bandit Invincible" document is the only reason I was able to prove with science that Butch went to Paris, France and had a facelift.

Our book "Hitler Escapes to America" has photos of Brent's "Hitler" collection.

We will do a book on John Fitzgerald Kennedy's assignation and Brent has shared some JFK items with us already.

The "Hitler" books and memorabilia, "Amelia Earhart's" leather jacket, goggles, book, and a hand written letter of Amelia's, as well as "Marilyn Monroe's" extensive collection and John Fitzgerald Kennedy items are all in Brent Ashworth's collection. Amazing! He even has "Elvis" items. There is an original photo and the shirt Elvis wore in "Jailhouse Rock."

We are friends and we all know how important all of his items are to our research. We are literally rewriting history.

A heartfelt "Thank You" Brent for your time and all that you do to help Story Teller Productions.

*Marilyn Grace*

Tres Cruzes. Feb. 16. 1908

C, R, Glass,

Dear Sir

Garberry leaves here for Sicasica on
18. he will be there the 20. I dont know
g he will be there but I will let you know
he leaves, every thing is OK here
far as I know.

Yours Truly

Gibbs

By the hut of the peasant when purity.
~~sleeps~~, And nigh to the throne of the King o
Clasr, Close to the cradle where infancy
sleeps, And Joy loves to linger and sing o
Lives a garden of light full of Heaven
perfume, Where never a tear drops in shed.
And the rose and the ~~left of~~ lilly are ever
in bloom The land of the beautiful dead

Santa Cruz. Nov. 12. 1907

To the Boys at Concordia.

We arrived here about 3 weeks ago. after a
very plesant journey. and found just
the place I have been looking for. for
20 years, and Ingersoll licks it better than
I do, he says he wont try to live any where
else. this is a Town of 18.000. and 14000
are females and some of them are birds
this is the only place for old fellows like
myself, one never gets to old if he has blue
Eyes and a red face and looks capable
of making a blue eyed Baby Boy.
Oh god if I could fall back 20 years and
have red hair with this compleclion of
mine I would be happy. I have got into the
400 set as deep as I can go. the lady feeds
me on fine wines. and she is the prettiest
little thing I ever seen. but I am afraid
Papa is going to tear my play house down
for he is getting nasty. but there is plenty
more, this place isnt what we expected at all
there isnt any cattle here all the beef that is
killed here come from Mojo a distance of 80
leagues, and are worth from 80 to 100 B$.
but cattle do very well here the grass is good
but water is scarse, there isnt any water in
this town when there is a dry spell for a wee

the people down in town have to buy water at
180 per barrel but they can get good water at
40 feet. but are to lazy to dril wells.

land is cheap here and every thing grows
good that is planted. but there is damd little
planted. every thing is very high it cost us
1300 per head! fed our mules! 250 each for our
selves. we Rented a house hired a good cook
and are living like gentlemen.

land is worth 10 cts per hectaria here or 10 leagues
from here and there is some good Estancias
for sale. one 12 leagues from here of 4 leagues
with plenty of water and good grass and
some sugarcane for $5000, and other just
as cheap, and if I don't fall down I will be
living here before long.

it is pretty warm and some fever but the
fever is caused by the food they eat. at least
I am willing to chance it.

they are doing some work now building a
R.R. from Port Suares. here and they claim
it will be pushed right through. so now is
the time to get started for land will go up
before long.

It is 350 miles from here to Cochabamba and
a hell of a road just up one mountain and
down another all the way not a level spot on
it big enough to whip a dog on. and most of

the way thick brush on both sides, but there is people all along and lots of little towns. I guess it is thickly settled. there is plenty of game on the road but it is so thick for it is impossible to get at it for brush. I killed 1 turkey 1 Sand hill Crain and 1 Buzzard. we could hear the turkeys every day and seen some several times but I only got one shot, it wont do for Reece to come over that road for he would kill himself getting through the brush after birds. we would of left here long ago, but we had a little trouble with the old mule Ingersoll hobbled her and tied her to a tree and wore a nice green pole out on her, but I didnt think he had done a good job so I worked a little while with rocks, between us we broke her jaw and we have been feeding her on mush ever since, but she can eat a little now and we will leave in a few days for a little trip south to see that country. I are looking for the place Hutch wants, 8 leagues long 4 league wide with big river running through it from end to end

we expect to be back at Concordia in about 1 month

Good luck to all you fellows
J. P. Maxwell

As Jim Kennedy sat in his office looking over his accounts one early fall morning; there was a look of deep worry on his face. Buisness had been very poor for the past two years, and the outlook for future buisness seemed very poor to say the least, Up untill two years before our story opens. He had been too quite successfull for four or five years, but a great deal of the money he had made had been put back into the buisness in the way of men and added equipment in anticipation of future contracts and consequently when the crash of the big depression came Jim found himself in a rather tight place financialy; and with all prospects of immediate contracts gone, owing chiefly to the sudden fall of prices in the metal market. As all of his work consisted of mining equipment.

As he arose from his seat preparatory to leaving the office, a friend Bert Ellis

312

entered,

Hello Jim! Just driving by and thought I would drop in and see how things were going with you, Have you heard the latest? The —— bank closed its doors, or rather failed to open them this morning, Lucky thing for me that I drew almost my last dollar out of there soturday.

Well I'll be —— I wonder what next will happen. It just seems that everything has turned upside down with me. I just *this morning* reived a check for nearly five hundred dollars on that bank. ~~this~~ and now that's all slot. This sure means another mess of troubles for me, to say nothing of the holdup of this check which I could use to a very good advantage this very days. Well with all my other troubles this is a fine start for monday the first of the month.

Ellie remained in the office but a short time, ~~and~~ as soon he left Kennedy took down the telephone receiver and called Kenwood four nine seven six

Helo, helo, is this you Anderson? have you heard the ~~news~~ about — bank has closed its doors? Just when is that note of yours due? it must be due in a few days; are you able to do anything toward meeting it?

I have a little money in the bank Jim, returned the vase over the phone, which I intended to use as a part payment and extention of the note, but I supose that is tied up now, and I will have to try and make some other arangement. it sure leaves me pretty well sewed up right now, but I'll git busy and do the best I can for I supose they will be crowding every one for settlement

Well Anderson I hope you will do all you can to raise the money for payment or make some satisfactory arangement for if they come onto me for payment just now it will put me high and dry on the rocks, as I am being crowded

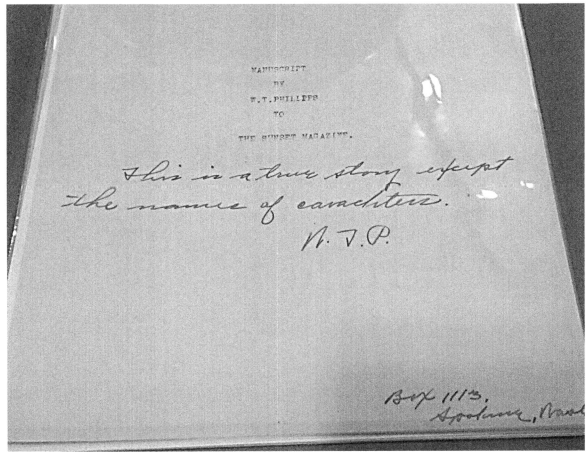

THE BANDIT INVINCIBLE.

This story is based entirely upon facts.  All of
the holdups herein described,were actually perppe-
trated by Cassidy,during the years of his life of
banditry,in both North and South America.  Several
of the minor holdups have been omitted,as space,in
a single volume,will not permit chronicling all the
episodes of his strenuous life as a bandit.

the way thick brush on both sides, but there is people all along and lots of little towns in fact it is thickly settled. there is plenty of game on the road but it is safe for it is impossible to get to it for brush. I killed 1 turkey 1 sand hill Crane and 1 Buzzard, we could hear the turkeys every day and seen some several times but I only got one shot, it wont do for Reece to come down that road for he would kill himself getting through the brush after birds we would of left here long ago, but we had a little trouble with the old mule Ingersoll hobbled her and tied her to a tree and wore a nice green pole out on her, but I didnt think he had done a good job so I worked a little while with rocks, between us we broke her jaw and we have been feeding her on mush ever since, but she can eat a little now and we will leave in a few days for a little trip south to see that country I are looking for the place Hutch wants, 8 leagues long to league wide with big river running through it from end to end

we expect to be back at Concordia in about 1 month

Good luck to all you fellows
J. P. Maxwell

Dedicated to

Heber M. Wells, who as Governor of Utah
gave me the protection which enabled be
abandon the bandit life and go straight.
        And to
Joyce Warner, my daughter, whose faithful
and intelligent aid helped so much in
bringing out this book.

Copy for back of Title page

The last of the Bandit Riders

Copyright 1940
        by
The CAXTON PRINTERS, Ltd.
Caldwell, Idaho
All rights reserved.

Printed, lithographed, and bound in the U
States of America at Caldwell, Idaho by
The CAXTON PRINTERS, Ltd.

                54778

Job No.

318

(2)

Chapter Titles for

THE LAST OF THE BANDIT RIDERS

XXVIII————————————— Robbing a Bank On a Bronco

XXIX————————————— Buried Robber Gold

XXX————————————— We See a Cattle War

XXXI————————————— Tracks that Bring Adventure

XXXII————————————— The Two Bar Holdup

XXXIII————————————— Slipping Through the Dragnet

XXXIV————————————— The Roslyn Bank Robbery

XXXV————————————— I Face Judgment and Death

XXXVI————————————— The Thunderbolt Strikes

XXXVII————————————— Betrayed and Sold

XXXVIII————————————— Buying Law With Robber Gold

XXXIX————————————— Jail Break

XL————————————— Gold Conquers Law

XLI————————————— I Reach the Cross Roads

XLII————————————— The Death Trap

XLIII————————————— Stealing Money to Buy Justice

XLIV————————————— I Pay the Price

XLV————————————— Between Good and Bad Law

XLVI————————————— How I strained My Pledge

APPENDIX: My acquaintance with Matt Warner
by Samuel J. King

*The End*

28559495R00193

Made in the USA
Columbia, SC
27 October 2018